Flights of Angels

ARSENAL
PULP PRESS

FLIGHTS... OF ANGELS

MY LIFE WITH THE ANGELS OF LIGHT

Adrian Brooks

photographs by Daniel Nicoletta

FLIGHTS OF ANGELS
Copyright ©2008 by Adrian Brooks

ARSENAL PULP PRESS
200 - 341 Water Street
Vancouver, BC
Canada V6B 1B8
arsenalpulp.com

Cover collage by Bill Bowers; cover and title page illustration by Karen Garry
Photography by Daniel Nicoletta
Book design by Shyla Seller
Editing by Brian Lam and Bethanne Grabham

Printed and bound in Canada

Library and Archives Canada Cataloguing in Publication:

Brooks, Adrian, 1947-
    Flights of angels : my life with the Angels of light / Adrian
Brooks ; with photographs by Daniel Nicoletta.

ISBN 978-1-55152-231-9

    1. Brooks, Adrian, 1947- 2. Angels of light (Theater group) 3. Gay
theater—California—San Francisco—History—20th century. 4. Gay
liberation movement—California—San Francisco—History—20th century.
5. Entertainers—United States—Biography. 6. Dramatists, American—
Biography. 7. Political activists—United States—Biography. I. Nicoletta,
Daniel, 1954- II. Title.

PN2287.B72A3 2008   791'.092   C2007-904501-4

For Hibiscus

Deranged by his own audacity, he plunged into a dark sea,
leaving indelible golden wings freely available to all.
And who would refuse his legacy or choose to remain earthbound?
Well, "Goodnight, sweet prince, and flights of angels sing thee to thy rest."

Also by Adrian Brooks

Novels:
The Glass Arcade (1980)
Roulette (2007)
Black and White (and red all over) (2008)

Plays:
Leni Riefenstahl (1982)

With the Angels of Light:
Paris Sites Under the Bourgeois Sea (1975)
Holy Cow! (1979; 1980)

Poetry:
Limbo Palace (1976)

Contents

"I don't want realism, I want magic."

—Tennessee Williams
A Streetcar Named Desire

Preface

It's impossible to encapsulate the truth about the Angels of Light. No one possesses this history any more than anyone could possess the history of Gay Liberation itself. Everyone who contributed to it may lay fair claim to a shard of a still unexcavated, undocumented culture. It is theirs to share. Or withhold. I choose to share and, in so doing, complete a long, long cycle of my life.

The story of the Angels, as well as the white-hot underground gay culture of the 1970s, has never been told in print. If left up to some, it would never be revealed for, even now, they presume that this is their turf. I have my own strong feelings as to what this history *is*, and what it signifies, but while admitting stout resistance, I see no way to write a memoir without full disclosure. Still, as full disclosure touches upon issues of character, it seems only fair to be at least as unsparing of myself as I may be to others. If that seems excessive or exhibitionistic, so be it, but how else to reveal what actually happened when, instead of serving proverbial life sentences as degraded and passive victims, society's most despised underclass dreamed and danced ourselves into liberated self-actualization?

I hesitated telling my story for many years and for many reasons. Over time, these were revealed as excuses. The time has come to drop the collusion and secrecy that obstruct truth and speak, simply speak, about the mad, dazzling circus that I come from, and the mad, dazzling circus that I plunged into. There is no way to avoid a paradox that to unveil one necessitates unveiling the other.

However transcendent or grotesque the truth may be in places, I hope that it contributes to nurturing *all* inclusive movements for equal human rights, and the LGBT community in particular. I freely acknowledge that deconstructing *any* secret society may denude iconic myths cloaked by legend or deliberately obscured. In all accurate tales of beauty and pain and dreams attained but lost, a candid narrator risks appearing to act out or even old scores to no good end. The extent to which I can be circumspect but keep faith with the truth rests with you.

—A. B.

Introduction

On December 22, 1970, gay rights activist and writer Carl Wittman published "Refugees from Amerika: A Gay Manifesto." The fiery essay condemned the gay community's mimicry of heterosexual society, oppression of self and others, and the dichotomies of gender, among other ills and grievances. The piece was talked about and reprinted everywhere; it soon became one of the most influential documents of the newly minted gay liberation movement. And thus an era was launched.

The decade to follow was a time of roiling upheaval and realignment on many fronts. Passion was thick in the air, fueling a robust political economy of rapid change. For the first time in human history, gay sons and lesbian daughters of the working and middle classes felt liberated enough to collectively step out of their dark closets of fear and shame. It was a social movement unlike any other, and its impact was soon to change the world in ways both vast and subtle.

While this seismic revolution of sex and spirit had many centers—what was happening in New York was being duplicated in Toronto, London, Los Angeles, Paris, Tokyo, Sydney, and many points between—there was one place, arguably more than any other, that embodied its heart. And it was to this city, more than any other, that Wittman's new breed of "refugees" came to in droves. Sleepy, small, provincial San Francisco was suddenly shaken by a jolt no less felt than the mighty tremblers that had rattled its foundations from the very beginning. This gay wave engulfed every aspect of life in the city, inextricably altering the course of families and commerce, city hall and the arts. Nothing would ever really be the same again.

I arrived in San Francisco the day I turned twenty-one years old. The move north from my hometown on the Monterey Peninsula was symbolic as it was *realpolitik*, for I had long sensed myself as a card-carrying member of the Stonewall Generation. My father was a plumber, and the morning I departed he waved goodbye with a mix of unspoken knowing and curious approval.

My tracks of discovery throughout the city were vertiginous, but somehow I kept a steady balance: there was just too much to see and do. I especially liked the theater (having once been a community theater ham myself), which was richly represented all over the city. Some would say that by the mid-1970s the best theater was the city itself, its streets densely populated by fabulously talented people from all over the world. It was out of this heady brew that the grandest queer troupe ever known was born: the Angels of Light.

It would be hard to pinpoint when I first came to experience their unique, effervescent, life-affirming magic, but I will never forget the impact it had on me. The morning I awoke after seeing one of their productions for the first time, I knew something inside me had been touched and mirrored as never before. It was as if a dream I had forever been dreaming was now out of my head and placed directly in my hands. The private made public became a palpable tool; all the more so when it was made real through the love of art—and the art of love, both of which the Angels blazingly embellished.

Not long after seeing that first show, I came to know several members of the troupe, a signal honor for me, and one of them told me: "The Angels of Light are an expression that represents an inward vision for us. It means a positiveness, an idea of sharing the things that are important in uplifting people." And uplift they did.

As is always the case with the abundantly gifted and under-appreciated, there are psychic wounds—those deep pains of the heart that insist on betraying the Self and those around it. Just because everyone exuded the fresh joy of newfound freedom did not mean we were exempt from the sorrows and ashes of personal pain. What the Angels did supremely well was to shine beacons into those dark, burned-out places. It was a courageous act of illumination that simultaneously personified the glorious present moment as well as offering a guiding light to the next day. In essence, their art insisted said: Awake and listen, be real about yourself but never too serious to make crazy love and profane laughter.

I can think of no other theater company that has had such an intimate relationship with its audience. This is no joke, as some readers of the story to follow might think after digesting tale after tale of deception, violence, and sexual escapade without boundaries. What I mean is that while there was a "fourth wall," as there is on any stage, here it was permeable and fluid, always adjusting and accommodating the Angels' own particular dreams and wishes. The Angels of Light were truly a "living theater," like that other famous troupe of the day.

The community always greeted the announcement of a new production by the Angels with much glee and anticipation. Sometimes the news came via chat at a party, other times a poster spotted on the wall of a laundromat or a signpost; this was immediately followed by the question of what to wear. Nobody in the know would imagine showing up at an Angels show without some hint of fashion. Glittery knee socks and half-breeches made from old tweed slacks, topped off with a dash of mascara, was my statement of choice. Others brought armloads of flowers, some appeared in high queer drag—a time-hopping, around-the-world pastiche of objects found and made, genders molded and merged, to become its own indescribable, indelible nation-state of selfhood. At the Angel's performances, the theater was not only on the stage, but also in the audience.

Adrian Brooks captures the light that shined both ways superbly well in these pages. After all, he was at the very center of the Angels' vortex for many years as the group's chief playwright-in-residence and one of its most visible stars. Adrian brought a considerable amount of craft and discipline to their enterprises, but also a determined sense of humor big enough to skew any obstacle. The pomposity of power and the conceits of the elite were two of his favorite targets. And when not writing the characters, he played them well too—it takes a certain roguish élan to portray a latter-day Marie Antoinette with a towering headdress featuring a toilet bowl.

Aside from the charm of those early performances, what I have most admired in Adrian over many years of sustained friendship is his dedication to issues of social action and justice. He was then, and remains today, a consummate teller of truths.

In telling his story of the Angels of Light, Adrian does not stint from reflecting on some of the darkness that went hand in glove with all that creativity and commitment. "Once upon a time" does not always mean a happy ending, as any reader of fairy tales will tell you. But in this case, I am going to collude with the myths that do impart joy, discovery, and wonder, the enduring qualities that the Angels of Light brought to me, and on extremely personal terms.

As a longtime chronicler of the gay movement—I was a writer and senior editor at *The Advocate* for twenty years, as well as the author of five books on gay history and culture—I've witnessed many remarkable things. Few were as original, soulful, or thrilling to behold as the Angels of Light. They were the tribal theater of my people and me. I can never forget, and will forever be in debt to, what I can unequivocally say is one of the finest, if not shiniest, theatrical troupes of this or any age.

—Mark Thompson
Los Angeles, 2007

Chapter 1

June 11, 1975
San Francisco

Backstage at the Opera House, footlights spread a blue wash on a scrim hanging behind enormous velvet curtains. It was eight p.m. Out front, our audience was roaring. Whooping and hollering were common at Angels of Light shows, but this verged on pandemonium. Even so, I was preoccupied.

Behind me stood a palace, *my palace*. The glittery silver residence faced slums on the other side of the stage. The contrast between the rococo and penury couldn't have been more explicit. Off in the wings, I could see props and huge masks: a carriage with prancing horses, plague monsters, a brilliant red starfish, giant rats, and icebergs.

I was alone. The rest of the cast was getting into costume or smoking grass outside. Their absence meant I would have the stage all to myself. An aquamarine haze resembling fountain mist rose from a prompter's box to the netherworld of a proscenium forty feet above my head. I held a white ostrich feather in glittering talons; the billowing plume wafted across my field of vision.

Was this my life? Yes. But I hadn't stumbled upon this circus by accident, nor were its elements unrelated to my childhood. In fact, they ran parallel and in tandem because my past had prepared me for what was about to happen. Growing up in a surreal household where works by world famous artists occupied every single wall and tabletop (and even a few ceilings), I was more than familiar with visual overkill. I was equally intimate with personal flaunting. Exhibitionism both paralleled and underscored our broody residence, with its medieval battleaxes in the high stone entrance hall and two giant black dragon andirons flanking the front door.

Inside, oblivious to his rank pits, my pungent, control freak father, who eschewed underarm deodorant as unmanly, sat around pontificating barechested and in lederhosen while unable to maintain eye contact when talking with anyone for more than a few seconds, my disarmingly chatty and strategically charming Diva Mother swanned around transfixed to the point of being stoned on the staggering booty that represented her true proof positive of existence. "We must be insane to own objects of such importance," she'd cluck, thereby drawing even more attention to the treasures.

Sometimes she would hint that reordering their priorities or getting rid of the fabulous things entirely was something they might contemplate seriously. But that was just a tease. All was for conspicuous display, such as their decision that, henceforth, we'd converse only in French at dinner—a plan that floated no longer than the *Titanic* when we children cautiously restrained ourselves to *Passez-moi le beurre, s'il vous plaît*, in addition to the requisite lessons, instructions, reading lists, and drills. But not to worry. In due course, we'd be amply "rewarded" for letting them define and influence if not control our futures and "participate actively" in the shaping of such offspring that our loins might yield up.

Control Freak Father was too busy to squander time, so he trained himself to shit once a week, on Sunday from one to two o'clock. So as not to waste this time either, he used it to manage the family stock portfolios. Diva Mother was too preoccupied ever to bother coming up to kiss us goodnight, but being left alone was actually a relief. Still, whenever our parents got their "fix" and felt appeased from whatever drove them to wrest or seize still more from the paltry and mundane world, my siblings and I might find a respite from their unpredictable moods. In such interludes, all might be warm good fellowship, with our brindle bulldog providing comic relief. But there was never any safe harbor. No one was allowed to intervene in our parents' multi-dimensional forced march of their children that passed for an altruistic upbringing. *No one*. The message was clear: our task in life was to bow to their agenda, and then get out in the world and dazzle.

Well, I sure was "out" and certainly had found a way to dazzle! But it wasn't exactly what my parents had had in mind though—who knows—maybe it was...?

From the time I was four or five years old, my mother drew me into her cozy confidences, solicited my advice on what to wear, bought me the dolls I wanted, and certainly didn't mind if I paraded around in drag. Neither did my father, apparently. So wearing flip-flops and half-slips and my mother's necklaces was just my normal reality. But one afternoon when I was seven or eight, I wandered outside, where my father castigated me in a belittling and contemptuous tone for...? Shamed for the first time that I recall, horrified and somehow sensing that I was unlovable and not understanding why, I rushed into the now suddenly darker, colder, more forbidding house. *How was I so bad? I was only being myself.*

I retreated. It was safer to play alone with little model horses and fashion tiny dolls, my companions in self-hypnotizing tales of palace intrigue, monasteries, or frontiers of my mind, where stallions galloped forever unbroken through the woods at our funky summer cottage or in the garden behind the big ivy-covered house. I had no friends. I realized I was alien and felt that no one my age could fathom my need for beauty, a hunger so intense that it superseded my parents' and teachers' admonitions to view my fellow students at school as my competitors in Life, and to "apply yourself, study hard, and get ahead."

Get ahead? Of what? Of whom? I didn't want to get *ahead*. Nor, despite parental admonitions, did I want to compete. Competitiveness seemed like killing to me; I didn't want to beat "opponents" any more than I wanted to get "ahead." I wanted to slide backwards, slip deeper into spellbinding allure that might bear out the veracity and worth of my sacred dream state, the only place I truly felt safe. I never looked for, or expected, allies. It was enough to feel warmed by a sense of serenity when conducting private rituals, like building tiny ashrams out of hydrangea twigs for two Chinese ivory figures that my grandfather gave me.

The silence during those times of solemn ceremony was an internal meditation. When, years later, there were hippies—people who looked as if they might have come true when I'd never imagined it was even possible *not* to be alone—I grasped for union. They were like me, people who had never received unconditional love and though I was accepted by them, it was not enough to assuage a child who'd never conceded loss but who had learned to pray in his own strange ways.

Still, God is a God of mercy. I'd managed to extricate myself from my toxic family, and had gone searching for something magical, even though I didn't know what it was, flashing through extreme scene after extreme scene until, ultimately, I found others who were also intoxicated by dress-up games before the mirror and the delirious refuge of "Let's pretend." None of us had grown up or been compromised; rather, we'd created safe zones beyond the reach of our controlling elders. This was the secret society and underground world of the Angels of Light, our theater group that might best be described as a fusion of Gilbert & Sullivan, Philadelphia's Mummer's Parade, the Cirque de Soleil, and Bertolt Brecht.

From inception in 1972, the Angels were the most outrageous theater group in San Francisco, a gutsy flamboyant troupe most notable for gender-bending drag queens. But in reality, we were a collective federation of all sorts of people—straight, bi, gay, undefined—living on welfare, mainly (although not myself), and pooling our money to stage extravaganzas. Moreover, most of the Angels (again: *not* myself) had been declared certifiable, yup, *legally insane*, so we were *literally* a group of social castoffs and misfits, pushing artistic and political extremism to the limit, and right over the edge.

Unlike Manhattan, where wannabes lined up outside Studio 54, hoping to be permitted inside to be part of a floorshow with the other "beautiful people" who were stoned out of their gourds, San Francisco was manifesting gay liberation in an entirely different way. Ours was no mere avant-garde; avant-garde implies social connectedness or possible future integration, like Andy Warhol's scene in New York. We were Underground, in a wholly different and distinct secret society that had not been tied to, absorbed, or even glimpsed by the mainstream. Yet this Beggar's Opera was the thrilling figurehead of a revolution advancing on artistic, political, and sexual fronts. Most activists worked from inside the system; we were the electric, provocative outsiders on a cutting edge so far out that, even in San Francisco, the planetary capital of gay lib, we set the pace: the fastest lane of the fastest lane. And now we were about to prove it, hands down.

As I stood alone backstage, I looked down and couldn't help laughing quietly.

My ball gown was pale blue lace and pink satin spangled with silver stars and violet velvet bows. Birdcage-like contraptions thrust my skirt to a horizontal width of six feet. My neck was sheathed in rhinestones, a virtual pillar of "diamonds." Amethyst drops dangled from my bodice and, as the Countess Flushette, I sported a toilet on my head.

That's right, *a toilet* rose from a grey wig festooned with tiny pink roses. From the bowl, a massive forearm thrust triumphantly upwards, its defiant fist clutching a pink ostrich feather. The headgear was three-and-a-half feet tall. I stand six-two. Thus, from my platform shoes to the tip of my imperial plume, I was six feet wide and ten feet tall.

How had a horrendously confused fellow achieved this shining moment just nine years after graduating from prep school? As a youngster, I'd been so lonely and felt so alienated that I used to call operators of hotels in foreign countries and ask to speak with their guest, "Adrian Brooks," requiring them to page me. Naturally, I was never there to answer, but for an intoxicating moment, I could imagine my name being echoed in a foreign accent in distant lands, projecting myself into the lobbies of The Ritz, the Georges V, or the Danieli. I laughed again, contemplating what we were about to unleash on our unsuspecting audience. *Well,* I told myself, *sometimes dreams really do come true.... Or is this karma?*

"Adrian! Adrian!" Someone was gesturing urgently from one side of the stage. It was Bo Arenberg. The strapping, garrulous blond in black livery and I were roommates. As I moved toward him, I grew more conscious of the thunderous hollering on the far side of the immense curtains. "Have you seen the audience?" he cried. "Look!"

Following his cue without crashing my headdress into the wall, I managed to peek out from the backstage peephole. For an instant, I couldn't really believe what I was seeing. Startled, I drew back and met Bo's excited eyes before leaning forward for another look.

Something has gone horribly, horribly wrong, I thought. *This is way, way more than we bargained for!* I glanced at Bo and tried to grin but my knees suddenly felt weak.

Herbst Auditorium was a neo-classical theater. Immense crystal chandeliers were suspended from the ceiling painted with cherubs and angels. Tapestries and murals adorned the walls. The seats of the orchestra pit and gilded balcony were maroon velvet. And those 1,100 seats were packed. Packed. Despite the throng, hundreds more crammed the aisles, trying to find a seat before the house lights blinked and dimmed.

In its entire history San Francisco had never seen such a crazy scene. Ever.

Naturally, the adoring gay community was out in full force. But all manner of others were also present, people who'd never—*ever*—crossed the boundary from normal social daylight into the subterranean zone of the sexual underground. Further complicating this surreal situation, no one group outnumbered any others. This meant that none of the contending delegations could stake a believable claim to being an indignant majority.

Mavens in black dresses and pearls sat beside bearded drag queens in black dresses and pearls. A bald man draped in a bright green sari sat next to a Marine colonel in full uniform, family in tow. Glittering transvestites sized up representatives from the Lions Club. Masons and Elks stared as black men in sequin dresses paraded in. Suburban station wagon families scanned bull-dykes in plaid shirts. Stoned-out hippies down from Humboldt and Mendocino Counties offered joints to veterans of World War I, some of whom had tottered in on canes, sporting medals won at the Marne. Studs in leather caps and straps, their bare buns hanging out of chaps, gazed quizzically at white-haired old ladies in flowery summer dresses and sneakers. They knit as cowboys strutted past Korean War vets and hairy gay "bears"; the pom-poms on Mexican sombreros bounced ever so gaily as a man giggled beside a tweedy, pipe-smoking type. His wife wore sensible shoes and tortoise shell barrettes; they huddled over the program to be sure they were in the right place as Latino queens and Chinese businessmen maneuvered for a spare seat next to stodgy museum types and blond androgynes in satin slips—hair braided with flowers and ribbons—beefy truck drivers and grand dames in fur stoles, diamond brooches, and chic hats with delicate veils. Octogenarians wheeled in by nurses clutched lap blankets, grinning in toothless delight, eyes bugging out of their heads. Every imaginable denizen of the Bay Area was out in full force and, by contrast, they were in drag, no matter how they were dressed. And no one knew how to construe or respond to the outrageous scene, or how to react to the fact that, hanging overhead like a pungent shroud, there was a thick haze of marijuana smoke.

How the fuck had this happened?

Chapter 2

September 1973
Inverness, California

The parking lot beside the red-shingled Victorian store was crowded with 200 people. Behind us, a forest of bay laurel rose to the Inverness ridge, 1,200 feet above sea level. Here, one could look down the peninsula—the largest wilderness area near a major city in the country—and see San Francisco, thirty-eight miles away. Facing right, the national preserve of deserted beaches, dairy farms, oyster coves, and rolling hills reached Bodega, sixteen miles north. Here, Tomales Bay met the Pacific Ocean.

A warm late afternoon wind gusted off the bay and high clouds scudded across the sky, but no one paid much mind. Everyone in our New England-like village was too busy having fun at a gallery opening. The artist having his first one-man show was Alex Bratenahl, the twenty-eight-year-old son of long-time summer residents, Alec and Roberta. Alec was a nuclear physicist once nominated for the Nobel Prize; Roberta was a political activist, ecologist, and member of the Pasadena City Council. Alex's sisters Laura and Millie were dazzling and radical. From the moment of my arrival in town a few years earlier, the whole family had adopted me.

Alex resembled a Marlboro cowboy with a twist: he was startlingly effeminate, brazen, and hilarious. ("You know how to separate the men from the boys in San Francisco?" he'd crow. "With a crowbar!")

But he was also drug-addled, soulful, and wounded, whipping up his demons and social outrage into a frappé of walking, talking psychodrama worthy of any Warhol "superstar." Unlike Warhol, however, Alex was generous and gutsy, a soul brother, art comrade, and friend. Thanks to him, I'd started to fathom an exploding gay consciousness, distanced from the east coast art world absolutism, and stumbled upon a new and exhilarating way to regard life: an approach that integrated humor with politics, and work with love and pleasure. Blissed-out Northern California had seduced yet another willing convert.

I was attending the show as more than a member of our tribe, though. I was covering it for *Artweek*, a journal for which I'd volunteered to write. With my art world credentials and writing skills, I could knock out formal criticism, and the editor, Cecile McCann, had allowed me to review Alex's show.

Inside the gallery, ten big canvases seemed to leap off the walls: candy-colored chaos populated by giddy idiot-victims crashing into plastic suburbia. The effect was hilarious and nightmarish. But how could I have imagined that, in Alex's wild carnivals and in his enthusiasm for a theater group called the Cockettes—who shafted social norms with their hysterical, over-the-top camp shows—my own future was beckoning?

Outside the gallery, young parents held children on their shoulders as they danced to salsa music. Little old ladies in sensible shoes joshed with hippy carpenters in faded overalls and plaid shirts. Leaning against an old truck, Andrew Romanov, the lookalike great nephew of Tsar Nicholas II raised in Windsor Great Park as a neighbor of the Queen, communed easily with John Francis. John was a tall, radiant black ecologist with flashing eyes who'd given up talking and who wrote on a pad of paper to communicate, if words were necessary. As a personal ecological statement, he'd also given up riding in cars and, for years, walked everywhere he went, no matter how far.

A rising breeze ruffled flowers strewn on the sun-dappled buffet table. Dogs angled for handouts from musicians, writers, university professors, and gay men in faded jeans and cowboy boots. In short, West Marin County had gathered to celebrate.

Like many artists with the jitters, Alex was spooked, so I spent the day at his side. Even so, I couldn't help noticing some unusual strangers. Though they were from the city, they might as well have lived on Mars. Most were men wearing bright clothes, plastic sandals, heavy eye makeup, jewelry, feathers, glitter, and nostril rings. Straight or gay—and I couldn't tell which, any more than I could imagine that my future had just rolled into town—they were certainly different. One particularly sexy man who looked like a model for Brooks Brothers but was decked out in a blue and white polka dot dress, a Malibu boa, and a beret, was dancing with Victoria Lowe.

Victoria was a ravishing nymph in a tight blue skirt and pink and black horizontally striped leggings. We'd met in New York when she was twelve; her mother, Jillen Lowe, had a fine art gallery in SoHo. Now we were all in California, where Victoria was bursting into voluptuous womanhood with the nuclear fission of a brunette Marilyn.

At some point during the afternoon, as guests enjoyed the oysters and salmon and white wine and marijuana (and probably a few toots of coke in the loo), Victoria took me aside to confide that the strangers belonged to a free theater group. "The Angels of Light," she smiled, adding knowingly, "and they're gay. Well, *most* of them.... Or bi...."

I made a mental note to check them out. I'd already decided to move to the city to fulfill three goals: to work on my poetry and establish myself on the literary scene; to find a way to contribute to the world in a politically constructive way through art; and finally, to find a soul mate.

In 1974, the poetry scene and gay lib were parts of a multi-pronged revolution changing the country in ways very different from preceding decades. The civil rights crusade of the 1950s originated in black churches under the oversight of preachers. The locus of the radical 60s began with the free speech movement in Berkeley in 1963 but intensified after the Kennedy assassination and Johnson's subsequent escalation of the war in Vietnam, when anti-war protests that first attracted alienated (white) college students became a common cause and national majority. By 1968, aggravated by the draft, radicals made alliances with increasingly militant black power advocates. As a result, disparate elements of the resistance came together with a power that Dylan had predicted when he'd warned, "The times, they are a changin'."

San Francisco, luminous and iconoclastic, was the capital of this revolutionary consciousness. Tens of thousands of flower children and seekers like myself streamed toward this tolerant oasis, yearning to cleanse old wounds and be reborn.

Dylan couldn't have been more prescient. As the 1970s dawned, advocates of women's rights, gay rights, the ecology, and the human potential movement saw these causes as true to the spirit of 1776. While Nixon self-destructed, we demanded an end to the McCarthy-style anti-"egghead"/arty/ "pinko" mentality. Out and-proud gay people now stepped up to oppose the military-industrial complex and Big Oil driving national policy at the expense of the environment and the founding principles of our country.

If the 60s had been about protest, confrontation, alienation, and collectivism, the 70s were about inclusion, integration, and introspection. In effect, the groundbreaking 60s set the stage for a fundamental re-examination of national priorities in the 70s. And this was *huge*.

I WAS BORN ON October 2, 1947. October 2nd is auspicious, being the same date that Gandhi and Groucho Marx entered the world. Think about that: Gandhi, Groucho, and me!

As a Quaker, I was raised to make my own decisions about the nature of God and Christ. Careful instruction guides Quaker children to heed "the Inner Light"—that which makes us feel personally/dynamically connected to God—and remain faithful to it. But like the other children, I was bored stiff during hour-long meditations on Sunday.

Quaker meetinghouses are traditionally Spartan, but ours—one of the oldest in the country, built in 1695—boasted a picture on its otherwise bare walls. The engraving records a true event when Indians on the warpath broke into a Meeting for Worship. Instead of reacting, the Quakers continued meditating; the warriors sat down, joined in, and eventually went on their way in peace.

I was hugely impressed by this story and by the idea that conscious intention might actually shape (worldly) events. Somehow, somewhere, could even *I* find a way to help bring harmony to the world? If that sounds like a stretch, let me explain: in the 1950s, little Quakers were taught to revere Christ, Gandhi, and Martin Luther King. From 1956, when Rosa Parks refused to budge from a "whites only" section of a public bus, Dr King was extolled as often as Christ and Gandhi, whose writings Dr King studied. King was also influenced by Quakerism, and vice versa.

I was too young to fathom nonviolence, but I *did* understand that Gandhi had stopped eating to make people pay attention. From this I learned that everyone has the power to change the world. Although my own world was scary and overwhelming, from an early age I wanted to find a cause that was so meaningful I'd be willing to starve myself for it.

However noble my ideals, in adolescence I was the artistic reject whose glasses got knocked off and twisted out of shape by bullies; I was the "loser" no one wanted to know (something so shaming I'd never admit it to anyone, certainly not my family). But I admit that I had always been unusual. Taken to Manhattan at the age of three or four to see the Christmas lights on Fifth Avenue, I summed up my experience, saying, "New York is red." About the same time, I was on a trolley with my grandmother when I noticed a hideous crone whom everyone was trying to ignore. I slipped away from my grandmother to approach her. "You are very ugly on the outside," I told her. "But inside, you are very beautiful."

Yes. Unusual.

My inner experience was one thing. But I failed to live up to it as I got older, a failure I can only explain as being that of a frightened, isolated kid. Still, a higher awareness existed, despite my parents telling us, "The real game in life is to decide what you want, cut your losses, and get as far as you can get without unnecessary baggage."

I didn't believe that. Nor did I believe my mother when, without contradiction from my father, she said, "Women are completely untrustworthy cats. They pretend to be sweet, but they're really in competition with each other to get a man and keep him." No, no.... Something was wrong here.

But how was I supposed to know it was? When he was nine or ten, my older brother was stunned to learn that "Squabbie," three years younger than me, was in fact our brother. "I thought he just lived here!" my older brother said. We considered this funny. And until Squabbie was six, he thought our (black) maid was his mother. He called Josephine "Mommy" and our mother by her Christian name. But why not? He knew that Josephine loved him. She played with him and took him home while he considered the white lady in the big house a stranger. Then he found out the truth. *Not funny.* And me? It was just fine to parade around in drag until, suddenly, I was attacked for it. It was all so confusing. But none of us were supposed to trust outsiders. Or look to them for help.

"Don't you ever do that again!" my mother scolded one spring after I took cuticle scissors to some crocuses in a neighbor's yard and presented her with a bouquet. "Never give people an excuse to talk about this family because we're better than they are and they resent it and if you let them know anything, they'll use it against you!"

Gee, I'd thought I was being nice, even if I was so young I'd snipped off the blossoms without including even an inch of stem. Wrong, wrong, wrong. Still, I didn't believe we were better. Or that women were "cats." Or that telling the truth would make people hurt me. And while I relied on my parents for survival and looked to them for as much love as I could find, my chief memory of childhood was of insisting, as I did, again and again, "You won't beat me and won't break me. Some way, I'll get away from you. And when I do, I won't ever come back."

What gave me the determination to shuck the grass-stained flannels of my past and end up onstage with a toilet on my head? Many years later and thousands of miles from home, I had what was the only honest conversation I was ever to have with my mother, a talk in which she finally came right out and spilled the beans: "All children steal and lie and you were no different, no better or worse. But somehow—don't ask me how—you saw right through adult games and always saw and spoke the truth. But our lives are built on so many lies it was too dangerous for us to have a child like you. Even if your needs were legitimate, you represented a risk we couldn't afford. If that meant telling you that you were sick, or cutting you off emotionally, that was a price we were prepared to pay."

Well, there it was. At last. Validation of sorts, though still too late for a little boy who had struggled to survive amidst a bewildering set of demands. Not only the need to be a Warrior and win the Great Battle of Life and prove myself to the Opposition, but to stand by silently, without complaint, while my parents posed and preened.

"Those aren't the ones I wanted," my mother sighed when my father came up to our summer cottage with some shoes; she'd asked him to bring her low-heeled black pumps.

He gave her a look. "Low-heeled black pumps. Yup. I went into your closet and counted one hundred and five pairs of low-heeled black pumps." Mother: Imelda.

Superficially, the dearth of healthy nurturing was lost in the sauce of great familial fortune; far from Quakerly reserve, our house was an explosion of treasures from all over the world, some with mysterious origins, such as the stone sculpture from India that appeared in a wooden crate bearing a custom's declaration for "grass mats and sandals."

The mind reels, even today. Last week, a superb Rothko owned by David Rockefeller was auctioned by Sotheby's for $72 million. *We* (funny, it was always "we" or "us" or "our," when what was really meant was "I" or "me" or "mine") had a superb Rothko. Last year, a great David Smith *Cubi* was auctioned for $22 million. *We* had a great one from the same series, in addition to thirty or forty other important art objects by Picasso, Miro, Leger, Calder, etc. On the basis of today's prices, my parents' full collection might be worth $75 million, $100 million, $200 million, who knows? But beyond a certain point, the numbers are irrelevant because the floorshow was just an adjunct to establishing a dynasty. Children were of no "interest," our value lay in who we might become. Therefore, in their obsessive-compulsive rush to churn out "winners," childhood itself was snatched away in their mania for us to grow up and prove useful.

"Dad won't even play catch with me," sighed Squabbie one day. Of course not. He was inside, busy disparaging those who failed to meet his exacting standards, particularly those who let emotional feelings or religion guide their lives. Frustrated, we children had to devise ways to get attention.

I came up with a good one: setting our summer cottage on fire, thus becoming the hero who discovered a blaze that was extinguished quickly and blamed on "spontaneous combustion." Another time, another sibling set our garage on fire, testing a parental order to stay out of the way for an hour. Fairly big fire this time; fairly substantial damage too. No hero, alas. But I had a good time. While watching our garage burn, a neighbor let me wear her emerald ring. Unfortunately, despite my fervent prayers, Mrs Paxton remembered to ask for it back.

Arson was a risky way to get attention; a more surefire method was via a salacious family ritual: the running dialogue between my parents and us about the objects that had been bequeathed to us "in trust," their relative financial value and, as prices skyrocketed, their relative worth.

Is my Calder worth more than the Leger? Is the Leger worth as much as my Picasso? When you die, can I have that? How much will I get? Are we rich? How rich?

Advantage and privilege was the leitmotif of the ceaseless discourse about what was esteemed or a useful asset. It went beyond objects, however. One day, while evaluating my future social prospects, my father noted that my hair was blond. (I have brown hair.) When I called this to his attention, he said, rather obliquely, "You're blond enough." *Enough for what?*

Somehow, I symbolized something particularly useful to them. My parents creamed over the fact that I was charming, witty, and "beautiful" (yes, that was the term), effusive in their praise and often-times bizarre encouragement. "I'd love to be Adrian's girlfriend and get flowers and poems," my father sighed to my mother one night. I was sixteen. Silence. What the hell did he mean? But getting no reaction, he reiterated his weird remark: *Yes, I'd love to be Adrian's girlfriend....*

I had reason to be wary. The flip side of being extolled and applauded for my grandiose ambitions ("When I grow up, I'll be King of France and live at Versailles. That should do nicely.") was secret torture, like the dark night my father and I were alone in his car. All of a sudden, he came to a stop and beat me up because I couldn't do basic multiplication. Afterward, he bought me a vanilla ice cream cone before driving home. I can still recall rushing inside, thrilled with my treat, never dreaming of telling my mother what he'd just done to me. Would it have mattered? No. But the thing is: I never even thought of it. Was I eight? Nine? Ten? When does one learn multiplication? I have no idea. Brutality, bribes for silence. Bribes for silence, brutality. Which came first? To repeat: I have no idea.

Blatant physical abuse was rare in my case (*although how often does it have to happen to mar a child for life?*). No, God knows, I didn't suffer the worst.

My gentle, gawky older brother was so terrified of my parents he gulped air constantly and farted a lot. During the eighth grade, which he was failing, a teacher suggested that he try a technical vocation rather than aim for college. My parents went ballistic and bullied, browbeat, and tortured him until he broke through or broke down. He started succeeding brilliantly at school but, in what he himself terms "protective mimicry," he surrendered his individualism. To attain immunity from savage persecution, he appeared to become a carbon copy of our father, albeit far kinder; he learned to say the right words, make the same moves, read the same books, admire the same art. As a result, his gulag not only ended, it was as if it had never happened at all; as if in some psychic Stalinist revisionism, he erased all conscious memory of his first fourteen years, including being "pushed." (That's what they called it afterward: *pushed.*) To this day he doesn't remember. I believe that if he could recollect what happened—what they did to him—he'd die. Or kill. No. Whatever others endured, he got it far, far worse. But he is happy; and remembers nothing ... nothing.

But I remember. Forty years would pass before I understood how I'd been damaged—depression, post-traumatic stress disorder, and child sexual abuse accommodation syndrome, to name three ways. While I wasn't actively molested sexually, it's now accepted that being denied safe boundaries and being forced to accommodate such warping, frightening demands causes the same clinical harm to children as outright sexual abuse. Even so, something inside me, something unknown, defiant, stubborn, desperate, willful, proud, and fantastical, made me resist.

I doubt that my defiance stemmed only from seeing my older brother attacked until he caved in. I'm sure part of my mysterious motivation was *my gay thing.* Years before it surfaced, and as conflicted as I was, being gay saved me. How could I have imagined that in my pain and despair at being an outcast, a target of bullies, I possessed a golden thread that would lead me through my darkness and allow me to achieve an authentic identity? Happiness and independence had never been presented as acceptable goals.

Like many 1950s parents, mine appeared to respect high ideals, so they sent us mixed signals: asserting that men were inherently superior to women, and that whites were more intelligent but not "better" than Negroes. They called gay men "fairies" while saying everyone deserves tolerance and, as proof thereof, gave me an anti-Catholic screed—*American Freedom and Catholic Power*—a book of rabid bigotry. In all the years of my youth, I saw only one black person at our dinner table.

But *I* was clear. At eight, I blithely informed classmates at Friends Central School that, when I grew up, I wanted to be a peacock. Bad me. The proverbial shit hit the puritanical fan and I was thrown out on my neurotic ass. So off went Adrian to scary public schools.

When I went back to prep school after a few years, the minister at Episcopal Academy told us a fascinating story. In the mid-60s, Margot Fonteyn was the greatest ballerina in the world. When she and the young Nureyev were appearing in *Swan Lake*, Reverend Trimble was invited to a dance studio to meet her. At eight in the morning, there she was, doing her stretches, alone. When she took a break, the reverend was introduced to her, whereupon he asked, "You're a prima ballerina. Why are you doing this?" She said, "If I don't do stretches in the morning, I'm not free to become a swan at night."

That was the first time I ever considered a connection between discipline and freedom. Even so, I knew people who proved that life can be the fulfillment of private dreams. From boyhood on, I had two great friends, both female, both short, both born in 1895, both autocrats. Dame Margaret Webster

Plass was one of the world's foremost authorities on African art; Dr Stella Kramrisch was the world expert on Indian art.

Margaret—my "Grandmère"—looked like the Queen Mother and behaved like Ernest Hemingway. She held me spellbound when describing her visit to the Oni of Ife, an African king; to reach his palace, she was escorted up the Niger River by torchlight one night in the royal barge, seated on a throne draped with leopard skins.

If lusty, gutsy Grandmère taught me about Life and gave me the love I felt starved of, Stella gave me validation. She also gave me love, but so gently it was as if it came upon me like a quiet snowfall from a woman who was tiny, imperial, and so calm that, when she lived in India, tigers used to jump her garden wall to lie at her feet. Later, when the British jailed Gandhi and needed a transparent policy to ban sympathetic (Western) journalists from interviewing him and further publicizing the cause of Independence, official policy declared: "Gandhi may see no foreign visitors ... except Stella Kramrisch." Such was vice-regal law in the waning days of the Raj; such was the force of an Austrian woman who spoke "just the customary sixteen languages," who saw I was an artist when I was eight and told me about yogis and exalted levels of consciousness.

In 1966, as I neared graduation from Episcopal, my classmates seemed to have settled on traditional goals. But all I knew for certain was that I didn't ever want to be as bored as I'd been growing up in the richest area in the country at that time and the *ne plus ultra* of the east coast establishment. Totally screwed up, as I was, I really believed I could charm my way through life. The fact that I was about to graduate sixty-seventh out of sixty-eight in my class (beaten out by my best friend Linwood Layton Righter III for the last spot) didn't dent my confidence. No. I had a plan.

Having decided that Trinity College might be worthy of my presence after Episcopal, off I went to be interviewed at that first-rate school, positive that I would get accepted. At first blush, this was true: the interviewer was so impressed with me, he took me to meet the Dean of Students who was also so impressed, we then went to meet the Head of Admissions, then the President of the college himself, who thought I was "perfect Trinity material" and, as such, fit to attend a Board of Directors tea being given that same day.

Ushered forward with pride as a shining example of the next class, I was introduced to a little white-haired lady who gave me the once-over before asking for my class rank. I mumbled a reply but that shrewd old bitch saw right through me and would tolerate no evasion.

"Sixty-seven?" she frowned. "Sixty-seven?! How many boys are in your class?"

Trapped, I had to fess up. Then all hell broke loose and I was out on my over-confident ass. I was supposed to be interviewed at Williams College the next day where my parents had pulled strings to guarantee my entry but, by staying for the tea, I'd missed my bus connection to Williamstown, Massachusetts, and thus lost my chance to screw up at that superb institution.

Once out in the world, I didn't know where to go or what to do. In fact, I was stunned to find that a girl I was dating smoked pot. I broke up with her at once. Two months later, I was a stoner. But fucked up as I was, I felt a genuine desire to serve the greater good. Still, no matter how much weed I smoked or how many anti-war rallies I attended, I had no idea who I was when I dropped acid, grew my hair, and became a hippie.

Throughout 1967, I floundered until I ended up at what was, hands down, the most radical educational program on the planet. The Friends World Institute was the whacked-out brainchild of a Quaker educator who believed that experience was the only true way to learn. By his logic, if a school with worthy social concerns wanted to truly educate—and what self-respecting Quaker organization would cop to less lofty ideals?—the best way to do it was to establish "centers" all over the world. To become "agents of social change," FWI students/nomads would rotate from center to center, jump-starting a lifelong commitment to address international social problems by acquiring a firsthand global perspective ... or so went the theory.

There was no academic program. In true Quaker fashion, students were free to devise their own curriculum with guidance from a faculty advisor. Put simply, FWI students could go anywhere and do anything for four years then be awarded a degree.

But with the startling genius unique to Quakerism's historic ability to deny reality, the deranged world-saving idealists who created FWI in 1965 just happened to set up every single center smack dab in the middle of an international drug route: Mexico, Africa, India, Nepal, Amsterdam. It goes without saying that FWI's faculty sternly disapproved of drugs. Also, it goes without saying that the (same) faculty was often found smoking pot with students, when not in bed with us. In short, FWI was a full-blown international circus. How could I resist? I joined up in February 1968.

The first night, the faculty urged my class to get to know each other; we had an orgy. The next day, the faculty urged us to try again; another orgy. So after a *supervised* orientation period, we first-semester students were told to choose a worthy project and go on a field trip. Alone.

The spring of 1968 was a heady time for a country at a crossroads. Martin Luther King had summoned thousands of poor people from the rural South to come to Washington, DC, by bus and camp out *and remain* on the National Mall in a shantytown known as "Resurrection City" until Congress passed legislation to end poverty in America. Forever.

My "worthy project" would be to volunteer for Dr King's Southern Christian Leadership Conference (SCLC). It wasn't because I thought of him as a god. LSD had long since dissolved my sense of boundaries. In 1964, at fifteen, I'd wanted to go to Selma to protest segregation and police brutality; I'd hesitated. But not now.

Like millions of others, I felt Dr King spoke to my soul so profoundly there seemed to be no difference between his proclamations and my conscience. Politics and even race aside, for me, Dr King's message boiled down to making every choice conscious and deliberate. My efforts to pry myself away from family were typically adolescent. Psychologically, I was a neophyte. Sexually, I was unawakened. Even so, the same inner resistance that guided me through childhood—augmented by Margaret and Stella's encouragement and example—assured me now that, somehow, I was on track.

I knew that progress required individual change, even as I headed to Washington to work for Dr King. Over the next few weeks, working as the assistant head of the food committee for Resurrection City at SCLC's headquarters at 14th and U Streets, I spent sixteen hours a day arranging food shipments and blanket deliveries. Still, I did manage to get to the Mall, where 11,000 people were living in lean-tos and shacks made out of tarpaper and salvaged wood. I remember being called "nigger" by black coworkers as a term of affection, something that shocked me. I remember riding the bus without fear to Crittenden Street, in the black northwest section where I had a room, and remember the rising sense of excitement at the office when we heard that Dr King would be coming on April 2nd or 3rd. Sleep deprived or not, the certainty of meeting him was a thrill, though we all felt disappointment upon hearing that his arrival from Memphis had to be delayed by a day. After that, I didn't have time to think. Eighteen hours of work became twenty-four, then thirty-six until I dragged my weary ass home, so tired that my bones felt cold as I got in bed and turned on the radio. That's when I heard the news.

It's a sick joke, I thought, switching to another station with the same news. *I have to get to the office; they may need me.* I got dressed and hurried down to the corner and onto a 14th Street bus. I remember light rain and deserted streets—unusual for early evening—as the bus approached the intersection of 14th and U Streets and stopped exactly in front of the locked and darkened SCLC office building I'd left an hour before.

The sidewalks were packed. Thousands of black people stood silent in the rain. When I stepped out of the bus and people saw me, I knew I was quite possibly the only visible Caucasian for miles. I wasn't afraid, but I knew I had to stand perfectly still.

No one moved. Then a low cry began—the prelude to my own murder, I knew—until someone cried out, "I know that boy, he work for Dr King," and another person called, "Don't hurt that boy. He a soul brother."

Those anonymous voices saved my life; the growl subsided and the crowd parted, allowing me to get to the door where I knocked and was then yanked inside. About ten minutes later, activist Stokley Carmichael appeared to demand that the crowd help him to shut down the stores that had remained open, "in honor of Dr King." At that, people started running, rocks flew, glass shattered, and sirens went off.

Four hundred American cities were in flames. As fires burned around the office, I phoned my parents to see if they were safe in their townhouse. My father was upbeat. "Yes, yes, very sad.... Us? Oh, we're fine, thanks. We're having a dinner party with John and Emma, Doug and Sandra...." I wanted to throw up. I hung up.

"It's like a party," a coworker said as looters hauled televisions from a burning store.

"A sad party," another sobbed.

We remained in the office for a day, windows shuttered, doors locked.

There were dead bodies in the streets. The police were absent; the National Guard was mobilizing 16,000 troops to retake the city when Peter Atwood, another white guy, and I decided to go out. I don't know why Peter did it. I know why I went, though: I felt I could never look another black person in the face if I didn't. When I left my place, I'd deliberately decided to wear a bright red sweater; the perfect target. I remember thinking: *Okay, my race killed Dr King. Well, if you want a white life in exchange, kill me, it's fair.*

Peter and I walked for hours. Looters warned, "You'd better get your ass off the street, honky," but no one shot at us. Back at the office, we slept on the floor. Then, just before dawn, I was awakened by a single file of thirty-five tanks clanking down U Street.

Once the National Guard took up positions around the capitol, rioting stopped. But the next day someone called to warn that if the whites didn't clear out, militants would start shooting at the SCLC building. I remember that when we were forced to evacuate and I returned to FWI, the cherry blossoms were in bloom.

BACK AT SCHOOL, a fellow classmate named Freddie and I were asked to represent FWI at a Quaker conference on improving communication. Here, Freddie was assigned to one group of adults and me to another: twenty people in a graceful library in a gracious old house overlooking gracious lawns that looked perfectly gracious in the mid-April sunshine.

When it was my turn to introduce myself, unlike the others who said where they worked and how many children they had, I said, "I don't know what to say. I was just working for Dr King and now that he's dead and this country is still killing innocent people in Vietnam, I don't know if I'm straight or gay and nothing makes any sense."

You would have thought I'd thrown a hand grenade into that room. A man started shouting, "My father made me play the piano! I hated it and I hated him!" A sobbing woman blurted, "My son looks like you and I sure hope he doesn't turn out like you!" People started fighting with each other and our discussion circle fell apart.

Freddie's too. She'd panicked everyone by hugging a man who was in pain. We bailed. But ten years later, I ran into a man who was there who told me that he and his wife still talked about Freddie and me. I don't think he understood why I found that bizarre.

Just after Bobby Kennedy's assassination in June '68, I went to Syracuse, New York, pursuing a crush on Kelly, a rascal from FWI who came from a wildly destructive family. By September, I was also involved with his younger sister who resembled Joan Baez; their parents were convinced I was a latter-day Dorian Gray sent from hell. The circus continued as I ventured on to FWI in Mexico where, seeing the immense suitcase my mother had bought me at Harrods on top of our VW bus, people asked if we were the traveling freak show that exhibited a corpse that had been dead for twenty years!

I noted it all in a journal I'd begun in late '67. Initially, it was comprised of stoned musings mainly because I was smoking weed all day. If I didn't keep track of where I was, I'd have no idea later on and, even if I didn't know who I was or what I was doing, it still seemed important to know where I'd been, at least. And with whom. If there was an unreal aspect to the FWI lifestyle, it would be the fact that I was more or less infatuated or in a loose love triangle with a brother and sister, and it didn't particularly bother any of us. We were all spirited, reckless, attractive, and, naturally, positive no one would get hurt.

But what we called "The Grand Strategy" got more complicated. My girlfriend said she didn't mind if I was bisexual. I wanted to believe that, but I was edgy. As a youth, I'd seen closeted homosexuals in the suburbs, yet when our family moved into a townhouse, the men I saw who were obviously gay made me feel conflicted: I wanted to be desired but I didn't know how to tell the truth. This went beyond childhood admonitions not to trust others. Or the fact that being in the closet isn't really about sex; it's about hiding, living a lie, and letting the Lie be the actual fact of your life.

Part of my insecurity had to do with my appearance and a lousy body image. Although people told me I should be a fashion model or a movie star, I felt too unusual and fat, regardless of my weight. When it came to gay men, I was freaked out by posturing queens with ghoulish eyes. If I was going to turn out gay, I wanted to be with a proud blond Viking; I wanted an Alpine mountaineer; or I wanted a Tarzan.

In short, *I wanted*. And at twenty-one, I was fixated on what *I* wanted, not what I had to give. Spooked, I concluded that running away far enough or fast enough might put ample distance between me and anything too scary. Or unacceptable. And so I ran.

Still, after attending the muddy soup of Woodstock in '69, I fell in love, *really* in love, for the first time. Peter Sopagee was a great rock singer: a quixotic, introverted bottle blond with a craggy face, a throaty voice, and a gravely Bronx accent. Others saw him only as a dangerously sexy star, but despite his black leather swagger, he was a whimsical soul who loved Tolkien and played Bach fugues on his keyboard until dawn. We adored each other, but were both so driven—he by speed and rough edges, and I by my self-doubt—that we romanced through a glass darkly, unable to decide what to do or how to handle it.

Not surprisingly, my girlfriend and I broke up. She went off to college; I stayed with Peter. But he was shooting speed, and neither of us could stop the ugly merry-go-round. Then, as he was crashing from speed, he said he didn't want to see me anymore; then my ex-girlfriend called. Pregnant. What to do? Peter didn't want me; she did. I didn't want her and she didn't want an abortion. But did anything matter if I couldn't be with Peter? I was fond of her, though, and besides, I was a gentleman and she was a lady. As such, it was unthinkable to get her "in trouble" and leave her in the lurch. Sacrifice was called for.

Immediately after the wedding was announced and both families clicked into gear—hinting at inheritance and all the social lubricant needed in order to put the best possible veneer on an unfolding farce—Peter surfaced from his speed-induced depression. Before I knew it, we were living together again, tripping and laughing, ignoring my engagement and sharing quicksilver dreams as September fell away.

Forty years later, I still remember the wet sycamore leaves, the yellow dabbing the sidewalks in front of the intricate Victorian houses bordering Thornton Park as Peter and I drifted along in a cloud, never thinking that anything or anyone could puncture our dream. Outside our self-induced trance, nothing was real, especially the various social columns describing the details of my pending marriage. "After the wedding, the newlyweds will be honeymooning in London … no, Paris, actually … or was it Kenya?"

I don't know where they got their stories, nor did I care, as those grey October days ticked down to the rainy and misty morning of November 9, 1969. Peter and I were kissing outside up to the last moment before the ceremony; inside, he played the organ during the service. We kissed again later too, during the chaotic reception, outside on the lawn until, realizing that no one had made any plans for what would happen afterward, good friends bundled my bride and me into their bright red jeep and drove us away.

November 15th. In London, my bride decided on an abortion. *Why had we married!?* And though I wanted to return to Peter, I made a private vow to stay with her for up to two years, no more. Why? Because a scandal would hurt her. *Why else?* Basic respect. Probably. I don't know. I just thought I had to.

So off we went to Kenya where there was a FWI center and, from there, on to a safari. A month later, we returned. The FWI center was actually a farm in the mountains. The nights are cold at 9,000 feet; you need a fire. One midnight in late December, Africans with torches and spears surrounded our cottage. Inside, stoned, we thought: it's the Mau Mau rebels. Deciding to meet our fate calmly, we went outside with admirable *sang-froid,* prepared to be chopped to pieces. The warriors brandished their spears as their chief approached us.

"Your king is here."

"What?"

"Your king is here."

"What? Oh, right, right! Thank you. Thank you very much. Merry Christmas!"

"Yes, Bwana, thank you. Yes, Memsahib, thank you. A good day for your king."

And then they started leaping into the air and shaking their spears and drumming.

Another day, a tribal woman appeared. She had traveled to ask us questions. Important ones. They had to be. She'd come far. We were stoned. This would take time. Things do in Africa. We sat down. And waited. And time went by. And the questions came, with the help of an interpreter: "Is it true that people from your country have gone to the moon?"

"Yes, that is true."

Big pause. "Is it true that your people brought back rocks from the moon with them?"

"Yes. That is also true."

Big pause. "Is it true that these rocks are getting bigger and bigger and that there is no way to stop them from getting so big that soon they will come here and squash us?"

Now, we hadn't heard that. How would we know? Anyway, it did seem nicer to tell her that it wasn't true so she went away, relieved. But soon after, we left Kenya abruptly.

The impetus for our departure was an article in *Time* magazine on SoHo, the new hip area in New York where galleries were creating a radical alternative to the stuffy uptown art scene. *This is what I want to do,* I thought excitedly.

Thanks to my background, I scored one of those chic, highly sought-after jobs as the front person for one of the galleries. In truth, it was about as thrilling as watching paint dry. But that changed abruptly one day when a friendly, rotund woman with twinkling blue eyes came in, looked around and asked, "Would you mind taking off your clothes?"

"Excuse me?"

"Would you take off your clothes?"

"Why?"

"For a book of cock prints I'm selling to MOMA."

Her name was Brigid Polk. I liked the idea of my cock being on display in the Museum of Modern Art, so I stripped. She inked up my cock and my nipples and made pressings of them on paper, then asked if I wanted to be in a Warhol movie.

"Andy's going to film upstairs and one of the actors flaked out so...."

"Why not?" I said, thinking, *in for a penny, in for a pound.*

WARHOL WAS NICE to me. Contrary to his reputation as an exploiter and social climber, with me, at least, he was somewhat shy and whimsical and had a gentle sense of humor. Brigid liked to rant that she could never get Andy to give her any money or pay her for anything, but that was just part of their schtick. The fact is they loved each other.

In the film, I played a corpse (nude again) in a scene with Brigid. It was intended to be part of *Trash*, but it got cut and inserted into another entitled *The Further Adventures of Brigid Polk*. I have no idea if it was released; I never cared. I'd been so bored in my job, it was just fun to be in that white cone of light while Andy sat off somewhere in the dark, surrounded by hangers-on as he muttered cues like "do that again," or "lean forward."

After filming, he invited me to the Factory on Union Square. I went over there a few days later. When I got off the elevator and walked past the giant stuffed Harlequin Great Dane, I found Andy in a tiny office. Close up, his skin was weird: rough pink and scraped raw. His hair sat on his head like a mop and his body posture was weak, passive, like he was waiting for something. Andy had trouble holding a gaze as if his eyes were too much pupil and not enough iris. But he was friendly as he showed me his big screening room, and told me I was welcome to stop by any time.

After that, Andy called me, or I'd call him for the most studiously inane conversations I've ever had. What made them fun was his delight in focusing on the most ridiculous, trivial details and staying with them, laughing breathlessly while testing me to see if I'd change the subject, I guess, or just start screaming.

"What kind of socks do you wear...? Oh.... White? That's nice. Always white? Oh. Cotton or wool too? Oh fabulous. Sweat socks ... uh-huh.... What about short ones? Oh, well, how tall? The kind you fold over? Do any have a stripe at the top? Thick stripes? What color? Oh ... blue ... oh, that's great. Are those the sweat socks or the other kind? Do they all match? Oh. Do you ever wear one sock with a stripe and one without...?"

If he thought I'd get sick of it, he was wrong; what I was sick of was sitting behind a front desk eight hours a day. But when I quit, Andy offered me a job at his Factory (sitting behind *another* front desk!).

"I'll pay you seventy-five dollars a week," he told me, knowing that I was married.

"We can't live on that!" I said; my wife and I *just* scraped by on a hundred a week.

"You'd meet a lot of people."

"I already know a lot of people," I countered. "And seventy-five a week is bullshit."

But Brigid gasped. "That's more than that cheapskate ever offered anyone else! He must really want you there."

Probably. I was young, both Gothic and sensuous-looking, sexually ambiguous, a scion of a well-known family. Even with hair to my shoulders and clad in overalls, I conveyed "imperial simplicity," as someone said. Andy was fun and Brigid was a hoot, but most of the people around him were passive hangers-on, looking for Andy to define them and promote them.

By now I knew enough to realize that it was alright to be happy. I'd seen how easy it is to drown in a socially sanctioned lie. If I had to fight my way out, I would. I'd grown up in a psychotic circus. FWI was a circus. My marriage was a circus. Andy's world was a circus. Okay, I like circuses. But there had to be some point. So I turned Andy down.

I wanted out of my marriage too after a year and a half, and my best friends professed to be "surprised." But if they were shocked, I was appalled to see that people who knew I'd only married under duress wanted me to stick it out. Confronting such cushy Babbittry, I was at a crossroads. If I stayed, I could fake my way through a tweedy Pennsylvania rendition of eighteenth-century English country life. *But it would be a lie.*

It wasn't easy to bail. There's a gentle beauty in the winding, leafy lanes and fieldstone houses of the Main Line. It's gracious, colonial, and old-fashioned in the nicest way with its creaky floorboards and beautifully settled landscapes. A part of me never wanted to leave. I loved the grab-a-sweater quality of that existence, the scruffy chic of old money, golden retrievers, and Christmas caroling. Furthermore, the Canadian estate on Lake Muskoka in Ontario, where my wife's family summered, was like a private country: mile after mile of pristine wooded shoreline, dozens of uninhabited, heavily forested islands. It took forty minutes by powerboat to reach Minett, the nearest town, where we did our grocery shopping. The entire way in, everything we passed was family property.

Had I remained married, my children would have learned to water-ski there, pulled along by the gleaming wooden Chris Craft boat, and played tennis on courts overlooking the lake. They would have turned out just fine, being children of a woman who was great with kids (though *I'd* have been a failure as a father). They'd have inherited a fortune from both sides; her grandparents—descendents of Protestant Anglo-Irish gentry—had what the

English call "serious money." (Fifteen years later, when I lived in London and was a guest at a stately home, I couldn't believe my ears when Lady Astor suddenly mentioned them with great respect.) No doubt about it, on the surface, at least, I'd married well and could have had an enviable life.

But who would I have been? I'd have been catting around, meeting tricks on the sly and probably drinking too much. Had I stayed in town-and-gown society, I'd have been a phony and everyone would know it. But it wasn't out of fear of "others" that I bailed; it was out of fear of who I'd be and become if I stayed. I'd redeemed my honor by staying married long enough after that postnuptial abortion—*something we never even discussed afterward.* So it was a simple question of core values when, neither for the first time nor the last, I pulled away from a circle, feeling that I had a life to catch up with.

There was one final farce to play out, however. At the time, I didn't realize the full extent of the symbolism at the precise moment when the sword cut the Gordian Knot.

Months before my departure, my wife and I had agreed to participate in a charity event held at the Institute of Contemporary Art, a freestanding square building located on the University of Pennsylvania campus. It is an independent institution, not bound by U of P regulations. For their fundraiser, the ICA hired outside caterers, offending the union contracted for the school's events. The union called a strike, and other unions joined in. The ensuing demonstration occurred on a lovely evening in early June; Penn students were mobilized and out in force, and police barriers erected for a classic confrontation. And because this was all happening at the prestigious ICA, friends of mine—artists, even former FWI students living in Philadelphia—were part of the crowd that surrounded the building as my wife and I passed through the barricades and went inside. I was in a coat and tie, of course. My suntanned wife wore a long backless black and white print gown. How perfect for a receiving line, greeting friends as they entered, knowing nothing, of course, of my departure.

"Lovely to see you. Now that it's summer, you've got to come out and play tennis."

"We'd love to."

Smile. Shake hands. Smile. Shake hands. This will all be over soon.

"... come out for a swim ..."

"We'll call next week."

Smile. Shake hands. Smile. You will never have to do this again as long as you live.

Demonstrators outside; the ruling class inside. Politics and money and art. The collapse of a fraudulent marriage, the beginning of a quest; the final moment before the ice breaks over a subterranean world. Four years later, all this would appear in a play I'd write for a San Francisco museum. But here, for the last time, I was nodding and bullshitting and just about to stop dying because, the next day, my best friend Linwood (whom I hoped my soon-to-be ex-wife would now get involved with) drove me out to a turnpike, where I held out a thumb and hopped into the first car that stopped. *I was free!*

California had beckoned. Again. I'd visited a friend in late 1967. A vivid memory of the Haight-Ashbury in its glorious heyday had remained with me. Now, at his invitation, I hitched west to spend the summer of 1971 sharing his cabin in the woods in Inverness. And once having tasted the glories of Marin County's wide, unpopulated beaches, soft fogs, avocados, funky trucks, and shaggy-headed youths of both sexes, suntanned and mellow, there was no going back for long.

Still, in September, I returned to work at a second gallery in SoHo, Paley and Lowe, before bailing in favor of going to India to become a Montessori teacher through the FWI program. But just after arriving in India, I was stricken with hepatitis. After six weeks in bed, it was too late to start Montessori training, so I traveled to Nepal and lived in a thatched mud hut in Swayambhu, a mile outside Katmandu and just below a Buddhist temple built in 250 BC. Here, hippies debated such burning issues as which cosmic spot they should select to regroup to usher in the year 2000 (this in 1972!) while clustering in dark little cafés to devour truly excellent lemon meringue pies.

After being in hospital, my experience of life was never the same: instead of feeling I was trying to control it, I felt I was flowing with it. California, golden and misty, was the irresistible gate through which I would pass. This time, there would be no turning back.

On October 2, 1972, I turned twenty-five. Basking in the sun outside a small chai shop, I realized that I'd spent the past twelve months in rain: all fall and winter in New York, a rainy April in California followed by monsoons in India, and a rainy Nepalese September. That day I met the Queen of the Hippie

Underground, Petra Vogt, a Valkerie who'd been a star of the Living Theater. Now attended by a surrealist photographer and poet-hopeful, Ira Cohen, Petra and I were soul mates, a tricky thing because the Nebuchadnezzar-like Ira was an attention hog. Still, when I shared a poem with them, he praised it and asked if I knew Gerard Malanga. "He's a poet, Warhol's right-hand man. He'd like your stuff."

In November, I flew to California. Back in Inverness, on March 6, 1973, I jotted the following in my journal, dedicating it to Linwood:

I, a poet, live in a poem.
Jet at my throat, amethyst and amber
I wait for ships to return
Fire on the deck pushing the sails home.

In a place with an ancient name
I imagine death a passage to the other side.
Wearing black, ivory and shell
I melt with rain, the only skies I've known.

This is my homage to you.
Take it from light into dark.

Chapter 3

It was hard to believe that I'd unearthed my true calling, but so many people in Inverness encouraged me, I kept working until summer. I was excited by my discovery, but restless, too, and in need of confirmation. Then an old friend from Pennsylvania appeared. He was heading east and asked if I wanted to go. Needing change or a cosmic sign, I jumped into his bright yellow jeep and we set off. Once in Boston, I moved in with Kelly, my now ex-lover/ex-brother-in-law. We'd remained on perfectly friendly terms, as had my ex-wife and I. But after saying goodbye to my friend who continued south to Philadelphia without me, I was puzzled as to why I'd bothered crossing the continent.

A week later, I went to see a gay Western movie, *Zachariah*, playing at a dinky theater in Harvard Yard. The lobby was crowded for the midnight show when a Husky nudged a handsome man who filled a paper cup at a fountain. As the dog drank thirstily, I approached. "Is this dog yours?" I asked.

"No," he said, "but he follows me everywhere I go." He paused. "My name is Gerard."

And suddenly, even though I'd never seen his picture, I knew, I just knew. "Gerard *Malanga*?" I asked, remembering the name Ira had mentioned. He nodded and I laughed.

The swashbuckling poet wore long scarves and carried his manuscripts in a beat-up leather post office bag. Of course, I was attracted to him, but after the movie we went separate ways. Within a day or so, we met again. When I read him my poems, he praised them to the skies and volunteered to serve as my mentor. At first I was confused. Did he want to...? No. He was in a relationship. But if I sent him my poetry he'd give me critiques. Affirmed and moved, I returned to Inverness and began sending off parcels.

Years later, I saw a self-serving aspect of Gerard. Being a hothead, I was too critical of him, which became a mistake I regret because, during that critical year, no one could have been more generous. Thanks to his guidance, I began to grasp not only my own voice but the lineage of nineteenth-century French radicals and rascals who used poetry as a goad. Freed by the open verse of T. S. Elliott, fused to common vernacular in William Carlos Williams, Wallace Stevens, e. e. cummings, and Beat Frank O'Hara, poetry got hip and jazzy with Allen Ginsberg. The spare lyricism of Billie Holiday and the Robert

Lowell brought an understated quality to a confessional voice. If deft images could fleck Sylvia Plath's hardscrabble truths, revolutionary art was possible. Or so I thought. But from the fall of '73, I knew I couldn't remain in this west coast Martha's Vineyard. Baghdad by the Bay was beckoning....

LET US RIDE AS if in a hot air balloon. As it ascends, we leave the sweet hamlet of Inverness and glean a bird's eye view of rolling golden meadows of bleached summer grasses set in valleys crowned by redwood, Douglas fir, madrone, and Bishop's pine. For ten miles, Marin County is virgin, but suburban density increases until the Golden Gate Bridge, that last mark of Western civilization before the Orient, and we catch our first glimpse of Oz.

Most people don't understand how San Francisco sits on the land or how a crazy quilt of neighborhoods is defined by its remarkable geography, but the "balloonists view" will reveal this complicated city of districts as a grid, like a board for tic-tac-toe. The top row of three squares represents the southern reaches. They have nothing to do with this tale. But the bottom row is interesting: let's call the bottom left square Chinatown, the largest population of Chinese outside China itself; North Beach ("Little Italy"), home of the Beat movement, City Lights Bookstore, coffee houses, and the neon strip of Broadway where strippers and jazz clubs beckon. The middle square is Nob Hill and Russian Hill: staid, steep districts. And the right square is wealthy, self-aggrandizing Pacific Heights and the Presidio, pristine forests and former army base, overlooking the Bay and the Pacific.

In the middle row, the left square is the downtown business section. Let's beat it; who cares about work? No, our balloon will hover instead above the two remaining squares of the middle row. Here, we can chart the course of gay liberation.

In the center square, imagine a street going north-south, from a renovated chocolate factory on Ghiradelli Square, overlooking the Bay and Alcatraz, and running south to City Hall. This thoroughfare is Polk Street. In the early 1970s, this ordinary street of shops, markets, cafés, and restaurants, represented the Boulevard of Dreams, the living parade. Once regarded as little more than the "high street" for the rich hilltop districts, it had become the hippest quarter not only to see and be seen but to *be*. And become.

Heading west from the tanned abdomen of Polk Street and across that hip-hugging belt of the city lay the faded Victorian glories of the Haight-Ashbury, its decrepit mansions in ruin; the H&O miniature train-set charm of the Castro, a village set on sunny hills; Golden Gate Park in all its elegant glories; and, finally, the sea.

South of Market Street, from the towered Ferry Building on the east shore of the city all the way west, is Folsom Street. During daylight hours, there was an eerie stillness in its light industrial warehouses. But come night, here, in the narrow alleys, bars, and bathhouses, the nocturnal creatures came out to play: the leather boys and bikers, the daddies and the cowboys, as well as the hippies, artists, and sexually adventurous nomads. Folsom was the southernmost frontier. Beyond there, there was no *here*.

IN 1973, SAN FRANCISCO reveled in the Glitter Age, its prevailing style coming from retro fashions found in thrift stores or salvaged from "free boxes." The original hippies had held a funeral service to bury the movement in 1968 when speed and heroin turned the Haight-Ashbury, home of "peace, love, and flowers" into a nightmare zone. Now, gay lib ushered in the "glitter people" as its sparkling figureheads, people re-created themselves as icons from past, or imaginary, worlds. No matter how outré or extreme, they found a receptive, appreciative audience for unfettered and exuberant exaggeration.

Polk Street was a catwalk for the psychic tryouts and reinventions flocking to the city; the range of characters was extraordinary. Peter Berlin, a blond German stud, turned Narcissism into art, strutting and posing in black leather, each cubic inch of his smooth, muscular body a sexual prod. Fe/male Joan Crawfords or Marilyn wannabes mingled with Brazilian bodybuilders, and the quaint, endearingly spooky "Cosmic Lady" wafted about in a crocheted cape of sky blue and puffy clouds. "Jesus Christ Satan," a pudgy, lipsticked, and bearded quasi-pilgrim dressed in a robe with bells, carrying a staff and accompanied by a little dog, was a benign apparition wandering by the skinny runaways, hustlers, slumming social types, jingling gypsy mamas, and pot farmers in from the hills.

In short, Polk Strasse was a circus. In its cafés and elegant coffee houses, a new culture was inventing itself. Always indolent, risqué, and sublimely freed from Puritan values, San Francisco reveled in it. The city had been both Strawberry Fields and Pepperland for the hippies; now the Magical Mystery Tour had taken off in a giddy new direction.

The city had always set itself gloriously apart. As Mark Twain said, "San Francisco went from village to city without stopping in between" and Oscar Wilde noted, "When good people die, they're invariably seen in San Francisco." Whether nurturing socialist politicos in the 1920s and 30s, Beat poets in the 50s, civil rights and free speech activists and anti-war protesters of the 60s, and gay revolutionaries of the 70s, this city, the first buildings of which were bars and brothels, stood defiantly outside the mainstream. San Francisco gloried in its badness, proudly trumpeting its trashiness and reveling in its checkered reputation. It made civic heroes and heroines of its libertines, nothing if not eager to usher in the next phase of evolution, positive that, sooner or later, the rest of the world would catch up.

One critical factor of our hybrid culture was that money was accessible. Not a lot, but enough. Welfare, unemployment, free clinics, and a plethora of other free services allowed people to live without working. As a result, hardly anyone held a straight job.

Bolstered by the anti-war and hippie movements, gay people had inched closer toward the closet door. Well-known meltdowns, such as the explosive confrontation at the August 1968 Chicago Democratic Convention and the Stonewall Riot in June 1969, not coincidentally in the same week that Judy Garland died, are famously part of that process. But recently, transgender activist and historian Susan Stryker made a startling discovery:

In the mid-60s, the shabby Tenderloin was home to many visible queers who met at "Gene Compton's Cafeteria," a safe base for those who worked as prostitutes or lived on the streets, and who were subject to police intimidation for wearing lipstick, mascara, or having buttons on the "wrong side" of a shirt/blouse! Complicating their precarious lives, a serial killer had murdered several of them and mutilated their genitals.

In the summer of 1966, Cecil Williams began his ministry at Glide Memorial Church. The African-American minister brought the fervor of the civil rights movement to the forefront of the city's consciousness. Seeing homelessness and the persecution of racial minorities and gay people as legitimate concerns, Williams applied for federal funds allocated for LBJ's "War on Poverty." This was the first time that rights for gay people were addressed as an issue involving Constitutional promises and American civil rights.

In July, drag queens and hustlers organized politically under the name "Vanguard." This revolutionary effort to confront police brutality came about during a period when one transvestite received sixty days of solitary confinement for refusing to let the cops cut his long hair! Vanguard never quite got off the ground. Even so, that fledgling effort, truly the vanguard of a force about to transform the country, had immediate positive results.

"Once you feel good about yourself, no one can hurt you," says one of the people Stryker interviewed. And while the police continued to arrest drag queens on trumped-up charges of "obstructing the sidewalk," when they pressured Compton's to close at midnight instead of staying open all night, things came to a flashpoint. Many patrons used drugs to help them handle the fear of beatings, harassment, or murder. Aggravating the already tense situation in August, police raiding the cafeteria became abusive. Upon being prodded with a nightstick, a drag queen threw a cup of coffee at the offensive officer. In a bizarre replay of the Boston Tea Party, revolution was born as sixty drag queens, transgenders, and hookers fought the cops. And in a harbinger of the White Night Riots after the Dan White verdict of May 1979, a squad car was trashed and burned during the first known instance of gay people actively resisting police brutality. Tiny but gutsy San Francisco had once again taken a pioneering step toward advancing human rights. And common decency. Thus, San Francisco and New York (via the 1969 Stonewall Riot) launched the first revolutionary assaults on heterosexual supremacy and American orthodoxy, and became the two most visible poles of gay liberation.

They were very different scenes. In New York, the avant-garde revolved around Warhol as part of both his social goals and marketing strategy. San Francisco, meanwhile, developed a true underground culture: a completely separate society that evolved with no interest in being integrated into the straight world.

San Francisco had a precedent for gay theatrics such as the flamboyant camp diva José Saria, who began staging one-person operas in the 60s. But by the early 70s and in contrast to "back to the country" hippies, the sensibility and aesthetics of the Glitter Age were unabashedly urban. And why not?

The city's penchant for experimentation had fueled the place from its inception. Apart from its longstanding love affair with writers from Jack London to Beatniks (local columnist Herb Caen coined the term), San Francisco had always welcomed romantic nomads. And outsiders. Therefore, we who grew up believing ourselves to be pariahs, losers, and victims suddenly saw not only allies, both straight and gay, but the possibility of being honestly ourselves and (wonder of wonders!), being *loved*. At last, people like us had a place to be visible. *And safe.*

But despite the open displays of love and tolerance, the early stages of the movement weren't merely pleasure-oriented. There was a phenomenal exuberance, vitality, and "rush" driven by a spirit of acceptance. An encouragement to stand up and be counted characterized this rising wave. It could not have happened without the invaluable contribution of activists who'd earned their spurs in other arenas, such as the civil rights and anti-war movement. Therefore, in many ways, Gay Liberation was the latest incarnation of successive crusades for social inclusion.

ON ONE EARLY foray to the city, I'd gone to the Stud, a funky sawdust-on-the-floor bar, where I met a man named Bob Arenberg, who presented himself as a psychologist specializing in transactional analysis. We went on to the Ritch Street Baths and spent a day together before losing contact. But a few months later, I ran into Bob, now "Bo," again. He and his new lover, a fellow named Roger who reeked of Aramis cologne, had met two days earlier and were now moving into the bottom flat of a two-story Victorian at 2153 Polk Street. The building occupied the end of an alley behind the Yacht Club, a dingy gay bar for middle-aged men with a penchant for white sailor caps and old show tunes. Generously and characteristically hasty, Bo offered me a room in their love nest. I accepted but, two days later, Roger moved out. The next day, I moved down from Inverness. Two or three days later, Bo hooked up with a hunky New Yorker named Peter Leone. With that, a gay commune on Polk Strasse was born with a total rent of $175 a month.

There was nothing unusual about a lanky blond, a swarthy Neapolitan, and a hippie androgyne in sandals and baggy clothes (me) living together, but one day, Jillen Lowe, whom I'd known since I worked at her gallery in New

Tony Angel (l) and Ralph Sauer, Angels of Light backstage, Castro Street Fair, August 1978

York, called to ask if her daughter, Victoria—who had brought the Angels to Inverness for Alex's show—could live with me while finishing her last year of high school at Galileo High, five or six blocks away.

Freud said the Irish are impossible to psychoanalyze, so rather than figure out the Why of it all, the Who boiled down to Jillen herself. Gaelic and lovely in a Vanessa Redgrave way, with manners polished in 1940s Scarsdale, she was haunted by multiple childhood surgeries, her father's accidental death/ suicide when she was fourteen, her mother's alcoholism, a sexual assault, and the accumulated baggage of a lapsed Catholic burdened by sexual conflicts, unrealized ambitions, "betrayals" by various men, and lingering rage at the ex-husband she despised with quasi-messianic fervor.

Despite her beauty, humor, grace, and manifold talents, Jillen was an ambulatory "might have been," snatching defeat from the jaws of victory. Married to JFK's private photographer, Jacques Lowe (the author of many books about the Kennedys), she'd "saved her life" at thirty by walking out of their five-story Manhattan brownstone, two little children in tow. From then on, as a single parent without much financial support, if any, from Jacques, Jillen caromed around the hip art scene of Greenwich Village.

Around 1970 at the age of thirty-nine or so, she met Jeff Paley, the adopted son of CBS chairman, William Paley. Jeff was an oral compulsive wannabe who could be relied on to seize upon the snarkiest Freudian analysis of any situation. But Jillen fell madly in love. Two years later, they opened Paley and Lowe, a gallery showcasing Jillen's superb taste and Jeff's famous surname and deep pockets. But while nominally in love with him, Jillen was wildly attracted *to me too.* Once I was hired, she was outrageous (making out with me passionately one night while Jeff waited for her at home), while denying it all to Jeff, whom she often accused of betrayal. In the limelight of SoHo where we were so visible and considered sooo glamorous, Jillen couldn't quite seal the deal romantically. Or professionally. A year after I decamped, she and Jeff broke up. In July 1973, she came to visit me and got swept away by California, then went east to pack up and return with her children. Once ensconced in Inverness, she avoided people her own age and ran around with my friends like a latter day Isadora Duncan, pursuing spiritual fulfillment and a series of twenty-somethings, only to carp and lament when they weren't ready for a serious commitment to her or chose women their own age.

Unfortunately, as Jillen caromed into her profound new calling in life—a turgid and highly autobiographical novel—her children had different needs. Her son Jamie was eighteen and able to fend for himself; not Victoria. Enter me, always willing to rush in where angels fear to tread. But it was more than a lark; Victoria and I had a compelling bond, albeit one that was complicated or shadowed by her childhood of unrelenting crisis due to her mother, the lovers who came and went without ever saying goodbye, and the fractious relationship between her divorced parents.

Without realizing it, in 1971 while I was in New York, I had become the surrogate father for a twelve-year-old desperate for love, reassurance, and nurturing. I never saw myself as a parental figure, but to Victoria, a beautiful and preternaturally gifted child with a vivid imagination and passion for the unusual, strange, and bizarre world of cabaret creatures, I became not only the hero figure, fantasy "daddy," and friend, but the androgyne of her dreams. Although her father didn't vanish from their lives entirely (Jacques bought a chateau in France where Jamie and Victoria spent their summers), I became the unwitting object of an extremely complicated projection, one component of which included her virginal desire. But that was still in the future, when in September 1974 Victoria came to live with me and converted a tiny laundry area off the kitchen into her personal Fantasia of ostrich plumes, glittering postcards, draped velvet, and veils.

Nearly sixteen, Victoria appeared alarmingly adult and bore an uncanny physical resemblance to Marilyn Monroe. But her breathless, endearing charm was absolutely genuine. And her style was unique: tight skirts, striped leggings, kung fu slippers, and quilted Chinese jackets. With her fingernails painted green, smoky eye shadow *à la* David Bowie, maroon lips, and adorned with a plethora of pins she fashioned herself—tiny enamels and miniatures—she rushed about with a pile of art books and drawing pads, her beret at a jaunty angle, her limpid eyes as lovely as those of a faun.

During those heady days, I was writing poems, and occasionally stepping outside onto Polk Street. Here I encountered Harry Hay, one of the first leaders of the gay rights movement and, later, founder of the Radical Faeries. But revolution takes many forms.

On February 4, 1974, Patty Hearst, heiress to the newspaper empire, was kidnapped in Berkeley. To encourage her release, her family sent fleets of trucks to appointed centers where blocks of cheap orange cheese were hurled into crowds of poor people. But in mid-April, Patty (now "Tania") embraced the Revolution and helped her erstwhile captors rob a bank while brandishing a machine gun. We cheered.

On Folsom Street, sailors and drag queens and leather boys crowded Hamburger Mary's, a restaurant that resembled a Christmas tree. Across the street, hippies beat tambourines at the Stud. Bathhouses were going full tilt. So were VD clinics. Instead of skulking in, praying for anonymity, clinic-goers met up with friends in the waiting room, many of whom had recently prowled the red light maze at Ritch Street or slipped into its inky orgy room, where there was always the certainty of action on a huge round bed.

But I was a monk, writing in my tiny room with postcards covering the walls. A single window. A double mattress with no box-spring occupied ninety percent of my room, leaving space only for a vegetable crate I'd salvaged to use as a desk for my 1930s Remington typewriter. But I felt I was in a palace as I curled up on my bed in a black and pink robe, surrendering to Erik Satie's "Trois Gymnopédies" while sipping Lapsang Souchong tea (see poem on page 227). It was tranquil, peaceful. Although San Francisco had a high crime rate, I never felt threatened. If anyone looked weird or out of place, it was the police who cruised Polk Street as I wrote in a two-line untitled poem in 1973:

From cars, the police say, "Keep moving ..."
Thorns on the midnight rose.

Aside from a sense of being supervised by authority, however, at no time did we feel intimidated. In fact, a manifestation of cross-cultural tolerance occurred in 1974 when gays challenged the police baseball team to a game. Hundreds attended the spectacle in which drag queens wielding pom-poms did their cheerleader routine to the appreciation of "our side." To everyone's surprise, the gays trounced the constabulary in what was to become an annual event. But the overarching feeling of that first game was budding and peaceful coexistence, and a good time was had by all so much so that, walking home, I was singing that jolly old song,

San Francisco, open your Golden Gate, you let no stranger wait
Outside your door...

I felt so comfortable in San Francisco that I went back east rarely because it was always bizarre, as was evident in December 1973, when I went to Philadelphia to see Margaret, my beloved *Grandmère*. I wanted to tell her about the scene but this time I didn't have to use words.

In 1972, the Cockettes had made a short film. *Tricia's Wedding* was a parody of the 1971 nuptials of President Nixon's daughter. In this deliriously trashy film boasting flagrant nudity and blatant sex, someone at Tricia's reception spikes the punch with LSD and the White House affair disintegrates.

By coincidence, the movie was being shown when I arrived in Philadelphia, and in the "city of brotherly love," the only venue that would screen X-rated entertainment was a porno theater. At twenty-six, I'd never been in one, but when I told seventy-nine-year-old Margaret about the Cockettes and mentioned that the film was playing a few block away, her bright blue eyes lit up.

"Darling, I think we'd better go see it."

Off we went into a warm afternoon for a late afternoon showing:

Margaret, in diamond pin and pearls, and I, clad in overalls and with hair flowing to my shoulders. At the Blue Boy Cinema, I slid ten dollars under the badly scratched box-office window and asked for two tickets. But when the sallow guy with reddish hair saw Margaret standing behind me looking like a dowager empress, his jaw literally dropped. Resembling a deer trapped in oncoming headlights, he motioned me closer to a perforated cutout in the glass.

"For you?" he whispered, from the safe side. "For this?"

"For *Tricia's Wedding*," I explained, wondering why he looked so nervous.

He gulped. "Does she know what kind of place this is? See, we don't want any ..."

"Yes, we want two tickets, please," Margaret said, stepping forward. "Thank you."

The guy shrugged. Whatever this lady was into, she was certainly over twenty-one. Anyway, what did he care if we were there to see *Tricia's Wedding*, *Convict Slave*, or *Leather Fisters*?

Inside the front door and past a thick black vinyl curtain, the Blue Boy reeked of sweat and poppers. There was barely enough light for us to see the seats. Soon enough, *Convict Slave* ended with some big flourish and *Tricia's Wedding* lurched underway, with lurid images of White House guests loaded on acid as Tricia Nixon's grand affair blew apart at the seams. But as the minutes ticked by, the other patrons of this sleazy dive realized that *they were not alone.*

No. However, instead of being horrified, Margaret was fascinated. Word of her attendance traveled fast and stupefied men emerged from the glory holes, hastily buttoning up their pants before slipping into vacant seats behind us, getting as close as possible to this genuine queen.

Margaret was used to being in the limelight—she was world-famous, after all—although I'd doubt she'd ever held court in a porno dive. But she certainly didn't mind if the guys were "making the world a more loving place," as she might put it. Besides, she was thoroughly engrossed, and not by the action in the glory holes a few steps away.

On screen, poor hapless Tricia was getting fucked with a baseball bat and screaming her idiot head off; stoned to the tits on acid and having a bad, bad trip, Nixon was dragging his sorry ass around, clutching a teddy bear and

muttering nonsense. But Margaret was riveted by the Cockette who paro-
died a benumbed Queen Elizabeth.

"Oh darling," she told me happily, "I know her and he's got her exactly
right."

"You know the Queen of England?" a guy behind us whispered, leaning
forward.

Margaret turned to regard him. "Hello, dear," she said kindly. "What's your
name?"

"I'm ... uh ... 'Joe'."

"Hello, 'Joe'," Grandmère smiled, accepting his alibi at face value. "I'm
Margaret Webster Plass. Isn't this a wonderful film?"

Well, if that didn't just beat all. Not only had this grand dame plunked herself down in the middle of the sex sluts, she was ready to make new friends!

"I knew her parents, you see," Margaret continued as Joe nodded in dumbfounded disbelief. "And before she and Prince Philip were married, they used
to come to my house in London. Because I'm an American, we didn't have to
observe court protocol. So they could sit by the fire and play records and be
like any other young couple."

When *Tricia's Wedding* ended, I helped Margaret into her coat as her ad-
mirers crowded in, asking to kiss her hand. How could they have imagined
that she found being there, *with them*, infinitely more interesting than being
at Buckingham Palace? And thus inspired, she delivered another stunner. "I
live at the Barclay on Rittenhouse Square," she told one and all. "And any
time you want to come over, just call and ask for Mrs Plass in 11A. We'll have
a wonderful drink. Thank you all for such a lovely time."

As we left, Margaret said she couldn't wait to tell her friends about the
wonderful film at the Blue Boy Cinema. Which she did. Yup, she was so
impressed with the Cockettes, she undertook it as her mission to urge her
friends to get off their staid Philadelphian asses and go see a groundbreaking
and drop-dead hilarious work of art.

I seriously doubt that any of her friends followed her advice and rushed
off to see the Cockettes. As for the flabbergasted patrons of the Blue Boy, it's
equally doubtful that any of them ever called Margaret. If they had, I know
that she'd have been delighted to invite them over; she liked all kinds of people. I can't begin to speculate how the boys from the glory holes would have

finessed the lobby at the Barclay—it was a bit like the *real* White House—but what the hell did I know? I straddled two worlds now, an insider in both, still trying to figure out how it all fit together. If it even did. But this was my life.

EARLY EACH MORNING, Victoria got up on her own and headed out for school down the hill. By ten, I'd wake, make coffee, and get to work. Bo worked until two in the morning as a doorman and Peter did lighting at the Cabaret nightclub on Montgomery Street off Broadway; oftentimes, they slept until noon. By then, I'd been at work for hours, beginning twelve-hour work days, sometimes as many as sixteen, extrapolating poems from my journal, a lit joint in hand as I typed, refining the silences in the sounds, changing a word, a line, which meant retyping the whole thing again and again. Then, every few weeks, sending off a packet to Gerard, awaiting his critique, absorbing his advice, reading and writing more, still more. It wasn't onerous; it was freedom. And I was a fledgling, opening my young poet's wings.

WHEN DAVID MEADOWS, he of the blue polka-dot dress in Inverness, visited and urged me to visit the Angels of Light commune on Oak Street, I hesitated. I'd seen one of their shows and, despite David's persistence, I wasn't sure I wanted to get to know them. Even after years in the counter-culture, they looked too freaky to me. But though I deferred a personal visit, I listened to what he had to say about the Angels because I was sexually attracted to him (and so naïve that I never realized that he was schmoozing me to get to Victoria-the-bombshell who was uninterested in him).

Seen through his eyes, the Angels embodied a heroic ideal. Not only did they live communally and share all their possessions, their shows were free of charge. Even voluntary donations were refused, so determined was the group to resist the polluting grasp of "Amerikan" capitalism and spread their messianic message: everything should be free; the purpose of art was to inspire people to come out and foment revolution. One early performance consisted of decorating their truck and participating in the city's first Gay Day Parade, an event with so many names over the years, I don't know what to call it. But their altruism co-existed with a psychotic sense of entitlement.

While materialism was *out*, as David revealed, the Angels had nothing against ripping off theater supplies, stealing clothes, or bilking the System for monthly stipends and food stamps. In LA, Patty Hearst's gang robbed a sporting goods store, "liberating money" in the name of the People. In San Francisco, despite their much-vaunted disdain for publicity and self-promotion, the Angels basked in the limelight: the undisputed stars of Bay Area slum-glamour. By now, they had a claim to it, thanks to a circuitous route that requires an equally circuitous explanation from me and a little patience from you:

From 1969 to 1972, San Francisco midwifed the Cockettes, a troupe of drag queens who staged deliciously campy and intentionally tawdry parodies of 1930s and 40s Hollywood musicals. Founded by the gorgeous Hibiscus (née George Harris), who was compellingly masculine offstage and anything he wanted onstage, this group was the toast of the town. Adventurers of all sexual persuasions crowded the Palace Theater in Chinatown to revel in the outrageous antics of such stellar talents as Divine, later the dog-shit-eating star of John Waters' cult classic film *Pink Flamingoes*, the disco queen Sylvester, and the endearing Pristine Condition, a human valentine. But Hibiscus was playing Trilby to a peculiar Svengali who hovered over the Cockettes.

Chicken-breasted Irving Rosenthal was a bearded and diminutive Byzantine padding about the periphery of the scene. A figure in his own right, as editor of the *Big Table Review* at the University of Chicago in the 1950s, he'd published a seminal issue that featured excerpts of William Burroughs' *Naked Lunch*, which he edited, and Allen Ginsberg's "Howl." Later, after appearing in Jack Smith's film *Flaming Creatures*, Irving penned a stylish novel, *Sheeper*, in which he famously attacked women, ordering them to cease reading epicene prose that might be summed up as a boiled testicle impaled on a Faberge hatpin. All style, no heart, it showcased a lacquered, brittle attitudinizing instead of risking vulnerability. Or humanity. Or, God forbid, a laugh.

Upon moving to the city in 1967, Irving became an arbiter for people half his age when he founded a commune: Kaliflower propounded utopian ideals and community-focused activities. It provided information on free food banks, medical care, clothing, housing, and local events. Not coincidentally, via a newsletter sent out to 300 Bay Area communes and collectives, Kaliflower proclaimed itself the *ne plus ultra* voice of conscience. As its pronouncements were shrouded in the anonymity of "the group," Irving remained discreetly offstage. Even so, as guru in residence, it was clear that he called the shots.

Youngsters drawn to Kaliflower were exhorted to do all for free while none too subtle pressure was brought to bear on individual behavior and rights, including those of private property, diet, toilet habits, and sex. To fathom such curious cult orthodoxy, it's critical to recognize their genuine idealism as well as the degree of oversight and monitoring that first reared its head in Kaliflower and, later, affected the Cockettes and the Angels of Light. Here are a few of the notable regulations, or accepted behavioral guidelines:

Beyond being vegetarian, men were encouraged to grow beards, private property was deemed illegitimate, and everything was to be shared, including household tasks. Toilet paper was disparaged; as an ecological alternative, people were urged to develop "asshole consciousness" and cleanse with water, like Hindus. Private bedrooms were unnecessary; monogamy was subtly discouraged in favor of all-inclusive sexual openness. But it goes without saying that the Wizard of this Oz was pandered to.

Much of what Kaliflower did was meritorious. In addition to community involvement and providing safe haven for lost souls. I can believe that, at his best, Irving functioned as a benign father figure. But he bears responsibility for fomenting a cult that was nominally devoted to revolution but which served his need to control or dominate others. From his solipsistic realm, Irving saw the Cockettes and the Angels of Light as colonies.

A stray fly drawn into his web was Mary Hyssen, heiress to the Kellogg fortune. Mary was sweet but neither hale nor hardy of mind; soon after meeting Irving, she purchased a big warehouse in the Mission District—Irving's name somehow wound up on the title—as a base for Kaliflower. Here, behind closed doors, Irving cast his spell over his troupe of brilliant and talented gay men such as Ralph Sauer, a sort of Celtic Dionysus who frequently performed naked, and Jim Windsor—a.k.a. Tihara—a comic totem. And Hibiscus. Each deserves attention because each played major roles in the Cockettes and as archetypical Angels.

Ralph was a curious man, sometimes reticent, sometimes charming, often-times fragile. A startling, dynamic presence born on April Fool's Day,

1943, he was quick-witted with a flair for verbal pun, dance, and burlesque. Never comfortable with rehearsed dialogue, he excelled at slowing down timing to enormous comic effect. Ralph's heyday came during the time when the Cockettes and the Angels derived their primal energy from gay male lust.

Tihara was born in Pampa, Texas, in 1950. As a little boy rodeo clown, he started off in show business by dodging Brahma bulls. Dark-haired and strikingly handsome with blazing blue eyes, he seemed to be a mélange of Buster Keaton, Emmett Kelly, and Lucille Ball. Tall in person, he appeared immense onstage.

"Are you six-one with heels?" someone once asked.

"I'm six-one *with anybody*," Tihara shot back.

At eighteen, the charms of working at a local phone company couldn't compare with those of his Latino boyfriend so they lit out for California, and were so paranoid about being stopped and arrested that they zigzagged and double-backed through five or six states. Upon reaching San Francisco on July 4, 1969, this self-described "cross between Jayne Mansfield and a telephone pole" became a fixture in the Cockettes. Imperial, opinionated, and drop-dead hilarious, Tihara was a unique and cosmic star who knocked my socks off.

Finally, the phenomenon with the startling capacity to inspire people to create not only groundbreaking theater but transformative identities: Hibiscus was a driving force of nature, an exuberant, incandescent, and gorgeous tornado. As glorious as the scene was, it cannot be overstated that there was something unique in the dazzling prince who refused to consider himself damaged or inferior because he was gay; he'd grown up in a family that supported him. As a child and teen, Hibiscus and his sisters performed in shows produced by Crystal Field at the Theater of the New City in New York. But he was certainly destined for other things.

Hibiscus glowed with unapologetic sexual confidence. After the chilly McCarthy era of the 1950s, when almost all gay people were made to feel ashamed and remained in the closet, he charged forward to hoist high the banner of unabashed sexuality. By doing so, this charismatic, physically beautiful, and ballsy man struck a mortal and intentional blow at American Puritanism. Hibiscus was not one for the martyrdom of Oscar Wilde, the implacable veneer of Noel Coward and Cole Porter, the self-torture of Tennessee Williams, or the toilets of Joe Orton. No. The fabulous Hibiscus was in-yer-face gay. And by God, the world was going to get up and dance in celebration of personal freedom!

Though he'd grown up the adored golden boy of a theater family, Hibiscus was looking for a mentor when he fell into Irving's sphere—a bitch's brew for this masochist who needed to be sexually abused and humiliated, a tendency that later grew extreme. Once in San Francisco, his charisma and spirit drew others to him, resulting in the formation of the Cockettes in 1969, thus launching what became the first cutting edge of gay lib theater.

But even before 1972, when the Cockettes went to New York and floundered in a debacle that led Gore Vidal to hiss, "No talent is not enough," the troupe had splintered. Sylvester and Divine wanted professional careers while Hibiscus was determined to create a free theater. Urged on by Irving (who, it might be argued, stood to gain from seeing Hibiscus go nowhere and thus remain dependent on *him*), Hibiscus quit the Cockettes in the autumn of 1971.

Ten or so former Cockettes who shared Hibiscus's commitment to free theater joined him in a new group that took its name—Angels of Light— from a little child's remark. And while impossible to distinguish a "proper" theater company from the hippies and the glitter people parading around in drag on the streets of the Haight-Ashbury, by 1972 the Angels had begun the first of three discernible major cycles.

Their initial shows revolved around bearded drag queens. There were no fixed boundaries between performers and audience. Many events began as shows but devolved into sex orgies involving cast and attendees in glittering, lurid improvisations that started off as full moon parties celebrating Halloween and Christmas.

The chaos was overblown and wild. Tihara told me of a show where Hibiscus played the Virgin Mary giving birth. Naked, he went into labor, and Tihara-as-Baby-Jesus crawled out from between his legs.

Another event encapsulated the group's magic for me. An artist wore a headdress of small plastic baskets, such as those that hold cherry tomatoes, glued together from end to end to create three "towers" that rose eighteen feet from a skull cap. Strung with white Christmas lights connected to a portable battery pack worn around the waist, the flexible construction blinked on and off while swaying gently. When I first saw a photo of that, I realized

Lily Tomlin, Divine, Sister Ed, and Pristine Condition, June 1975

the Angels were capable of godly transcendence.

In the early days, the offstage action merged with what was happening on-stage, such as the night when eight infuriated lesbians attacked Hibiscus for doing drag; they chased him around the theater, ripped his dress off, tore out his huge boobs, and trashed his wig. The gestalt was realism, exaggeration, and art, simultaneously hilarious and crazy.

Most shows took place out on the street, in parks, or in a huge space at the first gay community center at 330 Grove Street. But one production, a mock Chinese opera with pretend Cantonese dialect, was staged in Chinatown. *Madame Butterfly* featured Sister Ed, whose specialty was the classic sing-song dance form of Beijing Opera and took place in an alley to an audience of startled Chinese residents. They loved it.

But a show I saw in early 1974 was a numbing mess. After an hour in which nothing happened, someone walked a tightrope. Later, drag queens appeared and smashed some dishes, before quarreling and wandering offstage. By then, I was so bored I left. Once outside, it was edgy on the midnight streets. The Haight-Ashbury district was blighted by hard drugs, crime, and tense race relations. But I was glad I'd left the show when a beautiful man ap-

Dancing in Golden Gate Park, San Francisco Gay Day Parade, June 1976

peared before me in the lamplight. It was misty, and we smiled, then without a word, we danced and kissed before drifting on our respective ways.

Month by month, I was falling into a spell. San Francisco's effect on me was transformational: as a child, I'd been reared to detect social differences. Even at five or six, when being taught how to introduce one person to another, rules of hierarchy prevailed: the person of lesser status was *presented* to their social superior or elder with a cue to ensure that communication would flow seamlessly.

Memory fails. I'm not sure, exactly, *how* we were supposed to have the radar to know who "outranked" whom; we just did. But thanks to my years in the counterculture and my move to San Francisco, I felt aligned with others now, no matter how different-seeming I appeared on the surface. This was the greatest gift my journey had given me and I felt it even as spring 1974 arrived and two things transpired which had an important effect on my poetry.

First, after being put in touch with novelist Christopher Isherwood, who liked my poems and invited me to visit him in Santa Monica, Gerard suggested I telephone a local Beat poet. At fifty-six, Harold Norse was a stumpy ex-bodybuilder with a bad toupee and a huge chip on his shoulder about being overlooked. I loved his earthy New York humor and ballsy work. I also appreciated his praise, and his invitation to serve as the editorial assistant for his cutting edge magazine, *Bastard Angel*, which featured surrealists and celebrities like Jean Genet, stellar Beats, and on occasion, up and coming "unknowns."

Also at this time, I met two local editors central to the gay cultural scene; the contrast could not have been more extreme.

Paul Mariah, the poet and cofounder of *Manroot*, was the kindest publisher on the scene. Once jailed in Texas for seven years for having consensual sex with his lover who was technically underage but deeply in love with him, Paul wrote searing, scalding odes to prison tenderness and edgy sexuality. After his release, he moved to San Francisco. The whip thin, auburn-haired leather queen with freckled skin and bad teeth could not have been less bitter and less egotistical. In an arena characterized by competitiveness, name-dropping, picayune pettiness, and prickly reputation mongering, Paul was a prince.

Winston Leyland was the opposite: a pear-shaped former English priest with a perpetual sheen of sweat above his upper lip. He'd assumed control of the magazine *Gay Sunshine* from an original collective headed by cofounders Gary Allinder and Konstantin Berlandt. Pushing forty, he made *Gay Sunshine* the most visible west coast gay rag while insinuating himself into the lives of the writers he favored, who found themselves obliged to tolerate his grasping ministrations in exchange for exposure.

In 1974, Winston published my first poem with gifted poets such as Aaron Shurin, Dennis Cooper, and Robert Gluck. I admired all of them; Aaron for the tensile strengths of his early work, Dennis for his deft toughness, and Bob for his polished, elegant style.

With my poetry career thus launched, I became involved with Intersection, a church and arts center where I gave free poetry workshops. Once ensconced there, I considered reading in public, but feeling that going public was premature, it was a step I delayed.

Finally, after yet another invitation from David, I went to visit the Angels of Light. As I climbed the stairs of their Victorian house, I noticed stubbed out cigarettes and the headless trunk of a large nude doll. Perhaps there should also have been a flashing sign to alert me that, once I crossed the threshold, I'd be entering a palace of pathology. There wasn't.

Chapter 4

Once inside, I froze. My Quaker college had been bizarre, but neither it nor race riots, airless chats with Warhol, nor African warriors surrounding the house with torches and spears could have prepared me for such a sorry spectacle.

The long dark hall running from the front doors to the back of the house was littered with debris—a pair of crumpled-up tights, crushed beer cans, cardboard flats stacked against a wall. A black dog skulked through, her tail low to the ground. Off to the right was a small room with a tatty Oriental rug, battered paper umbrellas, and brightly painted masks. Things looked torn and threadbare, smashed up, shabby.

A guy appeared but sloughed by without saying a word. It was weird.

(Years later, Teena Rosen-Albert, amethyst-eyed, tawny-haired, voluptuous, and in my opinion, the most beautiful woman ever to appear with the Angels, shared her memory of arriving at the house for the first time. "It was insane," she said. "No one would make eye contact." Dan Nicoletta concurred: "The atmosphere was totally paranoid.")

I considered retreating just as David glided into view. Acting as if nothing was amiss, he offered me a tour.

Just beyond the small room to the right of the front doors, there was a bleak-looking dance studio, thirty feet long. On the right, bare windows overlooked a parking lot. On the left, a wall of three or four contiguous mirrors and a barre. One mirror was cracked.

Beyond the studio was a kitchen. I'd always regarded kitchens as the heart and soul of communes. Here, however, there were no loving touches, no homey tablecloths or flowers. Instead, there were forlorn-looking piles of industrial-sized trays and pans, some dirty dishes, and a sense of chaos.

Upstairs, a large bedroom looking out over the front of the house contained several beds separated by veils. There were smaller bedrooms too, most with more than one bed. Across the hall was a bathroom devoid of any human touches save a rusty can. "Asshole consciousness," David explained, ushering me down the hall to *the drag room*.

Imagine a thrift store in which a bomb went off. Here, in the commune's closet, clothes hung on long bars suspended from the ceiling or lay scattered around the floor: costumes, torn dresses, clothing pinned or patched, ball gowns, wigs, feathers, boas, bits of tulle, velvet, lamé—a chaotic jumble.

"This is our bus transfer collection," David said, drawing my attention to a file of paper slips that merits special mention. Passengers on MUNI—the city's public transportation lines—receive a timed-stamped paper when they board; these are color-coded, making it easy for authorities to see if the transfer is valid. Over the years, the Angels had collected a huge file of transfers, making it possible to go anywhere by using the correct "pass." It was an extraordinary urban subterfuge. Unlike the chaotic drag room and mind-numbing kitchen, the file revealed obsessive and impressive organizational skills.

"I want you to meet someone," David said, pausing outside a curtained bedroom door.

I was used to unusual rooms. My own cell was completely papered with postcards. But this was a first.

My first impression was of a spider web. Flats, veils, and shaded lanterns were strategically placed to create a *Cabinet of Dr. Caligari* effect. Reclining at the center of this chamber Jilala, a.k.a. Jet, exuded the air of being forty years older than he actually was—a turbaned, wizened man with a lean and hungry look who resembled Jean Cocteau imitating Marlene Dietrich. Jet was Irving's emissary to the Angels—he was never in the Cockettes and didn't perform with the Angels much, if at all—and a filmmaker with undeniable talent, though his footage was always out of focus. But however blurry, with their whorls of color and Rubenesque sensuousness, his films had panache. I think Jet saw himself as a courtesan or court eunuch; his fluttery discourse combined sharp insight and his rendition of aristocratic disdain for the hoi polloi from which he absented himself.

"Someone saw Angel Jack fucking Hibiscus with the handle of a hammer," he allowed, gauging my reaction. "Another time, I heard Jack whipping him." Finding me neither impressed nor disgusted, he turned to other topics: how the Angels went to see Marlene Dietrich in concert and presented her with a loaf of homemade bread that she displayed to the audience; how Allen Ginsberg had appeared in *Pickup's Tricks*, an impromptu Angels film in 1972, where he read poetry.

Jet may have been a legend in his own mind, but I felt as if I was observing a moth flutter against a dirty window in his cardboard Xanadu. As I walked downstairs, a blond woman hollered, "Bad wig!" as she hung out a window to jeer at a passerby. The black dog lay beside the woman's sturdy legs as she repeated the derisive taunt, "Bad wig! Bad wig!"

"What's that about?" I asked David.

"Oh, Beaver likes hassling this neighbor with a bad toupee." He grinned, but I frowned. Wasn't the whole point of gay revolution to be compassionate?

"Beaver" moved away, avoiding eye contact, but not before I'd seen her. Of middle height, slim on top but heavy-hipped, Beaver Bauer possessed a startling blondness and pale blue eyes. She reminded me of the alien children in that classic 1960 horror flick, *Village of the Damned*. She seemed insecure and had a shifting gaze, but her body conveyed raw power.

To portray this *extremely* complicated person adequately, one must proceed slowly for she will repel all efforts at analysis. And yet, not only because of her role in the Angels, but also because she and I became very close for a few years during which she told me her story, it's critical to attempt honest dimension. So bear with me:

Brilliantly talented and intensely driven, Beaver boomeranged between exalted visions of nobility and a voluptuous display of private demons. Her sense of shame must have begun early for she had a savage birthmark scarring the inside of her upper thigh. Moreover, as she told me, her Republican family was emotionally abusive and, some contend, also sexually abusive. Though wealthy enough for Beaver to have a horse, they derided and belittled her. The upshot was a smoldering welter of contradictions.

Beaver was seductive and secretive; charming but emotionally inaccessible; indirect but scalding on occasion; a fierce devotee of the Angels' aversion to promotion, she was, also, the first to muscle into the frame if a camera appeared. Often noble, generous, and self-sacrificing, she was also hypervigilant and quick to jeer at a faux pas. Astonishingly focused (I never saw anyone work harder), she was also, consciously or unconsciously in denial about issues of abuse, past and present. Extraordinary and sensitive, she was in such psychic pain that, at times, I felt she was in total shutdown. A vocal advocate of proletarian equality—always a popular position and an easy sell—she concurrently and none-too-subtly demanded special exemptions

predicated on her specialness.

All in all, she was one of
the most controlling and
complicated people I've ever
met. While art was her way to
achieve release and self-actualization, whatever she was trying to achieve release *from* was
"off limits" absolutely, possibly
because she didn't want to
know herself or couldn't bear
honest vulnerability. Instead,
she danced around the beast,
vaulting to glory in public
while spinning dervish-like on
some private hellacious edge.

As a girl in Ohio, Beaver
sought refuge in horses, but
by high school, she found a

(*l–r*) Gregory, Rodney Price, and Joe Morocco, San
Francisco Gay Day Parade, June 1977

sturdier ticket to oblivion in alcohol. When she left to go to art school in
New York, even before reaching Manhattan, she found psychic completion
with a man who accompanied her, a gay man who was, not coincidentally,
a substance abuser. And in falling desperately in love with the unobtainable
Rodney Price, Beaver turned her existence into a devotional but thwarted
hymn.

Born in Pittsburgh in 1950 of Italian-American descent, Rodney was handsome, dark, with a dancer's loose gait. I won't pretend I understood this gifted graphic artist who attended the Columbia School of Art and Design, but
beyond painting dazzling sets, he was a dancer/acrobat proficient in several
styles, able to execute flying somersaults and land in full splits. He was no
actor, but his onstage presence was mighty. An immense egotist, stubborn,
star-struck, and smug, one axiom held firm: Rodney would do whatever was
best for Rodney. I knew him to be disciplined and fairly modest about his ac-
complishments. But as one Angel put it: "Rodney was an airhead."

Rodney and Beaver's codependent relationship had a cosmic slum-glamor that might have come out of Hugo's *Les Misérables*. Reports of their time in New York vary; some say they both became alcoholics, running around in rags, panhandling and sleeping on traffic islands. Whatever the finer points of their hardscrabble existence, they decided to save themselves and migrate to San Francisco. Here, Beaver kept drinking, but Rodney appeared to arrest his downward spiral. And so, a long rising arc ensued, one that led him to attempt ever-greater artistic heights which, at his best, were truly excellent.

In California, the pair separated. Rodney longed to be a poet and moved in with Hunce Voelker, a poet who found Beaver so obsessive that he banned her from his house. Not for the first time or the last, she exhibited her sufferings like Saint Teresa; her role of shining victim became a hallmark and leitmotif for, in multiple ways, Beaver's sacrifices, Beaver's sufferings, Beaver's stoicism were issues for public consumption. They were on display as conspicuously as her altruism, creativity, and triumphs.

Now, with bases loaded, the last batter stepped up to the plate.

In 1971, Beaver met Brian Mulhern, the scion of a wealthy family, recently released from a mental institution. Physically handsome and blond, the hulking, muscular Saxon was brooding and unpredictable. Soon thereafter, Rodney and Hunce broke up. Now a critical passage ensued which defined their lives and shaped the Angels of Light.

Brian was in love with Beaver, but Rodney wanted him; Beaver certainly wasn't going to risk losing Rodney again. So when Brian got Beaver, he got Rodney too, despite the fact that, here-to-fore, Brian had been straight. So the long-term domestic tax for Brian was to be co-opted emotionally, and sexually exploited. Their design for living might have worked more smoothly if the tawny-haired, muscle-bound Brian had been well balanced, but he was an alcoholic and paranoid with a penchant for sudden and sick assaults. For example, at a party, Brian slipped into the hostess's bathroom where he found a big jar of cold cream. Uncapping it, he scooped out the lotion and took a shit into the jar and recovered it, leaving the lady of the house to unearth his time bomb at some later date.

Upon hearing this, I thought it was completely insane. Bingo. But far from being unnerved by psychotic episodes, most of the Angels seemed inured to perverse behavior and to their hypocrisy in ignoring it. For example, personal theft was decried, but stealing from big stores was approved of. Exhibition-ism and addiction were as customary as verbal assault, neglect, vulgarity, and hysteria, and states of emotional distress, mania, and paranoia. Hyper-bolic outbursts of rage, passive aggression, and vicious backstabbing were so frequent as to constitute normalcy. Screaming fights were conducted in front of little children, irrespective of the effects. It was so commonplace that no one paid any attention. I do not exaggerate.

When Beaver became pregnant in June 1972, she told me that she prayed the baby would be Rodney's. However, when Sham was born on March 2, 1973—and after the birth, in true tribal fashion, the Angels cooked and ate the placenta—it was obvious: Brian was the sire. That said, while Sham was adopted equally by Rodney and Brian, many Angels felt that Sham was "their" baby. He certainly needed family; Beaver's parents were horrified that Sham was born out of wedlock, and their shocked, guilt-tripping letters were read aloud to the commune with mirth and greeted with ridicule. But Sham's birth had far-ranging importance for the house; with the alpha female's baby on site, the wild energy abated ... a bit.

By this time, Hibiscus had quit the Cockettes in 1971, and when the group broke up in 1972, Tihara had taken off to travel in South America. The exo-dus continued in 1973 when, with babe in arms, Beaver went to London with Rodney and Greg, a young fellow who'd been living in San Francisco.

As a little boy, Greg figured out how to get what he wanted: by putting toy wood blocks inside his socks, he could make high heels. This should have been a dead giveaway, but it's possible his mother didn't notice anything so unusual. The tall, green-eyed, and pale boy had always been unusual. No one spotting the gangly child in make-believe high heels would guess that Greg was actually black. Black he was, even though his skin was white—whiter than most whites, in fact. But for all his constant talk about blackness, he associated almost exclusively with whites.

How could he escape wrenching doubt about core issues of identity?

All the glowworms tunneling toward Sodom waiting to be born sought an alternative "heightened" reality or parallel universe: We all needed a rich, magical-but-defiantly private realm because each of us had grown up feeling intimidated, and still felt threatened by, the Great Dread God of Normalcy. As youngsters, we conformed to survive the baseball bubblegum culture of mainstream America. Even so, we'd been searching for a wholly new way to identify (see poem "sHe" on page 235).

In 1969, Greg moved to San Francisco where he lived in the bushes of Golden Gate Park. In 1970, he met Hibiscus. In performing with Hibiscus, the nineteen-year-old Greg discovered his identity. And also learned what was theatrically possible.

"In one show," he told me, "the entire cast found itself in the wings on one side of the stage. For the show to work we all had to enter from the other side, but there was no way to get there because there was no backstage. So we told the audience, 'Close your eyes.' When they did, we all rushed to the other side and said, 'You can open your eyes again.' And the show went on."

In the performances staged at the gay community center on Grove Street, a building housing the Black Panthers on the first floor, the early scarification of Greg's life reached a pivot as he realized: *Art is survival.* And while his appearances with the Angels were sporadic and short-lived, in the summer of 1972, he went to Europe to perform with Hibiscus and Angel Jack, joined by Rodney and Beaver. After their tour was completed, Greg remained in Europe until the summer of 1974 when he flew to New York to perform with Hibiscus and Jack. Thus, two years after the group officially began, there were now east and west coast "wings" of the Angels of Light. No one realized it at the time, but although the two companies used the same name, from then on they would develop totally different kinds of theater.

In San Francisco, Beaver and Rodney rejoined Brian in a big Victorian house. While Hibiscus and Jack did high camp shows in New York (and got paid for them), the house in the Haight-Ashbury was the locus of the west coast wing that became magical and fable-oriented. Other Angels occupied other dwellings, communes and shared houses, but Oak Street was the center. Here, the Angels pooled their funds in a treasury, laying emphasis on group criticism and collective decision-making.

1974 was the era of drag queens. Even as they morphed away from their Cockette roots, the Angels still featured the totemic presence of imperious transvestites. Their importance can't be overstated; their presence onstage smashed gender roles—not because they portrayed the opposite sex, but because they played whatever gender they *decided to be*, whether or not they looked the part. Other drag artists tried to pass as women or "become" women, but the Angels were never interested in creating such illusions of "gender traverse," marking a telling distinction from the assumption that drag was only about concealment or posing as the "other" through transformation.

For us, drag was about fusion and exuberant play. Bearded men played women; bare-breasted women played men. And this was a first. Genderfuck marked a telling distinction between a traditionalist seeking to imitate standard sexual typing and a revolutionary subverting images; presenting an artist as a self-created, conscious invention willed into being and sustained as much by individual choice as by communal assent.

It was staking-out new psychic ground, but, aside from this fusion, there was a poetic "in-between-ness," a lure appreciated and shared by many in the group. Certainly, one of the few principles all the Angels could agree on was our absolute rejection of the tyranny of male power. Our drag queens weren't sexual substitutes but political activists, expressionistic, not naturalistic. Scenery-chewing shamanic drag queens were conduits as they pried the lid off of twentieth-century theatrical tradition—most notably Meyerhold's theory of the unity of time and space. Genderfuck was muscular, volcanic, lean, electric, unpredictable, and infused with sheer theatrical magic. Such was the ancient and divine gift of Dionysus, God of Theater; such were the Angels of Light exploding in bawdy, incandescent, spellbinding transports.

Until 1973, Beaver drank a fifth a day according to Tihara, often staggering onstage drunk or passing out backstage, unable to perform. After Sham's birth, she cut down her drinking but, if prenatal damage had been done, it didn't end with his birth. Sham was never inoculated against any diseases for, like many Angels, Beaver decried Western medicine and wanted him to grow up "strong." *Strong?* Didn't she realize that if he wasn't immunized and got those diseases he'd suffer terribly?

In the fall of 1974, when the baby developed eczema, Beaver bound his forearms in cloth and told Sham that these were his "puppets." He was in torment for months. But no one, including myself, criticized her or alluded to this medieval approach as neglect or abuse. *Why?* In hindsight, I think that I was afraid of her. I think everyone was. But I kept silent because I wanted to fit in. That meant not confronting her. Beaver wielded power and would lash

Beaver Bauer and Sham, August 1976

out with a vengeance if put on the defensive. Newcomers were distinctly conscious of being in an undifferentiated limbo. But insiders felt tentative too. "It was impossible for anyone to know where they stood," Tihara says.

Such were the "politics" and the dynamics in the madhouse. And a madhouse it was. Most of the Angels were designated insane and got ATD (Aid to the Totally Dependent): $300 a month, plus food stamps and Medicare. From their $300, each Angel had to pay their share of the rent, about $50, and about $100 to the commune's food budget. Subtracting a few dollars a day for lunch or miscellaneous items left about $50 to $100 per month. From that, each Angel had to make their costumes for mostly one-night-only shows that took months to create. Because there was no money to rent a theater, the life of the Angels meant putting everything into a show that burst to life and vanished just as suddenly. It also meant that, for each show, Brian and his crew—if there was one—had to transport and set up the show from scratch, then dismantle the whole thing the next day, or the same night. It was an incredible workload.

In 1974, I lived on $300 a month, the same amount as the Angels. But I got mine from a trust fund and didn't get food stamps or Medicare. Though I was unaware of it, many thought I was filthy rich. The opposite was true.

By failing to satisfy my parents' demands, they punished me, saying "No" to my desire to buy a house ($25,000 in 1971), rent out rooms and become self-sufficient. So like the other Angels, I eked out a marginal existence. And like the Jets in *West Side Story*, we felt oddly empowered by an underdog status we treated as a badge of honor.

SHRINK: This boy don't need a job, he needs a useful career.

    Society's played him a terrible trick

    And sociologically he's sick!

RIFF: *(cheerfully)* I am sick!

JETS: *(in chorus)* We are sick! We are sick! We are sick, sick, sick!

    We are sociologically sick!

Some Angels really did look sick to me. In particular, a trio who were particularly harrowing and formidable (although they were always nice to me).

John Apple was a skinny alcoholic and addict who tended to get blind drunk onstage. A blond with shaved eyebrows, he had a propensity to rip off his clothes, hog microphones, and spew vulgarity. He sold Angel Dust (pig tranquilizer that people smoked!) for Miss Tiddy, a dealer from Long Island. With black nails, a caracal coat, heavy makeup, and the affectations of a Jewish country club maven, Miss Tiddy was all nouveau riche pretense.

Jeremy came from Florida where he robbed pharmacies and banks at gunpoint. Because he was always in drag for holdups, "Wanted" posters proved useless as they bore no resemblance to this dizzy emu with a skinny neck and pointed Adam's apple.

Such were some of the characters. But I was offstage, not yet one of them.

Chapter 5

In June 1974, the Angels were invited to Stanford University's Gay Day festivities. Though not part of the group officially, I came along. Getting permission to go onstage was a nebulous thing, so, swathed in gold velvet, I hung around—feeling completely peripheral—as the Angels got into costume. But when the lights dimmed, I had a great seat for the spectacle that followed:

The Jungle Show concerned Lila Cortez (played by Tihara, looking like a movie star in black lace and a hoopskirt made out of his great-grandfather's ties that he'd sewn together and studded with rhinestones), who crashes into the South America jungle. Here she's wooed by Dickhead, the richest man in the world, whose entire cranium is a pink glans. Accompanied by four sailors and an aged spinster, they fail in their attempt to escape in a hot-air balloon, whereupon Lila is captured by headhunters, the Roho-Ohos. She and their chief fall in love but an evil monkey in love with the Chief takes revenge on Lila by poisoning her. The poison fails. Ultimately, the Chief is given a magic potion that turns him into a bird; Lila battles the soldiers of the monkey to save her lover. She triumphs and, as a prize, is turned into a bird and reunited with her lover.

I recall Sister Ed coming out in full drag to do his Beijing Opera dance, his hat crowned with three-foot-long partridge feathers and with a hubcap for a shield; but of all the eye-popping effects, the costume I recollect most clearly was the dragon.

A tall and rangy fellow named Muldoon, who lived in North Carolina when not in San Francisco, had spent six months creating the twenty-foot-long dragon. As he endeavored to get the creature on stage without enough help, he lost his balance and the dragon toppled in the wings, collapsing even before it ever came into public view.

Watching spellbound, I realized that the Angels had developed a full theatrical vocabulary. The visuals, the use of dance-drama, the masks, the blending of cultures and more, comprised an outrageous palette, as well as a launching pad from which absolutely anything was possible.

But how did this magic all come about? Where was it from?

First, because it was free, the audience understood that this gift ran

directly counter to the profit motive. The shows were sacred community of-
ferings, making them quasi-messianic, a dynamic that was then reflected
back to the stage from the audience. It was genuine phenomena.

Second, no one was trying to duplicate reality. And for spectators, watching performers self-actualize vaulted shows into the realm of dreams. Pre-
cisely because many Angels were not necessarily schooled, or in control of
their art, *or even themselves,* there was something fascinating and disturbing
about the shows to those who were accustomed to "normal human behavior"; traditional theater and core identities were being redefined onstage in
an outrageous *fata morgana* that was seductive, stunning, and, at times, repulsive or psychotic. But *always* riveting.

Finally, what we usually get from theater—despite the fact it is the closest
of all arts to ritual and religion—is not transport to another ecstatic plane.
In Western culture, one might have to go back to medieval mystery plays—or
even to ancient Greece—to find antecedents of such drama, for the Angels
didn't so much appear onstage as descend from above like wraiths, harpies,
and ancient furies, awe-inspiring and totemic, sweeping aside all nonessen-
tials with a spirit that was both unstoppable and uniquely gay.

By "uniquely gay," I mean that, in synch with the gestalt of the particular
happening or event, the Angels both exploded and explored gay visual coda:
the loaded psychological shorthand that gay people (as well as all imperiled
minorities) had been obliged to employ or decipher in order to survive. At
a time when homosexuality meant danger and fear, with the always present possibility of taunting, firing, isolation, beatings, and even murder, the
Angels' in-your-face ballsiness exemplified contempt for accepted "mores,"
and flew defiantly in the face of authority. There had been other wonderfully
valuable theatrical contributions from artists (for example, Charles Ludlam's
Ridiculous Theater Company or José Saria's operas), but those were oriented
around one star performer. In marked contrast, the Angels were a collective
with a political and social agenda: the flagship of gay liberation.

As an Angel-in-embryo, I felt the group was missing only manageable
form to unfold with some sense of order. It didn't have to be Apollonian but
it *should* be strong enough and clear enough to prevent mishaps like the collapse of Muldoon's dragon. The only way I could imagine collective cohesion
coming about was through a written script.

Ralph Sauer, San Francisco Gay Day Parade, June 1976

The crystallization of the San Francisco Angels in 1972 resulted in a creative contrast to Hibiscus and Jack's shows in New York. *The Jungle Show* marked another seminal moment because this was where I became actively involved in the troupe.

Joining the theater meant getting closer to an Angel who scared me until I realized that inside that manic New Yorker who resembled Captain Hook lay a heart of gold. Tony Jonopoulos, a.k.a. Tony Angel, was that rarest of all theater animals: a bona fide genius who couldn't care less about the spotlight. Of course, he performed and loved it, but not out of a desire for attention. What Tony cared about was how art was delivered. The more political, and the higher the impact, the better.

With a background in the Living Theater, Tony was an avid student of Antonin Artaud, Bertolt Brecht, and Erwin Piscater. From Artaud, he learned the shock value of "the theater of cruelty"; from Brecht, he derived inspiration from socially motivated drama; and, thanks to Piscater, he became an enthusiastic advocate of vertical staging.

Tony saw the Angels as direct descendants of Alfred Jarry, whose incendiary *Ubu Roi* opened and closed on the same night in 1896. Despite its electrifying wipeout, *Ubu*—inarguably the most outrageous play of the nineteenth century—paved the way for every extreme theatrical event that followed. Tony adored *Ubu* for its cast of masked and hooded creatures, its diatribe of filth and depravity, its rising anarchic breakdown, and its calculated insults on a piss-elegant audience, who staggered out reeling from the horror of being visually and verbally assaulted. For Tony, this was sublime theater.

"Be contemporary and gutsy," he crowed, though quick to add, "but no violence."

Tony propounded simple icons and symbols. He believed that an audience's "willing suspension of disbelief" was more than enough to justify shattering traditional theatrical norms. "Fuck Shakespeare," he muttered one day when a script meeting got bogged down. "Where's the action?"

"Hypnotic disks," he marveled another time, contemplating a new prop to use onstage. "We've got to have hypnotic disks!"

Tony was a nonstop laboratory, lean and punchy. As committed as any of the other Angels to free theater, radical art and politics, communal living, and vegetarianism, he was also a loose cannon. For all his powers, he was vulnerable. Alcohol and heroin were only two of his demons. The third was an unwise and unhappy marriage. His wife—and the mother of his daughters, Ananda and Kavita—meant well but felt unloved and unappreciated; she drove everyone nuts with her whiny complaints and ceaseless nagging and proclamations of perpetual exhaustion. When it came to shows, however, she wanted to be a star while investing minimal effort. More than once, the group had to issue ultimatums: to pitch in and work harder or be bounced from the show. Such dictums never got traction, any more than her efforts to elicit sympathy. Beset by her, Tony sought refuge through hyperactivity, with constant detours into the land of addiction and nod. At times, he could be wildly over-reactive, emotionally unpredictable, and difficult. But he was a visionary trouper and I adored him.

Outside our dream world, America was in chaos. Nixon resigned in August 1974. Six weeks later, Ford's presidential pardon confirmed that all institutions were questionable. The nuclear family was no longer the only model. Marriage was optional, as was heterosexuality. Any belief in our country as the best place on earth had been sullied. Acts of sabotage and anarchy were commonplace. The possibility of armed violence was increasing. And there were smaller tragedies, closer to home and closer to the bone.

"Did you hear what happened?" someone asked as I arrived at the commune one day. "Paul Darling overdosed. He's dead."

I'd glimpsed Paul only briefly—he was a pretty young druggie—but I was stunned by the cavalier way the Angels treated his death. In retrospect, this nonchalance seems horrific. But this was life in the fast lane and, for all the apparent chumminess, when victims fell, no one missed a step. Throughout the 1970s, the collateral damage accrued: the overdoses, addictions, breakdowns, and suicides were hardly unusual. It sounds awful, but no one suggested that we stop to ask: why were the hard drugs tolerated? What did the drinking portend? Where *was* the real power balance? The guiding ethos?

If pressed, I think all of us might agree that no one could risk questioning or tinkering with what we were doing. And so, for all its phosphorescent glamour and beauty, there was a murky and dangerous underside. The immense extremes of the arc, the exhilarating swings between the exalted and the base, the incandescent and the depraved, and the glory and degeneracy formed the razor sharp perimeter we'd staked out for our art. And ourselves.

Chapter 6

Compared to the often chaotic and nervy atmosphere on Oak Street which I witnessed more frequently after *The Jungle Show*, life on Polk Street was as calm as a Buddhist retreat. In 1974, Bo and Peter were still working late nights at the Cabaret nightclub and Victoria was attending high school by day and hanging out with the most outrageous drag queens in the city by night. I was writing, running workshops (for free, of course) at a North Beach arts center called Intersection, helping Harold Norse with *Bastard Angel*, and enjoying life as the littlest fish in the littlest pond in the world.

My perception of the Bay Area poetry cosmos was shaped by North Beach bars and coffeehouses like Café Trieste. The scene revolved around the City Lights bookstore, but the degree to which one had "arrived" in this tiny yet most egotistical of all art scenes, was how close one got to Allen Ginsberg or twee Lilliputian Bolinas, a coastal town south of Inverness. Against this yardstick, poets measured their importance. I found it ridiculous. For all its much-vaunted status as the coolest hotspot in the country, the San Francisco poetry world was sophomoric.

Even so, I admired the poets, well-known names like Jack Hirschman, Gregory Corso, and Diane di Prima, as well as lesser-known luminaries such as Jack Micheline, a poet and painter whose bellicose, belligerent manner and crudely fashioned verse—rarely edited—belied an unusual sensitivity. And in the background, Bob Kaufman wafted, a burned-out Beat star, like a disembodied ghoul out of Goya.

In the spring of '74, I decided to give my first public reading. Declining offers from friends who volunteered to come along, I went to the Coffee Gallery on Columbus Avenue, determined to succeed or fail on my own. My juvenile debut will not be recorded in any other book; the best I can say about it is that when reading romantic poems while clad in Greek muslin I was not hooted offstage. Even so, I learned a vital lesson: *if you want to play with the big dogs, don't pee like a puppy.*

But an hour after my flop, the city allowed me one of its magic moments in the red ballroom of the Cabaret, where I showed up early. Here, I danced alone under mirrored balls refracting spotlights. Then a young man in black leather who danced in exactly the opposite way, moved jerkily and

THE FALL EQUINOX FESTIVAL OF POETRY

GAY POETRY READING

WILLIAM BARBER
ADRIAN BROOKS
HARRIET FRANCIS
JUDY GRAHN
PAUL MARIAH
HAROLD NORSE
PAT PARKER

WEDNESDAY·SEPTEMBER·18· 7:30·PM·
Fellowship Church· 2041 LARKIN· NEAR BROADWAY·
LIVE MUSIC AND DANCING WILL FOLLOW
COURTESY of the Gay Students Coalition.
FOR FURTHER DETAILS CONTACT ADRIAN: 7718753

THIS EVENT SPONSORED BY THE POETS COALITION

Poster for first gay poetry reading, created by Victoria Lowe and Adrian Brooks, September 18, 1974

automatically toward me until we were dancing together.

He was German and came from the Black Forest region. But I *didn't* take him home. At twenty-six, I was still too inexperienced and insecure to relax sexually. As a result, not many guys were exactly hot to trot a second time after one night with me. I'd been in hiding since childhood. And as an adult, I'd found ways to elude my pursuers. It's a fact I recall with rue: during my twenties, I created barriers to being touched. Or loved.

Being fear-driven is a strange thing, especially if the trauma has origins in childhood (or infancy). Emerging from this interior half-light would only occur over time, and in stages.

In this long process, I identified with quiet, spiritual men. As for my female side, I identified with Garbo, *not* because I saw myself as female; I was—and am—a man, honest and true. But I was—and remain—spellbound by her, as fascinated by her lifelong vanishing act as I was moved by the understated play of a minimalism and charisma that no one can explain. I saw it as spiritual, absorbing that template so deeply that it influenced my own poetry, persona, and conflicting desires to participate in the world. As a consequence, my public appearances always led to periods of withdrawal. And even as one of the Angels of Light, I remained as invisible as possible.

I wanted love, but I was afraid of being hurt and was wary of being desired on the basis of my appearance. Quick approval made me suspicious. The only way I could know I was authentic was to master a craft. Poetry is a ruthless taskmistress. Still, it gave my life meaning and freedom (and, yes, a hiding place too) day after day, year after year, and decade after decade, as it turned out. Looking back, I believe it exiled me as much as it animated self-actualization. But come what may, I had to test myself in the fire. Being "nice" or "popular" was for kids. I wanted to be real and saw no viable alternative except working my way toward Identity.

Some men wanted me, but I found excuses to reject them while the strapping, shaggy-headed Vikings with shy or romantic souls whom I lusted after, were not looking for a glittering Angel. And no matter how many people told me how beautiful I was, I found faults with myself. Even when someone appeared on a magic night, like that all-too-willing lad from the Black Forest, I disengaged. And went home alone.

Stung by my dismal performance at the Coffee Gallery, I called the Fellowship Church on Larkin Street to ask if they'd sponsor a gay poetry reading. When they agreed, I put together a list of poets I admired: Paul Mariah, Harold Norse, Pat Parker, Judy Grahn, Harriet Francis, and William Barber. Dancing and live music would follow.

For the event on September 18, 1974, I wore street clothes, not muslin. One hundred fifty people showed up—a huge audience for a reading. My performance was adequate, not stellar, though I did well as emcee. But the evening was a success, not just because I felt I'd done something socially useful or because Winston Leyland said he wanted to publish a volume of my poems; it was because I met a lifelong friend and soul brother.

Mark Thompson (who wrote the introduction of this book) was born and raised in Carmel. There, the aquamarine-eyed blond first sought escape from an epically mad mother by watching old Hollywood movies at a local grindhouse. In doing so, he developed his photographer's eye. Later, as a film student and writing major, he met James Broughton, a sixty-year-old poet who mentored this introspective and profound young journalist, imbuing him with a keen appreciation for tribal ritual.

In 1974, Mark was the new lifestyle editor for *The Advocate*, the most important national gay magazine. We became friends immediately although we were very different. I was whatever I was while Mark seemed a bit cautious and tentative. But within that quasi-academic exterior beat the heart of a true sex slut and future black-leather explorer of the dark underbelly of San Francisco. Determined to know every aspect of his own nature, Mark shed his psychically cramped past and flung himself wide open to extreme experience and spiritual investigation. Put simply, he understood not only the white hot moment, but its place in some larger historical or cultural arc. Obviously, we were too young to imagine where this wild ride would take us, but we recognized one another and bonded. Whatever fate Oz held for us, be it glorious or sordid, we'd signed on for the ride, as was clear in the chilly atmosphere of my poem "How Long Has it Been Since the Circus Began to Win?" (see page 228).

Chapter 7

While organizing the gay poetry reading, I was also involved in a very different project, one that was to have an unexpected effect on the Angels of Light.

In New York, my gallery jobs had entailed greeting anyone who came in without losing my cool, be it John and Yoko or Jacqueline Kennedy Onassis just having a look, or some crazy who wanted to exhibit the sheets upon which she'd just had an abortion.

In autumn 1972, an artist had come into Paley and Lowe, hoping for a show. John Schueler didn't get one but I liked his nonobjective landscapes of Inverness, Scotland, where he lived. We kept in contact and, in the autumn of 1974, when I learned he was going to have a solo show at the Whitney Museum, I initiated a plan to bring him to Inverness, California, for a local show before the big event in Manhattan.

When John arrived, I gave a lunch in his honor. It never occurred to me not to invite Henry Hopkins, the director of the San Francisco Museum of Art, to a gay commune on Polk Street. But when Henry couldn't attend, he sent his wife, Jan Butterfield, who was just great: bright, enthusiastic, and positive. The event went smoothly; John's show was a success. *Artweek* published my review. John went on to Manhattan. And though I didn't imagine that this luncheon might prove useful, I now had an "in" with the museum.

In October 1974, I began attending meetings at Oak Street for the Halloween show, a spoof of 1950s teenage horror movies. It was exciting but nerve-wracking. For all their public outrageousness—and "out rage" is the perfect term—the Angels could be curiously passive. Muldoon, now in North Carolina, had sent a letter to Oak Street asserting that the Angels were under the thumb of Rodney, Beaver, and Brian; that people were afraid of them. But his letter was greeted with derision. Still, Tihara remembers this was when he began to question the direction of the group. At meetings, I saw there was no means to ensure that everyone's voices were heard, it was often a lopsided dialogue between the out-of-control queens and those who were prepared to listen and compromise.

Somebody Else's Children (Beaver's mother was responsible for the title) concerned a group of teenagers who have a party and wander into a graveyard where they rouse some ghosts. As rehearsals continued, Polk Street roiled. A friend was confronted by hate-mongers who shouted "Fag!" from a car. He retorted, "I'll do what I want with my own body!" whereupon they shot him dead. Meanwhile, the first annual "Hooker's Ball"—a huge fundraiser organized by ex-hooker Margot St James to raise money to change the laws regarding prostitution and to get political and social support for working girls—drew thousands, including the Angels, who got in for free. We showed up in trucks to party on down with the whores and the socialites. I couldn't tell the difference as was clear in my poem "Portrait of a Room" (see page 230), but I recorded my excitement in my journal on October 27, 1974:

> All the drag queens in the ladies room, hitting up on lipstick and girl talk ... all so many people I know   peacocks flying through a rainstorm: bedraggled angels breaking glass bottles and screaming all the way home. Tonight the cameras and TV lights were on me ... and I loved it: to be a member of this strange and glittering underworld of night creatures, this is my destiny, not just a passing fantasy. I know these moments as instinctively as I breathe or respond to a sunset.

HIBISCUS FLEW IN from New York during the last week of October 1974. I expected someone splashy, but with short hair and a tweed coat, he looked like a fashion model. As he prepared for his cameo role for *Somebody Else's Children*, I heard that he was trying to work as a legitimate actor, but was unsure how to replace a self-imprisoning role as a glitter bimbette with a new identity.

Victoria had created a poster for our debut—it would be her first show too. The Angels decided to meet downtown on Union Square for a meeting and to look for a location for the preview, as recorded in the following entry in my journal on October 11th:

> Beautiful day in the square. Benches of old people sit on the sides like patients in a geriatric ward. I wonder if they're ready for what's going to happen here?

I find myself conceiving of things in a political way these days with a much more defined sense of place than ever before, even in FWI years. The only exception to this being my time with Dr King, but this is art and that was social protest politics and—to a certain extent—chic. If I'm a revolutionary, I'm a revolutionary artist and hopefully a humane being 'cause there's no way I'm going to pick up a gun at this point. But the teeth and claws I've used on myself were inherited dentures, hand-me-downs from the straight world of breakdown and departure from that arena. Now I orbit where I always needed to be with the people I always hoped to find and I'm where I belong. I'm very sleepy but I want to say that the sky is blue and there are three pink roses in a glass jar on this wooden crate. On the wall—the black and red of my paisley (cloth) chase each other into another century of whirling color.

As rehearsals continued, Tony got everyone hyped up about one of his favorite themes: the insanity of the American Medical Association, which was a recurrent leitmotif in our repertory. Seeing that almost all of the Angels, with few exceptions (including Victoria and myself), were at least purportedly insane or had either been institutionalized or medicated in the past, there was shared contempt for Western medicine and a ready willingness to spoof it, as I wrote in my journal on October 17th:

> Today the rehearsal went beautifully. We all practiced jitterbugging and it was fun. Tihara came downstairs in outrageous drag: a 1950s fake leopard-skin coat and orange tits that stuck out forty-five inches or so, sunglasses, pearl drop earrings, pink high heels, and an orange jumpsuit that went *for days*. It was wonderful. I feel so good when I'm over there.

At the same time, a filmmaker who lived in the house on Oak Street was making 8mm movies. I found myself in something titled *The Maid Gets Laid*, and another one about hospitals. Perhaps being in a film explains why there were tattered nurse's uniforms lying around; little else can explain why I put one on and went down to Union Square on the afternoon of October 31, 1974 for our preview performance.

All I remember is that we climbed onto the stage in the square. I think there was a microphone and a cardboard flat as a background. Tony wore a white coat and a surgical mask and was shouting at shoppers emerging from the nearby department stores. They seemed shocked to be harangued by incredibly strange and bedraggled drag queen nurses.

Had the theater critic of the *San Francisco Chronicle* been present, I doubt he'd have reviewed our travesty of mad Dr Dash and his insane procedures. But we returned home in triumph to prepare our one-night-only performance. People were flying in for it. Any time word of a new show got out, producers would come up from LA to see what we did then steal our ideas. But, word of mouth traveled farther than Tinseltown. Over the years, I met people who'd come from New York, Bali, India, Nepal, and Europe. (In the case of *Somebody Else's Children*, if they had attended the preview, I'm sure some would have elected to stay home because nothing went as planned. Or maybe that was the whole point?)

The show was staged at the Farm—a corrugated tin-sided warehouse on Potrero Street. Four hundred people showed up in this drafty, primitive space for the spectacle with two last minute additions:

Greg rolled into town with Angel Jack—who'd tried to commit suicide by hanging himself just days before when he thought his affair with Hibiscus was over. Jack was dressed like Hibiscus, immensely over-bosomed in a pink sequined dress and huge blond bouffant wig. Onstage, Hibiscus lounged on a divan in a boudoir, singing a pouty number into a phone.

Beaver was a sight. For hours, she'd patiently applied strips of latex to her face. The final effect was of an old hag. Upon seeing her, Sham had a fit. "It's okay, it's okay," Beaver said, continuing to prepare. Everyone ignored his trauma. Myself included.

The show got underway as planned, at least until Victoria and I went out to do our jitterbug, an athletic act which involved me throwing her over my back and catching her; during an over-the-back-and-then-back-again-spin, something went wrong. We were right in front of the audience, people at our feet, when, suddenly, she was zooming past me, head first, body horizontal,

Audience members and (back row) John Apple and Miss Tiddy, *Sci-Clones*, March 26, 1978

at an altitude of about three feet. As her feet shot by, I managed to seize her ankles and yank her back onstage, amazed by our near miss.

Some time later, I slithered onto stage to sing my song (a capella) costumed as a glittering androgen in black and chartreuse.

> When the moon is high
> and shadows dance with shadows
> in your room....
> The night has many visits from the tomb
> Beneath Death's golden eye
> The night has many visits
> from the tomb/ is nigh....
> The night has many visits from the tomb

I felt glamorous when I went backstage to change for the next scene, when the juveniles visit the graveyard. However, shortly after we got onstage, someone gave someone else a cue and ... nothing happened. No one came out. There was just a big dead silence.

Suddenly, someone beckoned wildly from the wings, "There's been a huge fight and half the cast just walked out!"

"What do you mean 'walked out'?" Victoria cried.

"They're gone! And we have to take a vote on how to end this thing!"

"*What?!*"

"We all have to vote on an ending."

Meanwhile, cacophony reigned: Jeremy had seized the microphone and was stripping, leering and screaming at the audience. Victoria and I were desperate.

"Now go do something until we decide!" someone shouted at us.

"*Go do something. Go do....* Are you serious?"

The audience was bewildered. No kidding. While John and Jeremy, the two drunk drag queens, fought over the mic, Victoria and I were supposed to 'do something'?

Nobody noticed whatever Victoria and I had tried to "do" anyway because John's wig was sliding off his head while Jeremy was waving a bottle of Jack Daniels, shouting insults and sticking his tongue out. Mercifully, the Angels who remained regrouped in the wings, formed a sort of conga line, marched back out to center stage, pointed at the crowd, and closed the show by shouting, "You're under arrest!"

That was it. *You're under arrest.* And the lights came on. The crowd rose slowly, understandably puzzled. But—hey!—the Angels of Light Halloween shows were famously weird and it was time to go to the Stud for our victory lap.

Chapter 8

After Dark magazine reported, "The Angels fizzled and burned," but we didn't care. Okay, it was freakish to be onstage and not know what the hell was coming next, or watch Victoria shoot past me, but it was also exhilarating to feel such incredible audience enthusiasm (in spite of how the show had shuddered to its terminus).

Having witnessed both Muldoon's dragon collapsing and a full-scale walkout, it was clear the Angels needed to cooperate. But how? I had no idea.

Meanwhile, on November 3rd, Winston Leyland told me he'd publish my poem—"yes"—in *Gay Sunshine*. However, exacting his pound of flesh, he insisted that I attend a William Burroughs and John Giorno reading the following night.

I capitulated and went, my face pancaked white, glittering with a hundred rhinestones applied with a spot of Sobo fabric glue that held them to my skin like a living veil. Ushering me forward, Winston introduced me to Burroughs—kindly, rather shy—and Giorno, a warm man whose incantatory poems bored me silly. The event was nothing so special, but for the first time I saw that Winston was displaying me for his own status, something I found really creepy, as I wrote in a poem on December 29th (see page 232).

Throughout November of 1974, the Angels were in rehearsal. *Inferno Reason*, our next show, was slated for Christmas. It was initially conceived as our take on *The Lord of the Rings* because many of the Angels were reading Tolkien. I recorded in my journal entry of November 8, 1974:

> The Angels of Light are planning a Christmas show; today was the
> first meeting. We all sit on the floor in the dance room, on cushions
> or coats, and discuss ideas and themes. It is to be based on the Bible
> in a loose, interpretive way. A bowl of fruit is on the floor—today it
> is bananas—less messy than the customary grapes served in water
> which inevitably spills onto the wooden floor. A blue pottery vase
> with fresh pink roses is beside the fruit in the center of the room.
> The room is crowded. Anxious to avoid the trashy antics of Hallow-
> een, the Angels start discussing a wide variety of approaches to the
> Bible—duels between God and the Devil—a choir of angels, a dance

of the universe in creation. More and more ideas are piled onto the cosmic raft until someone asks, "Where do the drag queens fit in?" So there is the basic divergence of opinion between the spiritualists and the camp queens. I see magnetic fields wavering around each proposal as different approaches and a variety of aspects are considered. Basic constructions of theme and storyline are lost in a rambling shuffle of people trying to present sufficiently radical interpretations of the Bible through the lens of twentieth-century feminist politics. But there are good ideas in the air. People seem to connect chemically as their ideas parallel one another. But toward the end of the meeting, drag queens flutter in from other scenes— dressed to the tits with orange feather boas in their hair, tons of plastic jewels, and sequined pants with blue roses. The meeting gets too large and gradually disintegrates. But it's novel to be in on the first meeting and sense the wide divergence of energy and opinion from the beginning. I sense these philosophical differences underlie the forces that polarize the commune and maintain certain disruptive ideas. In other words, the trashy element or the burlesque gets right in there from the ground up and it's hard to structure the play and specifically avoid psycho-drama.

(More and more I felt a division between the Angels who were "out there" and the rest. Trying to capture it, I wrote a poem in January 1975 that concerned quiet rituals of preparation; see page 233.)

At this point, I want to pay homage to some of the lower-profile Angels who may not have seemed dominant onstage but whom I found personally endearing. It does them an injustice to skim over their portraits; their contributions were substantial. In fact, unlike the divas hogging the limelight, these were the truest, most tender-hearted members of the group:

Francine was a peachy doll with honey-colored hair and warm brown eyes. She was always sweet and upbeat, and wore beads and gypsy ruffles. A dancer and mime who had dropped out of high school to join the Angels, she lived in a commune separate from Oak Street in a dwelling she shared with Rose, Melody, and Much Obliged.

Rose was a large woman with topaz eyes. In those days, she was an earth

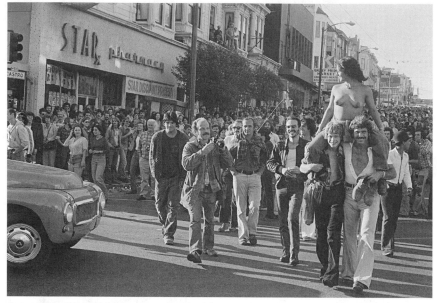

Castro Street Fair, 1976

mother who, like so many large women, moved and spoke with remarkable gentleness. She too was a dancer and mime, with the gift of making other people comfortable.

Melody, an ivory-skinned lovely with long cascading hair, possessed an airy femininity and sweetness. She was a dancer, actress, and mime; as with Francine, I never heard her say a mean word. Francine, Rose, and Melody bounced between the city and Marin County where they hung out with pot dealers and the Grateful Dead rock group.

Jessica Copen was truly complex, of solid build with beautiful crystalline blue eyes that reminded me of tanzanites. She was a dancer, singer, and mime, and level-headed too. Intelligent, driven, and sensitive, she was a hard worker. Some found her strident; not me, but I did find her haunted or dissatisfied in some way that I never did understand.

Much Obliged was the original, hip "bed head," a humorous cutie-pie who looked half human, half hobbit. An introverted dancer and mime with fuzzy hair, he was later known as Lichen.

Justin was an angular, feminine, and seemingly airborne introvert, endearingly gawky with a serious interest in the sitar. A dancer, mime, and musician.

Tufik was born in North Africa and always grinning; a delightful drummer and dancer. Good-spirited and always positive.

Walter Fitzwater was an architect with smoky eyes. He had a propensity to go to extremes but was always warm and kind with me. Another dancer and mime.

Cristin was an enchantingly lovely girl; dark-haired, dark-eyed, tiny, fine-boned, sweet. Back in the city after studying dance in Bali.

Indian was a hunky New Jersey number and butch act. He studied kung fu and was having an affair with Tihara but also fucking an Angel Dust dealer named Janice until Tihara flipped out and, brandishing a big pair of scissors, chased her out of the house.

These ten people, and more, met at the rehearsals throughout November. Cigarettes were always banned from the house and there was little, if any, drinking as we discussed the next show, often while enjoying vegetarian burritos and fruit juice. It was a fascinating process because, while working by consensus might appear to reduce things to the lowest common denominator, it also prompted passionate discussions about ethical portrayals and sexual stereotyping, for example.

In the end, we decided our next show would embrace the temptation of fairies and their choice between good and evil. Still on the periphery and insecure, I took notes, contributed ideas, and volunteered for several roles, one being part of an introductory trio of Angels who would explain our theme to the audience. Playing multiple roles was a staple of the group. With most of us doing three or four parts, audiences were often bombarded by over one hundred characters and creatures in one show. And though I looked forward to being a dippy Angel in the opening sequence, I was far more excited by the other role I'd landed.

Sent by the Devil to entice the fairies to hell, my part offered me an opportunity to hit the stage after a twenty-minute mime sequence where the fairies cavorted in Paradise. I realized that this sequence provided a showcase for mime artists, but I also realized that twenty minutes of innocence would bore even the most supportive audience silly. What a chance to charge onstage and shake the theater to its rafters!

As November tipped into December, everyone dispersed into separate spheres as they got to work: the dancers worked on their dances, and the mimes on their long sequence. Tony turned out masks in his muscular, expressionist style, and Brian designed lights.

A word about Brian's talent: although he had virtually no budget, he was masterful at creating gorgeous effects with the crudest of materials: stringing together lights in coffee cans, for example. When set pieces were few, he utilized the vacant space efficiently, adding to spatial dimension. When there were large sets with many props, he employed special lighting effects and mists of color to augment the beautiful backgrounds, caressing the performers and creating subtle cocoons to wrap the shows.

Tony's prop-making was equally fascinating: first, he would sculpt in clay before covering his molds with a wet, soft canvas-like material, "celastic," when dried hard, was lightweight, durable, and easy to paint or decorate with feathers, glitter, or rhinestones.

Sets were made by taping together huge sheets of cardboard. After the desired image was penciled on the front, the cardboard was cut out and attached to a grid made of slats of wood. In the final step, the facade was painted: kindergarten meets opera!

I had no trouble writing lyrics for my song and Tony generously offered to write the music, a process that took only about a half-hour because he was so talented. Still, I was stumped when it came to designing a costume. Aside from wanting to wear something extreme, I was lost until Greg handed me a book of costume designs and indicated a headdress shaped like an orchid. Such a contraption would rest on my shoulders; my head would be the stamen protruding from leaves surrounding my face. As for the lower half...? Well, "less is more," as they say.

INFERNO REASON WAS staged on four successive nights—January 9 to 12, 1975—at the University of California Extension Building at Haight and Buchanan Streets. Each night, a capacity crowd of 400 witnessed our parable about the fairies being led into Hell, where they rode a rollercoaster before finally choosing the Light and gathering together to sing a celebratory finale, "There's Gonna Be a New Day."

As predicted, on opening night the lengthy mime scene of the fairies didn't work theatrically. And accordingly, when a smoke bomb exploded in this prettily blissed-out Eden, the audience was desperate for something to happen.

Well ... yours truly was what happened.

Clad in my orchid headgear, fishnets, and silver platforms and clutching a pink ostrich plume, I charged onstage just this side of naked, Lust personified, bumping and grinding my way through a loud, driving song:

> One day you wake up
> With nothin' in your hand
> An achin' in your heart
> And a blood swollen gland;
> You can't read a book
> Saints are a bust
> You'll see if you look
> What you have is lust ...
> So
> stick it
> grind it
> suck it
> shove it
> squeeze it
> need it
> use
> abuse it
> ... *lust*

The audience loved it. And by the time the next scene started, the show had regained its footing as the fairies went on a rollercoaster to Hell where Tony, as the Devil, waited for them, an imposing figure in an immense red mask.

I loved channeling ferocious hard rock energy. It was the direct opposite of my offstage persona. But on this night, when I came down to earth with a jolt following my song, Tihara steamed toward me carrying some crudely decorated cardboard boxes.

"It's time to do the seven-headed dragon," he told me.

"What?" I frowned. I hadn't signed on for any such thing.

"Don't you remember? We said we'd do the seven-headed ..."

"Oh no, Tihara," I cried. "I remember the subject came up, but ..."

"I made these. *Here*," he said, giving me three boxes painted with beastie faces. "And cover yourself with this," he ordered, producing a plain white sheet.

Protesting was pointless. Tihara under full sail was a force to be reckoned with. So I surrendered, clapped a box on my head, and got down on my hands and knees. Not surprisingly, we couldn't see a thing; we got tangled up in the curtains until someone lifted them, setting us free. Tihara went on first; I followed, our heads covered and our bodies draped with sheets while we crawled around, snarling and growling. We were supposed to do this for three minutes—*three minutes!*—but, after one minute, I'd had enough and so I bailed out, leaving him to fend for himself: a four-headed dragon.

After *Inferno Reason*, my life changed. During my stint in the FWI and, later, with Warhol, I'd been a personality without a portfolio. But in the fishbowl of San Francisco, and as an Angel, I'd now been "discovered," as I wrote in my journal entry of January 9–10, 1975, after the show's premiere:

> I'm still high but it went well. My "Lust" number got people off.
> Later on, years from now, I may read these words in my journals
> with such a different attitude or approach but these feelings are
> real, for here, now, they exist and are part of me. A lot of people
> told me I'm the best thing in the show. All I know is that onstage
> I feel totally mystically connected. "Lust" made me an instant
> celebrity. Last night, at the bar, I overheard Tony say: "Suddenly,
> everyone is in love with Adrian!"

Harmodius and Hoti, Castro Street Fair, August 1975

San Francisco Gay Day Parade seen from City Hall, June 1980

Sister Ed and Lulu, San Francisco Gay Day Parade, June 28, 1987

Jerry Kirby and LZ Love in front of City Hall, San Francisco Gay Day Parade, June 1980

Ralph Sauer, Julie Petri, and *Holy Cow!* dragon, San Francisco Gay Day Parade, June 1979

FACING PAGE: *Tanlines* (performance art piece by Violet Ray), Castro Street Fair, August 1976

Much Obliged, Castro Street Fair, August 1975

Enchantra and Dan Nicoletta, San Francisco Gay Day Parade, June 1975

Lobby at Bimbos Club, October 1978

Tony Angel, Castro Street Fair, August 1975

Hibiscus, *Femme Fatale* (east coast Angels of Light production), September 1976

FACING PAGE: Hibiscus, *Femme Fatale* (east coast Angels of Light production), September 1976

Inferno Reason poster, created by Rodney Price, January 1975

Tihara doing a Balinese dance, *Inferno Reason*, January 1975

Fairies cavorting in Garden: (*l–r*) David Meadows, Gregory, Steven Brown, and Much Obliged, *Inferno Reason*, January 1975

Brooks ("Lust") with David Meadows, *Inferno Reason*, January 1975

Chapter 9

"Suddenly everyone is in love with Adrian!" Tony crowed at the Stud. Someone else might have loved hearing that, but when I found myself at the center
of attention, the hoopla disturbed me. As Winston led me to meet William
Burroughs, he told me, "The evening at Fellowship Church was the first gay
poetry reading there's ever been. You're one of the twenty most important
people in gay lib." Not true. I knew enough to know that. Even so, it was slip-
pery and disorienting. Becoming a performer challenged a monastic lifestyle
that included lighting candles at night to read the *Tao Te Ching* and doing
my best to avoid the limelight. Now, the limelight searched me out. It was jarring. And as events would prove, it would only get worse. In this, I was hardly
the first person to discover that success is bittersweet.

Part of my ambivalence was due to the poetry scene, that arena of huge
egos with so little acclaim. Suddenly, I was in demand. Harold Norse invited
me to illustrate poems by Jean Genet before giving me a full page in *Bastard
Angel* for my illustrated poem and putting my name on the cover alongside
major Beat poets. Gerard, who called me "the best poet of your generation,"
wanted to do a book featuring Robert Creeley, himself, and me. Paul Mariah
wanted my poems for *Manroot* magazine. Winston was including my work
in *Gay Sunshine* on a regular basis, and after I'd visited Kaliflower in November to elicit criticism for my poems, Irving had apparently told Tihara that
the Angels should hitch themselves to my wagon. (Irving had been gracious
with his time and praise, but I felt so uncomfortable in his environs that I
would never go back.) On weekends, I helped the gallery in Inverness orga-
nize another show called "Artists' Toys" which featured creations by stars like
Alexander Calder as well as locals. The gallery owner asked me to write an
accompanying book for the exhibit. I agreed, working for free, of course. And
the momentum continued to accelerate.

Because *Inferno Reason* went so smoothly, meetings for another show
began almost immediately. I now sensed I had influence on the group. My
first thought was that whatever we staged, as long as everyone got their moment in the sun, they were less likely to walk out. The solution? A script;
a structure that would focus everyone on a common goal. Given this, the
group might function perfectly.

My task was to get everyone committed to a story they believed in, then break down the plot into a series of vignettes. If each moment could "snap, crackle, and pop," a great show might be possible even without a director. And without anarchy or sabotage.

Lao Tzu counsels, *A leader is best when people barely know he exists. Of a wise leader, whose work is done, the people will all say, "We did this ourselves."* This would be my goal, leading us all to triumph before disaster.

In February, Harold Norse began a class for writers whom he considered had major talent: Jillen Lowe, Gene Berson, his wife Erica Horn, Neeli Cherkovski, Luke Breit, Michael Schwartz, and myself. On a bi-weekly basis, we met for Harold's lectures on modernism, readings, and group critiques. I found the course illuminating not only for the insights, but because I met a poet I considered the finest (coincidentally gay) rising star in the country.

Neeli Cherkovski, a biographer and sidekick of Charles Bukowski, was a hirsute and bespectacled roly-poly bear. He arrived on the scene in 1975 to assist George Moscone's mayoral campaign. The ill-informed might notice only his nervous tics and presume Neeli to be an absent-minded professor. But within his nebbish-like exterior beat the heart of Walt Whitman. And in his majestic, rolling verse, Neeli fused Whitman's soul with the searing jazz cadences of García Lorca.

In his mid-thirties at the time, Neeli had already grasped his major theme: the great longing heart in search of absolution. Gutsy and tender, romantic and forceful, he aimed for the stars with unapologetic faith in the centrality of love. I felt Neeli stood head and shoulders above all the poets of our generation. In my opinion, he still does.

In the spring of 1975, Paul Mariah and I shared the stage at Malvina's, a celebrated forum for poetry readings in San Francisco since the 1950s. Costumed and fully transformed into a glittering persona as The Painted Boy, my performance of high impact poems such as "Look Twice Before Crossing America" (see page 234), was all hard rock energy, totally fist-fucking the stale format of a traditional reading. The reading made me an overnight sensation. At last, I'd figured out how to make a poetry reading electric; it had to do with taking control of the moment-*as-performance*, filling the space with personal energy, and using the poems *as punctuation* in a reading that, out of respect for an audience's ability to truly focus, would be twenty minutes *maximum*. By doing so, I fused Irving's advice to give each poem an "iron skeleton" and Harold's admonition to "get them in the first line and never let them go." As a result of this formula that melded the two worlds I lived in, my tinsel star rose higher.

POLITICS INFUSED AMERICA in the late spring of 1975. The Vietnam War ended on April 29th. Of course, the Angels considered the Viet Cong victory a cause for jubilation. For us, such acknowledgment was not treasonous but a sign of ethical strength: that a healthy society could—and *should*—admit its errors and faults, expose high crimes and misdemeanors, and cleanse the rot and live up to the original and yet still-revolutionary intent of the most anarchistic and free-spirited Founding Fathers.

On a local level, there was a palpable coalescing of political consciousness. And these people warrant specific mention and high praise for contributing to the ensuing events:

David Meadows, who was now finally involved romantically with Victoria, had once been a member of the radical Students for a Democratic Society (SDS), the incendiary anti-war group that had resorted to violence. Hailing from a military family, with a face like a bright coin, this graduate of the Naval Academy at Annapolis was curiously gallant but wounded and confused. His good intentions were undeniable. Thanks to him, script meetings embraced poetic and political romance.

Tede Mathews, poet, politico, and performer, lived in a commune on Castro Street and was intricately involved with radical gay politics, both locally and as part of a pan-cultural outreach program to Latin America. In addition to appearing in the landmark gay documentary film, *Word Is Out*, Tede also worked at the first gay community center, and was part of the first faerie circle and an anarchist study group. Of all the gay men I ever knew, he was the most sensitive to women's issues. And of all gay men, he was the one I was the happiest to learn from; his shrewd criticisms and admonitions, which defied standard social typing and conditioning, was incisive, and he didn't spare the rod.

Dan Nicoletta appeared on the scene in January of 1975. Born in New York in 1954, he studied film at the California College of Arts and Crafts in Oakland before reaching San Francisco in 1974 with his darkly handsome and mysterious lover who resembled the hero of a nineteenth-century French novel. Introverted and seductive, Steven Brown (later, cofounder of the internationally famous New Wave music group Tuxedomoon) was a serious musician and anarchist. In August of that year, Dan met Harvey Milk and became one of his best friends and associates, centrally involved with his campaigns for a supervisor's seat at City Hall, as well as working at Harvey's store—Castro Camera—on Castro Street. I liked Dan enormously the moment I met him; he was thin as a rail with lively blue eyes and good will I found infectious.

In 1975, there was a longstanding split in the Angels about permitting photographers backstage access. (Lynne, a titanic member of Kaliflower, and a charming poet named Charles Rivers would get members to pose for pictures, as had photographers Crawford Barton and Marshall Reiner, but the general attitude toward the issue was negative.) Even so, I felt intuitively that Dan could be trusted to document our secret world without exploiting it, so I used my influence to ease opposition. Once granted entry, Dan's work and his character won the affection and confidence of the group.

Dan remembers it now as a time "when my paychecks were skimpy and immediately divided into three categories of utilization: rent and lunch food, beers at the Stud, and anything left over—not much—could then be used to buy rolls of film running through my camera." His job at Castro Camera allowed Dan the ability to shoot more film, thanks in part to the creative atmosphere cultivated by Harvey and his then-lover Scott Smith who managed the store, but the scene in the Castro was so vibrant that Dan required lots of film in order to keep up.

Dan came from a world of politics and politicians who appreciated radical artists. His work with Harvey and the troupe straddled two worlds, and his lifelong devotion to the preservation of that pivotal shift in the American landscape is a testament to the quality of his convictions and his friendship.

Silvertongue on Castro Street, July 4, 1976

Having been anti-war activists, Tony and I were determined to bring a gritty Brechtian consciousness into the new show. But a major concept for which Tony provided the sole impetus was that of the plague. Inspired by Artaud, in 1975, Tony saw the Plague as the primary metaphor of our time. To present the confluence of these political influences—the end of the war and our lingering sense of betrayal over Ford's pardon of Nixon—he advocated a show that used the Plague to emphasize global peril and also a condemnation of social depravity.

As I'd also been captivated by Versailles and French history since childhood, I saw theatrical potential in the fall of the *Ancien Régime*. As meetings progressed, I was thrilled to see the concept find collective approval. Sitting at scriptwriting sessions with my typewriter, I hacked out a script that drew on *A Tale of Two Cities*, allowing ample room for Tony's plague, David and Tede's radical politics, and a widely shared desire to celebrate the Viet Cong victory. As it started to jell, we suspected we were working on something extraordinary. But it really came together in part, due to two events: the luncheon I'd given for the Scottish artist John Schueler and the farcical last night of my marriage in Philadelphia in 1971.

At the luncheon I'd met Jan Butterfield, wife of the director of the San Francisco Museum. When I called her to ask if the MOMA would sponsor our show, that wonderful woman put me in touch with Bob White, the museum's director of education. Tihara and I went to see him. The result? For only the second time in its history, the MOMA agreed to support a free event! With their sponsorship, we got the Veterans Auditorium (later renamed the Herbst Theatre) for two nights in June *for a sixty-dollar janitorial fee.*

Shortly after this, Winston Leyland told me he was planning to include my poems in an upcoming anthology titled *Angels of Light.* I protested, but I got nowhere until I fibbed, claiming the group had copyrighted the name. Thus obstructed, he assigned me the task of finding an acceptable alternative. My sarcastic suggestion—*Angels of the Lyre*—was intentionally absurd, but Winston himself was too, so *voilà*: the title. His next anthology, *Orgasms of Light,* revealed how stuck for names he was. My estimation of Winston was tanking fast. Fortunately, I didn't have to see him much; he was busy with his live-in lover, a really sweet nineteen-year-old from Guatemala.

In March, Peter and Bo were fighting so much I sought refuge with Jillen, now back in town and living with Victoria on Bush Street. Two months later, in May, my father visited. I hadn't seen him since 1972; we'd been at odds since 1966 when he supported the war in Vietnam and just shrugged when, acting without a warrant, Chicago police burst in on the Black Panthers and, guns blazing, slaughtered seven people in the middle of the night ("If blacks wear Afros and behave badly, they should expect such things"). The topper was my father's dismissal of ecologists and anyone else who thought the country was being run by the military-industrial complex: "The one percent of the country who believes that are the dropouts who live in trees, and who don't count anyway."

But during his visit, he made an effort to heal past wounds, offering to lend me money for a down payment on a building where I could live and rent out apartments or run a bed-and-breakfast, thereby becoming self-supporting, something I'd been trying to achieve since 1971, when properties only cost $25,000. Although such houses now cost $65,000, he approved of the idea. It was an immensely important moment, convincing me that we could actually achieve a healthy and mutually respectful relationship.

Attending a rehearsal on Oak Street, my father made an insightful remark on my role: "Like Katisha in *The Mikado.*" But I had no idea what he thought of the Angels. Still, what would any parent surmise upon finding their offspring aligned with the most outrageous drag queens, a collective of people living on welfare and sporting nostril rings?

When he left, I felt we'd bonded, but there was little time to bask in an afterglow of incredible relief and gratitude. Our show was just around the corner. Still, *no one* suspected what was coming when the MOMA announced our free event with a carefully worded text that I'd composed for their June calendar, hoping to slip some cues in under the radar of the editor. To my astonishment, it worked:

ANGELS OF LIGHT EXTRAVAGANZA; PIÉCE DE RÉSISTANCE!
The scene changes from Paris, under the sea to the North Pole,
and to Paris again in the extravagant, outrageous, and zany Angels
of Light production. It is a fantasy of music, dance, mime, and
masque that draws from Chinese, Balinese, Hindu, African, modern dance, rock, and jazz idioms. The Angels of Light is a theater
collective consisting of men, women, and children who have produced many arresting theatrical events in the Bay Area, throughout the US, Mexico, and Europe. Free of Charge: June 11–12, 8 p.m.

When I submitted the copy, the show didn't have a name, but shortly thereafter, a title was found. And as was so often the case, it was Ralph Sauer who, with his unerring ear for puns, came up with the phonetic bull's eye: *Paris Sites Under the Bourgeois Sea.*

But as *Paris Sites* gathered steam, there was danger on the horizon.

Jeremy disappeared. Rumor had it that John Apple had him murdered by a Hell's Angel after Jeremy copped a deal with the police to expose John and Miss Tiddy's Angel Dust business. True or not, the bottom line is: Jeremy was never seen again.

Pausing to reread these words, they look astounding to me. Why didn't we do something? Had we lost contact with reality? Were we that dysfunctional?

For me, the answer was *yes*. As an Angel, I'd not only been reincarnated spiritually, I'd found a family. And if dysfunction underscored a bitch's brew of cult secrets, sexual conflicts, ostentation, exhibitionism, Narcissism, self-professed altruism, and self-promotion attending obsessive-compulsive ambivalence, xenophobia, lopsided power abuses, and dazzling displays of glitter, *what else was new?*

"Life in the Angels was savage," Greg allows. True. But all of us had learned to compartmentalize in this "other world" that allowed us to live and simply *be*. The process of recognizing ourselves while coming together as a group was not only a means of survival, it also represented individual spiritual commitment to our highest ideal.

That ideal wasn't simply about free theater, but it was our sustaining credo. Given the price we'd already paid to survive the weirdness of the 1950s and early 60s, every one of us was subsumed in the relief of participating in shows that embodied our best selves and which functioned as sacred ritual, identity, true culture, and refuge.

To some extent, "subsuming" involved closing our eyes to the darkest, most freakish elements. But that was the shadow that made the Angels so luminous. As the beautiful Teena Rosen-Albert asked rhetorically, years later: "But isn't it always that way with great art?"

THE CONCENTRATION OF creative energy was so intense in those last weeks of May and first weeks of June, I felt I was living inside a city workshop. Night after night, we worked on sets. Beaver was creating an underwater scene complete with coral reefs and a life-sized whale; Martin Wong, later a famous artist, painted the grand hall of the palace and a boudoir with three thrones. Chuck Drees, a newcomer and brilliant artist, built the first scene, the streets of Paris, and I made a carriage pulled by prancing horses. Dan Nicoletta created a cartoon film of a submarine going to the bottom of the sea to be shown just before intermission, adding an entirely new dimension to an Angels show. As for the underwater scene, Greg created a chariot for his brief appearance as a mermaid, and obsessively upholstered it with tiny pearls that no one could possibly see! Tommy Tadlock and Steven Brown composed original and progressive music. From this point on, each major show had not only its own look but its own sound as well.

As opening night neared, there was a tidal flux of people coming into the city. Some came from the far side of the planet. Pot farmers like my squeeze, Mountain Bear Splendor, arrived to pass out free joints or pot brownies. Free daycare centers were set up so parents could attend. There was free food, free places to stay, and free you-name-it provided to hundreds of friends, fans, and well-wishers. Kaliflower had printed a handsome poster for the show and Rodney designed a program with text that put show in context:

Once upon a time, there was grumbling heard in the streets. Rats roamed in the streets and ruled the palace. A riddle is revealed to the people:

> *"Search for the maid who hears with her eyes*
> *She will unravel countless lies*
> *Travel inside a steel-bellied fish*
> *Beseech the captain to do as you wish*
> *Under the land of blue, black, and white*
> *Where the water is hard and birds have no flight"*

Enough is enough. Out of their desperation and anger comes new energy; turning their anger into love. They are filled with the spirit of Courage, Good Fortune & Vigilance.

Inside the palace, the Court prepares for festivities. Alas, the people of the streets invade the party, spies reveal the secret plan, which takes them under the Bourgeois Sea, while others stay behind caring for the victims of the plague.

Inside the Belly of the Fish, a mutiny takes place and the tables are turned. The answer to the riddle charts the course to find a cure for the plague.

Intermission—ten minutes—

We pause at the Polar Paradise for plenty of plush pink party poopers and prissy pastries. The big freeze in the fire of fever breaks the ice.

The sea cools the heat of the plague and from a faithful love comes the answer: the cure. The power of the Spirit makes the transformation. Thereafter, joy was to be heard in the streets. Listen.

There were hassles even before the show began, however. Irving sent word that he wanted to photograph the cast in costume at four o'clock, four hours before curtain time.

"No way in hell," I said. The idea of getting made up and in costume that early was absurd. Up to the last minute, there were always hundreds of last-minute details.

I can't claim my refusal influenced anyone, but I do know that, for the first time, the Angels refused to accommodate the High Palooka. He was forced to wait. Later, once in court regalia, I gladly let Irving take a picture then hurried off to get ready for the show—something that I tried to capture in the poem "Backstage Angel: Incandescent Under Blue" (see page 236). On the far side of the curtains, the audience was roaring. *And isn't this where you came in?*

Chapter 10

Act I, Scene 1: Paris.

Starving peasants curse their fate. One finds a chicken and rips it apart, eating it raw. A carriage runs over a child. The people scream; jowly, impatient Countess sticks her head out the carriage window.

COUNTESS: What was that bump? And why have we stopped?

PEASANT: A child is dead under the wheels of your carriage!

COUNTESS: Well, you should have thought of that before you over-populated. But you have absolutely no sense of social responsibility. *(To coachman)* Drive on!

The carriage shoots away. The people gather to sing an anthem of defiance:

CHORUS: We're tired of being hungry and poor
   Crusts of bread satisfy us no more
   We're tired of being forced to beg and to steal
   Soon you aristocrats will know how we feel.

The poor go off to plot. A window in the palace opens, revealing a beautiful young girl, Nostalgia Flushette, the daughter of the Countess, who is mesmerized by a Pierrot who does a mime piece, calling to political—and romantic— liberty. Nostalgia replies to his woos by throwing him a red rose. Afterward, she paces in the street. Her mother enters. They argue about the poor.

COUNTESS: *(singing)* Let them eat shit! *Mangez gâteau!*
   Especially baked at our country château.

Countess ushers her sullen daughter inside to prepare for a surprise guest.

Scene 2: The Dressing Room.

Three countesses primp on towering thrones crowned with grinning skulls. Each sports a gargantuan headdress: a toilet, a pearl en-crusted cone, and a Putti holding his penis. En masse, the assembled trio is eighteen feet wide and nine feet tall. The front of one gown is a Peugeot car grill, four feet wide. The dialogue is phonetic; the countesses squawk like demented hens. Countess Flushette reveals a secret: she has a submarine in the garden. If there's an uprising, she'll escape. The Putti-topped countess embraces her. As the ladies kiss, her Putti shoots pee into the Countess Flushette's toilet. The three ladies swoon with delight as a servant girl sneaks away to join the revolution.

Scene 3: The Palace Interior.

In a set painted in sharp, declining perspective making it appear like a vast gallery, two counts sniff cocaine while discussing the slave trade. Rankly effeminate, the de-sexed nobles swap stories until heralds announce the ladies. Once assembled, the nobles summon Nostalgia and inform her of her surprise betrothal. She watches horrified as her fiancé enters: Prince Mince, a wheezy, wobbly twerp. Gushing hosannas, the nobles welcome him, ordering their lackeys to display his payoff: Nostalgia's dowry. The Putti-topped countess goes into raptures.

COUNTESS: Oh! I just love money! The older and smellier the bet-ter!

Baskets of money are hauled in followed by a ballet featuring the servant girl/spy and her lover, Harlequin. As they finish, Nostalgia regains her wits and storms forward.

NOSTALGIA: I won't do it!
COUNTESS: What?!
NOSTALGIA: You heard me! I said: I won't do it! He's disgusting!
COUNTESS: But everything is all arranged!

NOSTALGIA: I don't care! I'd rather die than marry him! You people
   make me sick!

A SERVANT: *(shouting)* The poor people are storming the palace!

COUNTESS: Quick! Let's eat while there's still time!

*The aristocrats stuff their faces, but invading diseased peasants,
giant plague monsters, and rats crash the reception. Sword play
ensues until a freeze action.*

COUNTESS: Get out! Get out! You aren't on the list and you weren't
   invited!

*Pandemonium resumes until the next freeze-action, when one of the
afflicted exposes his ass, screaming, "Fuck me!" Countess Flushette
flees as Revolution engulfs France.*

Scene 4: Submarine.
*A motley crew is put through its paces in an absurdist satire of naval
spit and polish. Countess Flushette enters and orders them to sail to
the Riviera, but the servant girl appears with an old clairvoyant who
reveals a cure to the plague will be found in a distant land "frozen
and white." The Countess kicks the old woman to death. The crew
mutinies and begins a quest glimpsed through a porthole (a white
disk in the set) upon which a cartoon film is projected.*

— Intermission—

Act II, Scene 1: The North Pole.
*With icebergs in the distance, penguins waddle into view, chattering
alliterative dialogue (written by Ralph) in which every word begins
with the letter P: penguin polar pies—primping, popping, plumply,
purple, popular. The penguins tap dance exuberantly but their giddy
revelry comes to an end when The Countess appears. Mistaking
them for servants, she scares them away.*

[Note: Up to this point, all proceeded as written, but while I was onstage, several people signaled to me and whispered: "Adrian! The show is too together! There was a vote and people decided you have to fuck it up!" Trusting them and familiar with backstage revolt, I shed my skirt to give an a capella rendition of "Stormy Weather." After my impromptu act, the show continued.]

A Kabuki dancer/blizzard spirit freezes The Countess to death. As she dies, the servant girl dashes in, pursued by Harlequin. The ice breaks, she falls. Harlequin plunges after her to be united in death.

Scene 2: Under the (Bourgeois) Sea.
A mermaid sings a siren song on a chariot drawn by seahorses. Behind her, a life-sized whale hovers. A glowing red starfish is a striking counterpoint to a coral reef. The drowned servant girl and Harlequin—both now sea spirits/reincarnations—reveal a miraculous rose. Thus, through sacrifice, the martyrs find the cure for the plague. A diving bell appears. Two deep-sea divers emerge and claim the prize of their quest, then return to the mother ship.

Scene 3: Paris.
In a wild finale—a Chinese banner dance augmented by Vietnamese and Viet Cong flags—the joyful citizens of Paris celebrate their deliverance.

—End—

Inside, we were deliriously happy as we stood onstage basking in the adoration and love of our audience. But unbeknownst to us, there was a startling scene taking place outside, one that had been going on for over three hours because, even before the curtain rose on Act I, someone reported screams inside the auditorium. We were stunned to learn that fire engines and police had been dispatched and local news teams sent reporters who heard the police feared a riot. So news team helicopters hovered above the theater, their searchlights revolving in the sky, as a fire marshal and police debated how to evacuate the theater without triggering pandemonium.

But mayhem had already erupted inside, not only due to our show, but because of the insanely diverse audience. Unbeknownst to us, the calendar listing our show was also sent to war veterans, as the "Veterans" Auditorium was technically the property of the United States Army. So veterans, veterans groups, Lions, Elks, and Masons got wind of it. Having no idea what the show was, they, along with their suburban families, waltzed into a crossfire of the right and ultra left over a show dedicated to the victorious armies of North Vietnam. *And they loved it!* Even so, this was just too much, even for San Francisco, which is why someone called the police. Having no idea that the screams were screams of approval, upon arriving at the museum, the Chief of Police and Fire Marshal decided it was too risky to order an evacuation, and they hoped for the best while the show unfolded inside and helicopters whirred outside.

Paris Sites Under the Bourgeois Sea poster, created by Kaliflower commune, June 1975

Paris Sites was a phenomenon: the apex of our Glitter Age, an event so outsized and outrageous that, even thirty years later, it defies description. People of all stripes screamed and shouted and could not believe their eyes upon witnessing a fusion of talents so extraordinary that words fail to describe it. Here we had a group of certifiably crazy outcasts, not only creating a new form of art, but also hoisting high the banner of anarchy from the stage of a major American cultural institution. In short: in every way, we'd triumphed.

As the show's star and swirling Big Meanie incarnate, I felt fused to the immense wave of love and enthusiasm rushing over me from our audience.

This was the actual dynamic of gay revolution; its irreducible heart and soul. At last I understood who I was. With this absolute commitment, I could be subsumed while fulfilling myself, giving my all and having it received beyond all question or doubt. It was electric, gorgeous, and so transcendent and utterly satisfying, *I would never need it again. Ever. But I would never be the same again either.*

In heralding the advent of the plague seven years before AIDS, in drawing a definitive line between the consciousness dividing the haves and the have-nots five years before the presidency of Ronald Reagan, in celebrating the victory of underdogs over the world's greatest superpower, and in launching this iconoclastic people's opera infused with a gay sensibility, the Angels hit their zenith by depicting the most immense drag queens ever, before toppling them in anarchic ritual madness. *This was revolution!*

Within days, thousands of people were phoning from as far away as Portland, Seattle, and Vancouver, asking how to make reservations or buy tickets. The museum was also reeling over the explosive show, however, an emergency meeting of the board was convened the following Monday morning, bright and early.

Bob White, through whom we'd scored the auditorium, gave me an insider's view of what happened when the Powers That Be met to discuss what we'd just done.

"At first no one said anything," Bob said. "Everybody just sat around, waiting for someone else to go first. Finally, I said, 'Well, I don't know about anyone else, but I liked it.' Then someone else turned to me and said, 'You did?! So did I!' and, one by one, they all admitted they'd been shocked to high hell but had had a wonderful time."

Okay, we weren't going to be sued, but we sure as hell weren't going to be invited back. Fine. We'd triumphed anyway and were ready to move on. But where? How?

Paris Sites Under the Bourgeois Sea program, created by Rodney Price, June 1975

Countesses in the Boudoir: (*l–r*) Gregory, Adrian Brooks, and Tihara, Paris Sites (Act I. Scene 2), June 1975

FACING PAGE: Adrian Brooks singing "Stormy Weather" in North Pole, *Paris Sites* (II.1), June 1975 .

Randall Denham and Beau (Beauchamp) as Counts, *Paris Sites* (I.3), June 1975

Steven Brown, *Paris Sites* (II.2), June 1975

The Hospital Show, summer 1975

Chuck Drees in Healing Yourself Dance finale, *The Hospital Show*, summer 1975

Marc Huestis singing "Someone to Watch Over Me" (minus the infamous bottle he flung into the audience), August 1976

Ralph Sauer with two of the many youngsters who participated in the shows, 1978

Teena Rosen prowling the Tango Palace, *Sci-Clones*, 1978

The Tango Palace, *Sci-Clones*, 1978

FACING PAGE: *Sci-Clones* poster, 1978

Art deco tap dance, *Sci-Clones*, 1978

FACING PAGE: Indian, *Sci-Clones*, 1978

(*l–r*) Elo Kent, Ralph Sauer, Tony Angel, Beaver Bauer, and Jessica Copen, *Sci-Clones*, 1978

Machine Worship mime piece (created by Beaver Bauer), *Sci-Clones*, 1978

(*l–r, from back row*) Melody, Radha (Madeline) Bloom, Francine, Janet Sala, (*l–r, front row*) Jessica Copen, Beaver Bauer, *Sci-Clones*, 1978

Chapter 11

Depression follows a closing night. This was no exception. An emotional void soon eclipsed our feelings of exhilaration; we suffered from a collective listlessness and sense of letdown. Nothing brilliant exists without shadow. The fellow who played limp Prince Mince died from alcoholism. And without knowing it, I was slipping into an abyss from which would take three years to emerge.

After the celebratory parties, someone invited the Angels to participate in a "Healing Festival" the following weekend at the Live Oak Theater in a leafy section of Berkeley. I have no idea why. Possibly they were gulled by our sweetly angelic name?

I'd spent the weekend with my new lover, a lithe, taciturn man with cat-like green eyes and a great body. Sidney Hushour was squatting in an apartment at the elegantly shabby and abandoned Casa Madrone on Frederick Street in the upper Haight-Ashbury. Home to Marilyn Monroe at one point in the 1950s, and Janis Joplin in the 60s, Casa Madrone sat inside a walled and gated garden.

Preternaturally gentle, Sidney revealed that he'd once robbed a bank and dabbled in heroin. Did I run for the door? Nope. At twenty-seven, I'd never had great sex before and because I was so hungry and wanted love so badly, I fell and fell hard, as evidenced by poems I wrote at the time: "Daydream— Color in Dissolute Blues," "More Justifications," "Rubble," and "Life on the Cutting Edge" (pages 237–242).

At Oak Street for a meeting about our new show, I was appalled. By now, I was used to all kinds of whack jobs showing up and wanting to be in our spectacles, but this time the wannabes just beat all: pre-op transgenders who were also certified mental cases institutionalized in the psych ward at San Francisco General Hospital, the lowest rung of the city's health care system. How they got out is anybody's guess, but "out" they certainly were! Besides being on and off anti-depressants and anti-psychotic drugs, they were gobbling up everything they could get their hands on: LSD, speed, grass, you name it. Further complicating the issue was the fact that some of them couldn't decide whether or not to go through with gender reassignment. The upshot was beyond nightmarish.

At Oak Street, they found the stash of ragtag nurse's uniforms. Costumed, they came downstairs and started marching around the rehearsal room in a preposterous conga line, shouting and singing as they splashed through a huge puddle of warm beer that had spilled from one of several kegs. Even so, in keeping with the Angels' open-door, anyone-can-join policy, they were allowed to stay.

"Who are you?" one demanded of me.

I replied, trying to figure out if this person looked more like Faye Dunaway or Marlon Brando, "Who are you?"

"Ginger." But a day later, Ginger's mood had changed wildly. So had his name: "Frank," he said violently. "I'm Frank! Don't ever call me Ginger!"

I beat a hasty retreat. And quit the show.

LIFE WAS ACCELERATING, my mother was coming to visit for four days. Because Peter and Bo had reconciled, I was back at Polk Street when David Meadows phoned to promise that if I rejoined the show, the pre-ops would be banned; their mental zigzags had freaked everyone out. So I agreed to return, with only five days left to create a new show.

When my mother arrived the next day and found me living in a room at the end of an alley behind a seedy gay bar, she sat down on one of the cushions on the kitchen floor and covered her eyes, possibly hoping that, by not seeing, she could make the situation go away. In this, I doubt she was the first parent stunned by a Polk Street lifestyle. But by this time, I was so used to my environment that I saw nothing unusual about it. Life had become a blur. And though I wasn't aware of it, it was about to get even more surreal.

Anyone with any experience of codependency will understand why I waited so patiently while Sidney stopped by a creepy house in the Haight-Ashbury to score Angel Dust from Janice. But when he went cold turkey from heroin and became physically ill, I panicked, went out and scored for him, *just trying to help.*

Meanwhile, the new show, which was set in a hospital, was developing at breakneck speed. Unlike *Paris Sites*, it was improvised—there was no time

Prissy and friend, Valencia St. storefront theatre, April 4, 1981

for a script. Still, the discipline and focus of recent months was helping. And we had an amazing talent bank.

"Okay, nurses," Tony barked. "You stand here, and in comes a junkie who collapses. You flip out, then check his pockets, and steal his wallet and all his drugs. Then you pop his pills until he comes to and puts the make on you. Got that? Okay! Let's do it!"

Improvising "real life," Tihara had concocted an amazing/appalling drag persona: "Zedda Kay"—a visual nightmare clad in a bright orange stretch pantsuit salvaged from a FREE box. The pants extended to a mid-calf and had fucked-up ruffles, and he wore bright orange stiletto heels. To the hard shell of a brown bouffant wig, he added white plastic cat's eye glasses, immense pearl-drop earrings, and a matching pearl necklace. But the crowning touch, the eye-grabbing *coup de grâce* emphasizing his cinched-in waist, were the two traffic cones on his chest that zoomed outward like missiles. With his dark beard and mustache and his bright red lips, it was—hands down—the funniest drag I ever saw. But not everyone approved.

"Don't you know there are children in this area?" a woman on Haight Street shouted, seeing Tihara cruising along like a freakish cartoon, a transistor radio in one hand, the bright orange lozenge of his purse in the other, and Prissy—his new acolyte—in tow.

Paying homage to Tihara, Prissy's drag—a pastel suit—was loaded with trinkets and jewelry, all the accoutrement of shameless and tasteless American spending capital.

In addition to creating Zedda Kay, Tihara also painted the set for Act I: a suburban living room at a forty-five-degree angle, as if on a sinking ship. Against this perilous list, I was to play a big baby in diapers; Tihara was my mother and Chuck Drees was my father. Tall, muscular, with a babble of blond curly hair, Chuck was one of the funniest people ever to appear with the Angels. Of all those I ever shared a stage with, he and Tihara were my favorites. Both were drop dead hilarious. But while Tihara was essentially nonverbal, Chuck fired off lines with ballsy zeal.

Born in New Jersey in 1951, Chuck came into the Angels just before *Paris Sites,* for which he painted that brilliant street scene in Act I. Although he also sold Angel Dust, somehow he was granted immunity from the group's condemnation of hard drugs.

As the show coalesced, Tony was happier than a pig in shit. Medical subject matter provided his favorite forum for satire. As Dr Dash, he'd supervise a hospital theater—the second act—and while masked and wearing surgical gear, he would conduct an operation.

I was so busy with preparations—I was to be a nurse in the second act and had to learn a song and blocking—I didn't think about how my mother might react. But she had a few surprises up her sleeve. One night, she took me out to dinner, and as previously stated, told me I'd always been thwarted in my desire to buy a house for being "rebellious" (such as not letting them run my life) and for telling the truth(!). When I asked her to explain why that was wrong, she replied that it was because "our lives are built on so many lies that it is too dangerous for us to have a child like you." She added that my father was "a pathological liar" and explained that, given his love of body contact sports, he was "very possibly homosexual."

Startled more by her nonchalance than the concept of my father's closeted desires, I asked if that would upset her. "Well, I'd rather he got what he wanted directly than by fighting," she shrugged. Okaaaay, whatever. Maybe he *was* a macho closet case who'd attacked me to cover his own conflicted self-hatred? True or false, the bare-chested poseur in leather shorts (lederhosen) was *o-b-s-e-s-s-e-d* with being a man. *Why try so hard?* But I let that explosive cue pass, wanting things to stay on a healthy, healing track, whatever their particular sexual intricacies. But she hadn't finished her star turn (was it a competition with my father for Most Successful Visit?) because a day or two later, she sounded more than mildly curious when she attended a rehearsal at Oak Street and asked, "Can *anyone* be in a show?"

"Uh sure," someone told her. "Why not?"

"Well, maybe I could do something?" she ventured. "As a doctor's wife, I've certainly been in enough hospital waiting rooms."

"You can do anything you want," said whoever that was.

Permission-granting is a wonderful, wonderful thing, but also very, very unpredictable. *You can do anything you want.* I think my mother had waited her entire life to hear those words because, without further ado, she joined the Angels of Light. It's fair to say that, in the entire history of the group, she was its most unusual addition. Even the Angels were stupefied. We were used to schizophrenics, welfare cases, junkies, bank robbers, pre-op transsexuals, whores, cross-eyed speed freaks, and bald women with piercings. *Not* ladies from Rittenhouse Square, Philadelphia.

But not only was the new cast member unusual, she had a credit card, one she used to rent a U-Haul truck, which I drove to chauffeur props, set pieces, and cast members from San Francisco to Berkeley for the first of two successive performances. As the others in that truck were thanking my mother for renting the vehicle, she turned to them and said, "Do you know how strange this is for me?" Then from a line they had seized upon and repeated like a mantra until it became a classic in-joke, they replied, "I'm from Philadelphia. I don't talk to anyone unless I've been properly introduced."

"You can be in our shows any time," Beaver said.

It took a while to set up the show in Berkeley, but it was still light outside when I saw my mother staring at Tihara and Prissy as they took off to hit the local bars, in full drag, naturally.

"Where are they going?" she asked.

"Out for a drink."

"Like that?!"

For the first and only time in my life, I saw her lose control and laugh so hard she could have peed her pants. Tears streamed down her face. I thought, *Well, that's a good sign,* understanding how this might look to someone who came from a place where men wore suits and women still shaved their legs. But why dwell on that stuff? It was show time!

THE *HOSPITAL SHOW* OPENED with a living room scene crudely painted as a coloring book, in bright red, green, blue, and black. As the lights came up, I, dressed in diapers, lounged around on a cheap couch watching television. Chuck—"Daddy"—wore long johns and hiking boots and, on his head, a porkpie hat and big rimmed glasses. And instead of a normal human nose, he sported a giant green pickle that curved toward his chin.

We bickered until Zedda Kay breezed in with a cheery, maternal call, "Mother's home!"

A family quarrel ensued as Prissy entered and screamed, "Oh! You have a cat!" Prissy started running around, spraying everything with room freshener to cover the stench of a litter-box, then "Daddy" got abusive, and "Mother" intervened. They went at it mano-a–mano, until—gasp!—Daddy had a heart attack. So off to the hospital we went.

The hospital set was divided into three parts. Stage right was an operating room where heroic "Dr Dash" performed miracle surgeries. At stage center in a reception booth, Valiumed-out "Nurse Edith Hasgas" (Beaver) wasn't far from where my real mother sat onstage in a folding chair, dressed in suede, cashmere, and pearls, playing the "Lady Sitting Around in the Waiting Room" who worked on her embroidery and ignored absolutely everything going on around her. Dr Dash had four nurses (including myself) to assist him in an emergency operation when he realized that my daddy did not have a heart attack but rather a gigantic pinworm up his ass. Naturally, this must be extracted. As the procedure progressed, Dr Dash seized the head of the seven- or eight-foot worm; we, his loyal team of nurses, pitched in to help tug and tug at the creature. To accomplish this heroic feat, we had to climb up onto the operating table. And one by one by one, we climbed onto it ...

... until it fell down ...

... and hit the set ...

... which then collapsed ...

... landing the entire cast...

... and the set ...

... on the floor ...

... face down ...

... a yard or so from the footlights.

Raising my head, I found myself staring at 400 shocked audience members. Behind me, the entire show had fallen down, cast and set, except Edith Hasgas's booth. And my mother, of course. No, she hadn't fallen flat on her ass. She was just sitting in that waiting-room chair. Embroidering. Not even looking up. Just ignoring everything.

"This is no way to run a hospital!" I improvised. "Get that table up! Put that wall back! Come on! *Move!*" Clapping my hands briskly, I behaved like an annoyed professional as we put the show back together; when the operation continued, my mother continued to sit there, paying no attention.

Then two newcomers descended: a fellow named Groovy and someone else. They were playing junkies who staggered into the hospital on ODs, or looking for heroin. But in real life, they *were* junkies and, to get into the proper spirit for their roles, they'd just shot up in the wings. Now all they had to do was stumble out to center stage and fall down, but when I saw them totter out from the wings, their red-rimmed eyes rolling back, I thought, *They're going to collapse and die.* But they *did* manage to hit their mark. And fall down. And as Edith Hasgas fired off questions—"Do you have dental coverage?"—they nodded out as my mother adjusted her tortoise shell glasses and kept right on with her thing.

It was time for the nurses to sing "Overdose Mountains," a country-western number with an anti-drug message. Was it the theme of the show? I have no idea.

We say don't wander Overdose Mountains
If you're lookin' to get high
We're sure you'll find a better way
To that great bye and bye.

I can't remember if anything else happened. I do recall that we'd never figured out a good ending. Someone had painted a set for the finale—a huge sun with spiky rays—and I'd written a dippy poem about healing yourself. So that had to be it, unfortunately. Clad in velvet harem pants and wearing a wreath, I read my ridiculous screed while Chuck, now painted gold and clad in only a gold loincloth and a wreath of purple plastic grapes, did an absurd interpretive dance that supposedly symbolized cosmic unity. Or harmony. Maybe it did. I sure hope so....

On our first night, the audience loved the show, collapsed set notwithstanding. They shouted and screamed and cheered. So we were pretty happy with that. On the second night, we performed almost the same show to another crowd of 400, but this time the reaction was stony-faced silence. Afterward, they filed out without even bothering to applaud. Were they disappointed that the sets hadn't fallen down?

In any event, we'd found a way to have fun after the marathon epic of *Paris Sites*. The *Hospital Show* was a perfect antidote. And following her debut in the underground where she'd established her star, my mother returned to her circus life in Philadelphia where, naturally, she'd say nothing about the one that she'd just participated in. I understood that. After all, if she hadn't seen a thing, how could anything have happened? Right?

Chapter 12

In late June, the Angels participated in the Gay Day Parade and wound up on a stage in Golden Gate Park where, by popular demand, I did my "Lust" number for a huge crowd. No big deal. Big numbers sound thrilling, but this was just another daytime performance. In fact, the event hardly made it into my journal entries as these became fragmentary during that summer of 1975 when I found the city increasingly weird.

1

Day burns off into night,
Night remains always anyway
Day is the question of choice

At the window in a penthouse
Midnight burns towards dawn
Champagne toasts / new stars

A galaxy of creatures
Young men with black lips
Women with garnet eyes

2

It's early afternoon in the asylum
A white tiger prowls linoleum halls
Pads past nurses and orderlies

Past nuns and technicians
He searches a mate
Searches a mate

At this time, the FBI was still hunting Patty Hearst; rumor had it she was in the area. At the People's Temple, a cult-gulag devoted to their apocalyptic guru Jim Jones was practicing dry runs of mass suicide they termed "White

Nights," which came to tragic fruition in Jonestown, Guyana, in 1978. Few saw the writing on the wall.

Having existed in glorious isolation from the rest of the country since 1849, San Francisco had seemed to slow down after the 1973 Arab oil embargo. With a nationwide recession, more and more hippies left town, choosing Mendocino and Humboldt counties to grow marijuana. Under mounting pressure, Alex committed psychic suicide. He quit painting.

Closer to home, Irving's criticism of *Paris Sites* was read aloud to a house meeting. In it, he likened me to Hibiscus. He meant it as a rebuke but I was flattered. But no one paid any attention. The split from Kaliflower was way overdue. We didn't want Irving or his impotent spy (Jet) monitoring us; the success of *Paris Sites* had removed any need for parental oversight and besides, people were just sick and tired of Irving's diatribes. For all his holier-than-thou posturing, the man was a crashing bore. Personally, I was glad to add my weight to the schism and so I wrote Irving on June 21st:

> The criticism read aloud at today's meeting would be more impressive had you actually seen the show. May I suggest that, in future, you witness the performance instead of concocting opinions from a hall off the backstage area? Or is it possible you were peeved at not having the cast pose for you four hours before show time?

The break between the communes was significant only because, in the absence of any remaining restraints or oversight from other parties, "the moist quivering triangle of desire" (Greg's phrase for Brian, Beaver, and Rodney) became a triumvirate.

During that summer, everywhere I went, people were oohing and aahing over me, half-expecting me to be outrageous on cue and provide another glimpse of the hyperbolic, scenery-chewing Countess Flushette. Poets, hungry for a chance to be *outré*, cozied up to me, wanting to share the limelight. When I balked at doing readings, they resented it. But there was one poet I was glad to get to know.

Francesca Rosa lived in one of Casa Madrone's abandoned apartments. At twenty, this innocent with dark curly hair and eyes like peridots had been in the Bay Area since 1972; now her ragtag existence featured hand-me-down clothes and silks salvaged from FREE boxes. Upon hearing from Sidney that I was a poet, she told me that she too wrote poems and asked if I'd take a look at them. I agreed, having no idea that she was a powerhouse with an ability to cut with words, like a latter-day Emily Dickinson cum Sylvia Plath. Her work knocked me out. When I found she didn't even have a typewriter, I bought her an old portable so she could edit more effectively. Though I was scraping by, it was a pleasure to do it because I was so bowled over by her ruthless and glittering poems.

At the time, Francesca was involved with another of Sidney's pals, Sandee "Charade," a rail-thin dyke and ex-con, used-car salesman, and coke dealer and addict with an ugly jagged scar from a knife fight in prison that had sliced her left cheek into incongruent zones. Emaciated, glib, and seductive, Sandee held us spellbound while chipping pink rocks of Bolivian "Mother of Pearl," the best cocaine, in which we indulged freely. I was so naïve, I never saw it as dangerous, though I was agitated and just couldn't get comfortable and didn't understand why—I never imagined it might have something to do with the drugs. Or Sandee. Or Sidney using "China White," the best heroin. At twenty-seven, I didn't believe in evil, although things just didn't seem to jell. The Angels were notified that they were losing their house on Oak Street. They seemed passive and directionless and stranded too. In July, I wrote a poem trying to capture my sense of fragility and fatality:

> Glitter falls in a shimmering wind
> bewitching San Francisco
> where young men roam—
> silver ink on the wings of a burning moth

In August, we did a show at an old-age home. It was an afternoon entertainment for the residents and there was almost nothing remarkable about it. *Nothing.*

For this occasion, Tihara turned himself into a noble black church-going woman of fifty in a beaded dress and Afro wig. But the *coup de grace* was his skin. He painted it a dark brown epidermis, accented with warm reds, salmon, and gold. Except for the fact that he had a full black beard, blazing blue eyes, and stood six-foot-six in heels, the transformation was perfect.

"What is that?" an old lady warbled when, hands folded in front of his skirt, Tihara launched into a demure gospel hymn. Squinting, the old geezer rolled her wheelchair closer to this spectacle and then, eyes popping, she started to laugh like hell. It was heaven, although behind closed doors, the Angels were in crisis.

Being evicted from Oak Street galvanized a longstanding plan for the Angels to acquire a theater and home. Tihara found a great possibility: an old synagogue with a seating capacity of 1,500 was in the offing *for only $39,000.* It should have been a done deal after the group managed to borrow money for the building, but it soon devolved into a mess.

After the agreement was in place, Enid Sales, the city bureaucrat in charge of the building, demanded $120,000 more as a fund for security and renovation. At this point, without any input from anyone else, Brian told Ms Sales that the Angels didn't have enough money and that the deal was off. Tihara said that such funds weren't a legal requirement but were based on what he saw as Ms Sales' homophobia. In any case, Brian's decision to torpedo the acquisition was neither his first nor last sabotage.

Rodney and Beaver refused to confront Brian. Faced with their resistance and his suspicion that the Angels were losing their revolutionary zeal, Tihara called a meeting to discuss this topic. As he told me, although everyone wanted a stable home and theater, he was the only one out looking for available buildings. But at the meeting, Angels member Madeline Bloom told Tihara, "We think we'd be a better theater without you." Others wavered, yet some appeared to agree. Tony tried to be a voice of moderation, suggesting that Tihara just take a break for a few months. But shocked by the others' lack of support, and intuiting that the group was heading the wrong direction, Tihara quit the Angels of Light. This was a mega-disaster, although, in retrospect, it was also inevitable. And thereby hangs a tale:

For years, Rodney and Madeline had attended dance classes, and their training resulted in the ballet in *Paris Sites* and an Indian dance in *The Jungle Show* at Stanford. Rodney needed a female partner, but while Madeline was a competent student of various dance idioms, she was just that: competent.

A word of explanation: when I was little, my siblings and I were taught classical music by the Curtis String Quartet, and my two lifelong friends, Margaret Webster Plass (my Grandmère) and Stella Kramrisch, were world-renowned experts on art. Put simply, I'd been thoroughly "wired" not only to comprehend but *feel* the distinction between the good and great, the passable and original, the serviceable and sublime. I admit there's a barbarity to rigorous aesthetic drilling, but the result was why I was hired by galleries in SoHo and could write philosophic analysis and informed art criticism.

"The soul selects her own Society, then shuts the door ... and closes the valves of her attention ... like stone," wrote Emily Dickinson. Admittedly, Americans too often confuse high standards with snobbery but it's simply a commitment to achieve excellence and an awareness of its often harrowing essential nature, no more, no less.

The Angels were great. But its dancers "doing" charming renditions of a rigorous discipline that requires a lifetime to perfect were never the heart or soul of the group. What made the group magical was its spirit and its incandescent process of transformation, not the technical and artistic proficiency of adepts, however talented they were.

Of all those regularly featured, I felt Madeline was the only one who lacked a guiding vision. But Rodney would never dream of sharing the spotlight with another male dancer and, because he hogged all romantic leading roles, Madeline got to partner him by dint of default. Always adequate but a bit humorless, she couldn't quite mask—or chose not to let slip—faint discomfort with gay men. There's a perceptible difference between committed artist-activists and opportunists who hop on the bandwagon. I sensed the latter in this darkly handsome, *very* straight Jewish-American Princess. Conservative identity seemed far more important to her than anything radical or personally risky. And for her to inform a uniquely totemic presence like Tihara that the Angels would be "better off" without him was as revealingly obtuse as a Sunday painter telling Matisse to buzz off.

House meetings being closed, I couldn't attend and defend Tihara. His exit was an irreplaceable loss. Superficially, I may have seemed to take up the slack, but no one had Tihara's humor and charisma. In his wake, shows would revolve more and more around Rodney, backed up by Beaver and Brian. And Madeline.

In rapid succession, I did a poetry reading at a gay salon where Harvey Milk gave a talk, the only time we were ever on the same bill, and another in-house party/salon where I read again. Here, I laid eyes on a frightful person

Victoria Lowe and Winston Tong, August 6, 1978

who would play a major part in the Angels in years to come. High on Angel Dust and naked—green lights making her pudgy body truly repulsive—she emerged from a bedroom, out of her mind and cackling: imagine the worst qualities of a buck-toothed and frenetic Mickey Rooney (minus the talent) mixed with a slattern. Shake well and—*voilà!*—Janice. I shuddered.

August felt listless, dry, and hot. Sidney said he loved me but I felt brittle. Victoria seemed changed too, lost and unsteady. At an Angels party in the country, I took a Quaalude (always an aphrodisiac for me), hauled some guy into a darkened bedroom—where, unbeknownst to me, Victoria was passed out in the big bed—and fucked him, whereupon she woke and—for whatever reason which may include being high or loaded herself—she insinuated herself into a sexual encounter with me, something that I'd *never* have permitted if I'd been clear-headed, though I knew she longed for intimacy with me.

It was a horrendous breach of my boundaries and horribly wrong for her too, for it changed what had always been a safe, trusting relationship into something that touched upon her deep-rooted need for a loving father. I'd fulfilled the role, though I never saw her as a daughter. But however adult she appeared, she was terribly impressionable and vulnerable. I realized that she loved me and that I was her hero and a bit of a dream figure too. But as remarkable as she was, as beautiful and sweet and tender and creative and sexy and exploding with potential, Victoria was a child. Crossing the line, even by accident, couldn't help but instill in her a hope or desire that I'd be there for her in ways that simply weren't possible. The scenario passed; we didn't discuss it. She went to France (with her brother), neither of us knowing that this incident would cause problems down the road. Besides, there were so many problems dead ahead!

In crossing into the netherworld of the Angels, I'd maintained a strong relationship with the people in Inverness, believing I could participate in the underground without losing my bearings. In hindsight, I realize how stupid that was. By now, the certifiable Angels seemed normal to me. Being in love with a bank robber wasn't unusual. (After all, Sandee had robbed a bank, and so had Jeremy.)

Once suspended, normal rules or standards of accountability are not easily resurrected and, at the time, I wasn't interested in returning to traditional mores. I hate to admit it because I can see so clearly how I spiraled down, past the point of no return. But the fact is: even if the summer of 1975 felt dead in San Francisco and everyone, including myself, looked disconnected, we had accomplished a lot of work in a very short period of time. And I'd established my star, albeit a tinsel one. But hadn't that been my intention?

I blamed my malaise on creative burnout. Oh yes, I needed a break. It wasn't because I was among drug dealers, bank robbers, prostitutes, heavy drinkers, and addicts. It wasn't that most of my friends were welfare cheats or scamming the System. It wasn't because for ten years, I smoked marijuana from the minute I woke up to the minute I crashed. And even if it *did* have something to do with my discomfort at being considered a "star"—and it did, that part was true—why, I thought, I could make all that go away by going away myself!

I decided to leave town. I knew there was a poetry scene in Katmandu. When Sidney said he wanted to go too, I believed we'd share a romantic adventure. I'd be the one paying, but that wasn't important. I wasn't the only Angel eager to get out. In addition to Victoria going off to France, Greg was flying to Paris to help Hibiscus and Angel Jack stage a new show. So, in June 1975, leaving for a while seemed harmless.

Things to do: Twenty-Six Essentials to Pack
1. a coat of silver foil
2. a white plume
3. a fringed wig
4. green velvet harem pants
5. pink ostrich feathers
6. fringed collar
7. black satin headdress
8. tasseled g-string
9. fishnets
10. Egyptian wig
11. silver platforms
12. silk flower wreath
13. rhinestone collar
14. paper umbrella
15. blue glitter claws
16. silver ankle bells
17. eyelashes
18. silver bracelets
19. solitaire (ring)
20. pearls
21. veils
22. lavender tassels
23. pink boa
24. velvet bows
25. gold lamé fan
26. scents and oils

A few days before I left, Winston Leyland called, upset about his young lover, Miguel, a native of Guatemala. Winston had sponsored his entry into the country so Miguel could attend college (a great plan as long as Winston didn't withdraw his support. If so, Miguel would have to go home). "Talk to him," Winston urged. "He's depressed and needs help. He likes and respects you. He'll listen."

When I called Miguel, the beautiful lad broke down sobbing. "Winston threatens to send me back to Guatemala if I don't do everything he says. He won't even let me play music in the house. I'm Latin. I need my music."

Knowing Tede Mathews wasn't only into Latin American politics, but Latin music too, I gave Miguel his number. The next day Miguel called, thrilled. Tede and all of his housemates loved him. So Miguel now had wonderful and interesting new friends.

Then Winston called in a rage. "How could you do what you just did?"

"Because you asked me to help you," I pointed out, suddenly wondering why I was even bothering to talk to this pathetic and sadistic sleazoid.

"But Tede and his friends don't like me," he fumed, furious at having lost control of a trophy boy whom he'd bought and paid for, fair and square. "And if you ever want me to publish you again...."

Thus ended my association with Winston Leyland. I couldn't have cared less. Before long, Miguel lost Winston's sponsorship and had to go back to Guatemala. But I was unaware of that development, for in September 1975, I left San Francisco with Sidney after writing some final poems, including "Testimony and Stage Notes" and "Music for Limbo Palace" (see pages 243-44).

Behind us, Patty Hearst had been captured and was claiming to have been brainwashed by her kidnappers. Heading out on our world tour, I never stopped to consider the parallels. If I'd seen the 1944 film *Gaslight* in which a supposedly caring husband deliberately tries to drive his wife insane, I might have been better prepared for what I was getting into. But I was in love. And I hadn't seen that movie. Yet.

Chapter 13

A zigzag line drawn across the world would indicate the places that Sidney and I went, where I received acclaim for my work while he hung back like a cobra. In Boston, I read at the Fag Rag Collective and met the Good Gay Poets. In Philadelphia, I read on a revolutionary gay radio station, infamous for employing "four-letter words"—gasp! But when I visited my parents and showed them my slides of the Angels, my father sighed disdainfully and said, "This too shall pass," as if the Angels were unfortunate "fairies" that no one could possibly take seriously. But I was so happy that we had negotiated that loan for a building—one he now confirmed and agreed to hold open while I made up my mind between Inverness and the city—I let it pass.

Sidney and I flew to bleak, dull Casablanca. Here, he withdrew a bit and further tested me by saying he wanted to pick up boys to fuck in our hotel room, an idea I nixed. In Paris, I read at the legendary Left Bank bookstore Shakespeare & Company, and we spent a week in a place located in front of Notre Dame. Then to London for my reading at Cambridge University. But by the time we reached Nepal, our romantic idyll was a nightmare, and I was taking Valium to negotiate the days.

"Do you hate me *yet?*" Sidney smiled, then urged me to try smack, promising our sex would be better if only I'd shoot up. My refusal led to sullen zingers. I tried to ignore them, smoking opium and designing a book of my poems and drawings, which I entitled *Limbo Palace*. But matters only got worse when a local drug dealer from Britain fell for me. "Archie" confided that he could never return to the UK, not as long as he lived. *What had he done?* Even in my Valiumed-out state, alarm bells were ringing. Archie hadn't left Nepal for years, but incredibly, he could always get his visa extended when no one else could, and his price for hash was even lower than the Nepali dealers.

Archie claimed to be in love with me, and explained how we could get rich. His plan went like this: we'd swallow opium in balloons, fly to Bangkok, sell the opium, buy heroin, ingest that, return to Nepal, and make a fortune. But people who did business with Archie got busted sooner or later, and everyone knew that Interpol had a secret agent in Nepal. I had no interest in the heroin trade, but I was so confused and disoriented with Sidney on one side and this new, shady man on the other, I felt paralyzed.

Outwardly, Sidney seemed so caring, I never imagined he might take active pleasure—*sexual pleasure*—in torturing. I'd never believed in evil, being a good little Quaker; I'd assumed people were basically good. Now I knew better. I knew it because I was in love with someone who was gently tinkering with, and gradually diminishing, my ability to trust my own mind: by telling me ways we could have better sex (heroin would guarantee it); by saying how much he loved me in public but then treating me to cold silences and caustic jabs at home. Living with a maniac, I got so brittle, some perceived *me* as the nut case! Not surprising. My ability to function became so severely impaired that I reached the point that I decided that doubting Sidney's love would be proof that *I* was insane! Yes, Sidney knew what was best. He had my welfare at heart even if I couldn't be rational. Sidney was the good person, stable, loyal, and honorable. And me? I was just a grasping basket case. I had to trust Sidney, I had to trust Sidney … I had to.

Then one morning as I was shaving, he assaulted me. An icy shudder ran through my body. I turned, prepared to cut his face, but an inner voice cautioned: *You are holding a razor.* I put the razor down before punching that sick bastard in the nose. He went down in a heap; I jumped on top of him and, to my surprise, my voice was calm as I warned, "Don't try that again. I'm stronger than you." Then I gave him money for airfare home, rented a cottage in a courtyard garden in the middle of Kathmandu, and ran a hippie bookstore while my book was being published (see poem, page 245). That day he assaulted me was the first time he tried to assert physical dominance. Until then, he'd employed steadily accelerating psychological torture. I have no doubt that if I didn't fight back, he'd have murdered me.

I may have been free of Sidney, but Archie circled around just as two potential means of rescue appeared. One took the form of a red-bearded American Sufi in a white turban. Travelers grow close quickly in the east and, within days, I shared my doubts about Archie with him. My new friend promised to investigate and said that, if my suspicions proved right—and they would be checked *very carefully*—Archie would be "taken care of." Would he be murdered? I didn't know and didn't want to know because the second form of rescue appeared—a communiqué from San Francisco:

Adrian Adrian Flash Flash Important Important Urgent
Urgent

BO AND TORIA ...TORIA AND BO HAVE BEEN ASKED TO DO
THE ANGEL JACK AND HIBISCUS ANGEL OF LIGHT EUROPEAN
TOUR ... SAN FRANCISCO, LOS ANGELES, NEW YORK, LON-
DON, AMSTERDAM, PARIS, ATHENS, OR SOME SUCH PLACE IN
GREECE. ABSOLUTELY BLOWN OUT IN SAN FRAN. PUH-LEASE
ARRIVE IN SAN FRANCISCO IMMEDIATELY, IF NOT SOONER.
YOUR REPUTATION HAD PRECEDED YOUR ARRIVAL AND
THEY ARE INTERESTED IN YOU BEING IN THE PRODUCTION
... HIBISCUS AND JACK HAVE BOTH EXPRESSED INTEREST
IN YOU BEING IN THE SHOW BASED ON YOUR INESTIMABLE
REPUTATION FROM THE PARIS SHOW AND FROM GENERAL
WORD OF MOUTH (YES ISN'T IT WONDERFUL MAJOR WORD
OF MOUTH FINALLY GOT HIS PROMOTION—SOMETHING
ABOUT BLOWJOBS TO THE PRESIDENT OR SOMETHING) OH
ADRIAN HOW CAN YOU LET TORIA AND I GO TO EUROPE
WITHOUT YOUR ACCOMPANIMENT ON THESE STRANGE
EUROPEAN STAGES ...WE MUST, WE MUST, WE MUST GAZE
INTO EACH OTHERS EYES IN AMSTERDAM AND PARIS AND
GOD KNOWS WHERE ELSE THINK OF THE SOIREES ... THE
CHAMPAGNE ... THE BALLROOMS ... THE GOWNS ... SOLID
SEQUINS! WHAT MORE CAN ONE SAY OR DO? WE PLEAD, WE
CAJOLE, WE DEMAND YOUR IMMEDIATE RETURN TO THESE
FOREIGN SHORES. REHEARSALS HAVE BEGUN BY THE TIME
YOU RECEIVE THIS.

FLASH   FLASH   FLASH
COME COME COME COME
YOUR DEMANDING AMORES: VICTORIA, BO, FRANCESCA

God knows, there was no reason for me to stay in Nepal. Rail-thin at 157 pounds and clad in black satin, I left Katmandu and flew west as the tall ships sailed toward New York Harbor to celebrate the US Bicentennial: July 4, 1976.

Chapter 14

Bo, Francesca, and Victoria met my plane at the San Francisco airport as if I were a returning hero. Kicking opium was shredding my nerves. As we sped into what appeared to me as an overly bright city, I sensed something way, way off kilter. Now, I grant you: coming off opium is no picnic and I was in no shape to be objective, but to me, the three of them appeared frightened, lost. Francesca was jittery, Victoria seemed depressed, and Bo's eyes looked scarily dead. And as the days passed, it seemed that they weren't the only one in the ozone.

Bo and Peter Leone had broken up. The Polk Street apartment was vacant, desolate, our little commune a thing of the past. Still, the rent was paid through July, so I crashed there with Victoria. Francesca and Sandee were another casualty; their affair had been brief, for not only was Francesca actually hetero, she'd been totally unnerved by Sandee's sordid ways. Francesca was a sensitive, spiritual soul and whatever fascination she'd had with Sandee had the same boomerang effect on her that Sidney had on me. As for Sandee "Charade," now living on McAllister Street in a house of recently paroled ex-prostitutes, she was buried up to her septum in coke while fantasizing about opening a head shop on Haight Street. Having landed but reeling from culture shock and in denial, I wrote "Cocaine Love Charade" (see page 249).

The Angels were in stasis too. They'd found a new home—a large house at 18th and Hartford in the Castro—and they'd rented a studio on nearby Valencia in the Mission; it was a long storefront, suitable for storage, rehearsals, workshops, and live performances. But they hadn't done a show for the entire year that I was away.

I went to see them. Eighteen people were sharing three flats for a total rent of $750. There was an eerie feeling in the house. But where the Angels were concerned, there was always a tense undercurrent.

One example: a young mother in the house had had a nervous breakdown. She bound her children in blankets and tried to drown them in a tub. The others in the house knew what she was doing but ignored it; *only one person intervened.* Afterward, no one took action or reported her to mental health authorities. The incident was allowed to pass.

In the strange way that Life can imitate Art imitating Life, the nightmare

Lenore Vantosh-Howard holding Kavita Jonopoulos, (*background right*) Rodney Price, and (*foreground right*) Prissy, August 1976

affected me too: desperate for sanctuary, and wanting to work again but needing a safe zone in a sane community, I flew back east to accept my father's offer of a ten-year, interest-free loan to buy a house in Inverness to run a bed-and-breakfast inn and thus become a self-supporting artist. But once in Philadelphia for a face-to-face meeting, I got the shock of my life.

"I never promised you any such thing," he sniffed. Appalled, I pointed out that he had, both verbally and in a letter. He adamantly denied it. And at that moment, I felt that there was no safe place for me and never would be.

The rupture that ensued would define our relationship forever because, when I told my mother about it, she said dismissively, "I think it's time that you start thinking about what you can do for us rather than ask us to do things for you."

I returned to San Francisco wondering if we would ever—or could ever—recover from this betrayal. Once there, I tried to wrap my head around the situation and figure out why things felt so lifeless.

By 1976, punk rock had arrived with a vengeance. To my surprise, many of the Angels had jettisoned the gentler ways of glittery hippiedom to embrace tough anti-social music and the hissing, spitting stance that accompanied it. From my point of view, this was the first time that San Francisco was importing a culture from the outside rather than creating something new and original. Moreover, the new idiom was hard-edged and pessimistic. But in multi-ethnic, multi-racial California, I saw it only as a sexy new trend with local headquarters being a club on Broadway: the Mabuhay Gardens. Even so, one thing was clear: the Glitter Age was over. Okay. But, if so, what was the relevance of the Angels?

Fair question. In a strange parallel to the 1974 *After Dark* magazine remark that the Angels were "yesterday's news," at some point while I was away, Edmund White had visited the studio on Valencia Street. In his nonfiction travelogue *States of Desire: Travels in Gay America*, he describes a bleak, burned-out scene populated by zombies. No doubt he had reason to comment as he did. In epic shows, the Angels could present the most incandescent, poetic images of beauty and dazzle. But when unfocused, one caught jarring glimpses over the edge of an abyss. Sadly, White saw only the latter.

Harold Norse told me Winston Leyland was now publishing porn and we had a good laugh, but aside from seeing Paul Mariah, I didn't want to venture anywhere near the poetry scene. Aaron Shurin had published a fine chapbook, *Woman on Fire*, but when I asked him what was important for poets to say, he had no answer. I didn't either, frankly, and it disturbed me though I didn't even want to publish my poetry anymore and stopped doing so then.

Even the gay scene had changed. At the Gay Day Parade, I saw a world that was once imaginative and experimental turn into a showcase for clones and beefcakes (see page 252).

Flying into San Francisco, Hibiscus wanted to develop his new show, *The Shocking Pink Life of Jayne Champagne*. He called and invited me to join, but when I went over at the appointed time he was asleep, so I decided to see the show before making a decision.

The performance was numbing. Hibiscus was beautiful and radiant onstage. But his overblown, big-bosomed bimbette just wasn't funny. Put simply, *Jayne Champagne* was a one-trick pony that everyone had seen once too often. Nothing that I wanted to be in. Nor, I imagine, was it a show that he really enjoyed doing because, offstage, Hibiscus was spinning out of control: hiring hustlers and, occasionally, working as one himself.

In a fascinating parallel to Japanese artists who, traditionally, take several names throughout long careers, George Harris, a.k.a. Hibiscus, now developed a third persona: Brian Wolf, clean-cut actor. There was a clear-cut distinction between his all-American "good boy" and the outrageous Hibiscus of glitter and drag. Each was a desperate effort to find sanctuary, but a hunger for limelight drove them both. Hibiscus ruined his own shows by rushing onstage during other people's numbers. "There were eleven songs in the show and Hibiscus sang twelve of them," Tihara joked.

In New York, when in drag, Hibiscus had easily gained entry to the elite Studio 54; the nightclub always welcomed outlandish characters who provided a surreal background for the likes of Liza Minnelli and Elizabeth Taylor. But Hibiscus was thrown out for rushing celebrities and inserting himself into photos of their grand entrances. His mania was a desperate cry for attention; he didn't know where to go or what to do with himself. The tragedy is that while there were hundreds of men eager to fuck him, there was never an equal to help him to focus and refine his extraordinary vision.

But what to do? Great talents were imploding all around me and I had no safe base. So when Sandee offered me a room in her flat, it seemed sensible, though I hardly knew up from down when I moved in. I felt like a snowflake falling into a pizzeria, still adrift, and still reeling from the aftershocks of Sidney and a sense of cultural dislocation which I tried to capture in my journal that September:

My crown is an invisible ring of light, an aura at a table.
It creates an illusion of Paris, Berlin, anywhere you want.
It is created with the wave of a hand, a decision to believe.

A month after my return, something stirred: the first impetus for an Angels cabaret. I don't know if my returning had anything to do with it. More likely, after a year of inertia, the Angels were bored stiff. Whatever the reason, I was delighted to get to work and when meetings got underway, I was there, pen in hand, helping to write the show and recording in my journal:

Free Theater: What Could Be Plainer Than That Secret World?
COME SEE OUR SHOW! MCs with Brechtian nostrils, pudgy with

ill-gotten profit of pre-Nazi decadence, anti-Semitic upchucking packets of paper bills, drowning in pea-green whirlpool of war to come.

THE AUDIENCE GOES MAD! Drink in Expressionistic mask, mime, and femme fatale swooning onstage, caught by penniless American wandering waterfront Hamburg.

REMEMBER! OH RECOLLECT three crowds standing and screaming at the end! *Oh Girl! How rude! Where'd you get that dress?* as we crash the visual barrier and jab ostrich feathers into the soft flank of America.

The West Coast farts with glee! Another seismic giggle scientists can barometerize with television satellite dish public instant press via their white courtesy telephones to scream "EARTHQUAKE!" Meanwhile, flaming Amazons, cowboys, obsidian queens, and Nile emissaries scratch the door of their long green hall with leopard claws. The scars glow in the dark; the green halls grow darker. Trucks roar across tin bridges, the moon squats to pee as the dancing grinds sawdust to bone marrow bar floor pulp of life.

The night with an electric anal cable over-amps into this wild version of *Decameron* crossed with whatever untold Arabian Tales remain. Outside in cooling midnight breezes of the Mission District, people light joints and prop against VW vans. Black eye-shadowed creatures in ermine coats, nefarious diamonds, pearls. Inevitable night sweats onto jade-colored silk cools with marijuana plumes, reapplies lipstick in oval standing sessions....

Mind Kamp Kabaret was enchanting. It featured a series of songs and dances connected by a simple plot: the relationship between a suicidal American sailor named "Joe" and a glittering femme fatale of the Berlin streets, "Fräulein Schnauzer." After she saves him from leaping off a rock and drowning, they fall in love while she tries to persuade him to stay alive by introducing a variety of songs and dances. Tragically, Joe loses interest in her. The Fräulein attempts suicide (by jumping from the same rock) but Joe stops her and they resolve their crisis by agreeing to share custody of the rock—a cinderblock—for which each now tenders a sentimental attachment.

Spliced into this tawdry melodrama and framed by vignettes of doomed romance was a catalogue of torch songs (such as Jessica's winsome version of "I Cover the Waterfront"), tap-dancing penguins (a tap dance by Rodney), and a satirical number by Bertolt Brecht and Hanns Eisler, "There's Nothing Quite Like Money"—a mix of music and taped dialogue that was Greg's contribution to the ever-expanding experiments with sound.

Doing another show gave me a renewed sense of purpose. And there was no trace of underlying anxiety in my journal of September 1976:

Tap-dancing penguins fuck country western singers in a Berlin 1921 cabaret with black-sequined Fräuleins evoking stern ghosts, a stomp of leather heels, hypnotic disks in red, psychedelic whirling sets, Kabaret by a sequined sea, ladies in green silk roses, Negro snakeskin thigh-high boots giving, much hot number, baby.

For this moment, the plumes and headgear pile in the spotlights, walls of paint, Tower of Babel, blessed Gomorrah of California's modern age of Sodom—inhabitants puffing cock, this oriental pipe, pathway to diamond sidewalks contorting beneath applied magic, split-second costume changes behind cardboard flats populated by stray dogs, fresh diapered babies, and fabulous transvestite Overload.

Confetti sticks to sweaty cheeks. Behind, stage/hands grasp perfect ass as trapeze swings performers back on/stage velvet curtained safety and whispers, "You were great!"—as applause foams over high heels. Behind the scenes to dressing-room gin, a blowjob tucked in a rack of costumes below Harlequin.

The conductor in white silk is bathed in blue lights at the end. The cheers won't quit. The city creams in its tight satin pants, the gypsies return for bows, the queens curtsey, penguins stand gawky/masked, dancers drift out for curtain call, an invisible hand underwrites a swirl of red, gold, blue, pink, black, and silver. An invisible veil descends as the stage is swarmed, a hail of roses and popcorn and yes, my dear, the Angels are *legend*.

Ananda Jonopoulos and Chuck Drees, August 1976

We staged the show at our new studio on Valencia Street (for which we all chipped in to cover the rent). Chuck Drees played Joe; as usual, he was perfect. I was nifty in the only glamorous drag role I ever did: the glum Fräulein Schnauzer, who was joined on the hard streets of Berlin by a prostitute named Escarita Maloche, played by Reggie Dunnigan.

Previously a Cockette, Reggie had an endearing sweetness that he combined with the wonderful aura of a worldly streetwalker. Tall, fluid, with satiny brown skin and the eyes of a doe, he was gentle and dependable despite being tweaked on speed all the time, and sexy in lurid green satin and thigh-high silver platform boots.

From its debut, the cabaret was a success. We could only play to about 200 people—the studio was small—but the show had "legs," as was clear in a poem I wrote that week, "Back On Stage with Angels" (see page 247).

We planned to play every weekend for a month, but on the second or third week, the fire marshal received an anonymous complaint. Of course, we didn't have fire exits or a license or anything else theaters were supposed to have so he closed us down. And not for the first or last time, the Angels were the victims of jealousy. And sabotage.

The anonymous caller? Angel Jack. Hibiscus's lover. With his shifty eyes and the chip on his shoulder, it was easy to see that he lived in the shadow of his stellar partner and derived his identity by serving him. And abusing him. Tihara recounted how Jack would take something Hibiscus treasured and threaten to destroy it while Hibiscus got on his knees and begged him not to, tears streaming down his cheeks. Edgy about his status and insecure artistically, he could be incredibly vicious. Still, there was no reason to turn us in, that is, until the next night, when someone dashed backstage with bad, bad news: "Marc just threw a bottle and hit someone's head and the audience is freaked out!"

Marc Huestis was a bona fide "case." While he did do constructive things (such as cofounding the San Francisco International LGBT Film Festival), he was a minor figure. And therein lay the rub. Aside from having little talent, the guy was an out-of-control "rageaholic." Lulu told me that Marc's parents never picked him up when he was a baby. Lulu reckoned that Marc spent his entire life hoping for love. If so, his behavior undermined any chance of that. When annoyed, he became insanely hostile, sputtering insults at any target of his wrath. Physically short but with a nice body, the poor guy had been scarred by terrible acne and beset with a nervous tic that made him rock constantly, like a human metronome. The disorder underscored his palpable difficulties and punctuated his out-of-control hysterics. Driven by a need for importance, Marc's identity came via symbiosis: attaching himself first to local stars (the Angels) and, later, erstwhile B-list Hollywood actresses who agreed to appear at the landmark Castro Theater for wheezy "tributes."

To quote Churchill, Marc had "much to be modest about." Now, to top it off, he'd assaulted the audience! Yup, while grinding out a tortured version of that old saw, "Someone to Watch Over Me," this none-too-passive-aggressive had (accidentally?) hurled a whiskey bottle into the crowd and smacked someone on the forehead. Hard.

Reggie and I sailed out onstage. Calming a frightened audience was a tall order but, working in tandem, we managed to smooth things over. Still, it was an abrasive incident.

The air cleared a bit the next week, until we took our show to the shingled hamlet of Bolinas in Marin County. Located on an estuary, fiercely xenophobic Bolinas was fixated with its own perceived specialness, despite having

Reggie Dunnigan and Adrian Brooks, August 1976

long since lost the war to tourists, with cute shops and the quaint cafés that had also commercialized and spoiled Carmel. Now, this narcissistic town that prided itself on being ultra-hip was about to face an acid test: hosting the Angels of Light.

Things began well enough. The show went smoothly. But in "downtown Bolinas," the local yokels at Smiley's, a combination bar and pool hall, got real uptight upon finding themselves outnumbered by bearded drag queens eyeing their crotches. The tension in the air was just beginning to subside when Victoria, in one of her feckless moments of heedless unconcern, jumped onto their beloved pool table to dance in stiletto heels, gashing the green felt surface. This led to my confrontation with a cocksure young redneck, as recorded in my journal on September 23, 1976:

> Bolinas cowboy came reeling across the sidewalk, beer in hand.
> 2 a.m. The bar was closing and the main street was clogged with
> glittering circus troupe in satin, sequins, and tap shoes. Angels had
> invaded country/mellow heterosexually repressed regions with
> fantastic guises, dances, and sinful city charms. We'd wooed and
> won the night which erupted on the misty mesa along the long

foggy roads, but, most especially, at Smiley's—a pub founded in 1850 and still serving beer to mostly men. With last call, the crowd oozed onto the street with tit-bouncy ladies crazed on after-show high, whoopin' and whirlin', sweaty with perfect art and gin. Dubious townsfolk tagged along, trying to keep cool, keep in rhythm, maybe get lucky, trying to pierce it all, trying like hell to fathom.... One approached. Couldn't quite figure me out, I mean, I sorta looked normal but who could tell anymore? So he chugged his beer and asked: "Are you one of them?"

"Yes," I said, stone cold sober.

"Are you straight?" he blurted.

"Of course not."

"You mean you're gay?!"

"Yup. Are you?"

"Hell, no!"

"You sure?"

"Course I'm sure! I only fuck women."

"Well, that must be nice."

"Nice? It's great! Christ! I'd go crazy without pussy!"

It was late.

I took him home.

He loved it.

Chapter 15

Back in town, Sandee told me Sidney had been flown in by Peter Hartman, a former member of the Living Theater. Rumor was that Sidney had done "something awful" to a child in Kathmandu. Whatever it was—and I didn't even want to know—it was so bad that Peter had to get Sidney out of Nepal real, real fast, before he could be arrested.

A few nights later, Victoria visited. Coked up and captivated with each other, Sandee "Charade"—the ex-con car salesman—and Victoria—a helpless Marilyn—engaged in a mutual seduction. As Sandee doled out the coke and the charm and Victoria acted flirty-helpless (and neither of them being aware that I was onto them), they upped the ante. Victoria cued Sandee in a very roundabout way that she was terrified of me *with me sitting right there, watching stupefied.* The scenario got even weirder when, via an equally roundabout code, Sandee alerted Victoria to the fact that she had a loaded gun under her pillow and was ready to shoot me at the drop of a hat.

That's when I said, "I'm so stoned I'm having trouble saying this, but I believe you're talking about a loaded gun under the pillow."

They both looked stunned, having assumed they'd been so subtle that I couldn't possibly have untangled their game. Victoria flat out lied, claiming total ignorance; Sandee, on the other hand, said that she and I had always been in "a cosmic duel" and then revealed that she'd invited Sidney to live with us! Upon hearing this, the thin ice upon which I'd been standing cracked and split. I moved out immediately, but it was too late; I spun out and went off the rails.

Each hell is unique. Mine felt like a bed of blisters where everything was connected and paranoid-making. I had no safety net and everything seemed to confirm my ugliest fears. I was too far gone in a world where I was a star to get out, and there was no way to get back (and to what?). The dark path I'd been on for a year and a half now looked like a series of burning bridges to nasty, polluted countries populated by psychopaths.

Desperate, I consulted a psychologist for the first time (voluntarily, anyway), but the therapist told me I was a woman trapped in a man's body and that he wanted to dress me in drag and take me to Las Vegas to gamble. I may have been on the ropes but I wasn't insane. I quit therapy at once.

In October 1976, I wrestled with my sense of slipping away from myself and the world I had so adored:

> What becomes a human life more than loose transparency? More than editors and acrobats careening in fog? If I can't answer that, I'll surrender my tin foil throne and wander in confetti. The dance hall is empty. The music is far away. I wear a gossamer crown. It all sounds so plausible: Beats to hippies to us.... A tribe ricochets in reverse. Gypsies to poets, in theory, one electric endless instant. Still, the Voice comes through witness consciousness. This game is no game. Maybe books are consumed by archive or fire; no matter. Movement continues. It is passion beyond possession and only now I begin to grasp its implications.

Mind Kamp Kabaret had been a lark, but the combination of coke and Sidney lurking around made me edgy. The situation grew worse when I drank champagne before a poetry reading at the Hula Palace. I got off to a marvelous start and had an enthusiastic reception, but I blew it by going on too long and losing my audience. Totally my fault.

I was chagrined by my inebriated wipeout until my brother Squabbie, who was staying with a friend in Berkeley, suggested that I meet a film director/friend. Paul Aaron was in the city on business. At forty, he looked like a nebbish, but he was a clever, clever man. He listened to me read my poems and did the "come to Hollywood and I'll make you a star" spiel. Normally, I wouldn't have given the idea any consideration but at that time, I was searching for something—anything to escape the stultifying sense of oppression and dread that I hinted at in a poem entitled "Autumn" (see page 250).

To this day, it's said that I was the impetus for the 1976 Halloween show. I don't know. I do recall that no one seemed particularly motivated about doing one as late as mid-October when Chuck and I cooked up an idea and wrote the script together.

Séance for Sore Eyes revolved around pathetic Phil Cantlay (me), a blind clairvoyant who lived in a trailer park with his wife, Magnolia (Lenore Van-tosh-Howard). Magnolia, who was deaf, supposedly did tarot card readings but, unbeknownst to Phil, her real forte was whoring. Aside from a huge hearing aid receptor dangling between her breasts, Magnolia flounced around in trashy Frederick's of Hollywood style negligees that she covered with a coarse blanket whenever Phil was nearby. Their next-door neighbor was Eunice Cycle (Chuck), Phil's sister, who owned the trailer park. Eunice was a surreal frightful sight, a day-glo, hatchet-nosed combination of Phyllis Diller and Olive Oyl.

Lance Plunger—a client who needed to contact his dead mother to find information allowing him to collect on a huge inheritance—came to consult hapless Phil in hopes of cashing in. Of course, everything turned into a mess.

As for the rest, I have a confession: I can hardly remember the show. For me, it was all a blur because I was tranquilized. Heavily. I had to be.

About an hour before curtain, Sham (Brian and Beaver's child), aged four, had decided to go exploring, so off he went, down the vast flights of steps zigzagging from Buchanan Street to Laguna Street a hundred yards below. When Brian realized his son was gone, he took off after him, racing down the stairs. And when he caught him, he beat the fucking hell out of him, landing fifteen or twenty hard, *hard* blows. It was insane, excessive, and so reminiscent of my own childhood traumas, I felt nauseated. Seeing Sham dragged up the stairs—screaming and terrified—I knew I couldn't do the show. Not in that state. But it was a pivotal moment for me. What to do? Walk out? Go home?

"Does anyone have any drugs?" I asked out loud. Someone had Valium. I hated Valium. But there was nothing else. I took it, not caring what happened, not caring about a damn thing except getting through the performance and getting the hell out.

While Sham wailed, Brian disappeared and Beaver was busily doing her makeup and getting into costume. I wanted to scream at her, "Your child just got the shit kicked out of him! Why don't you help him?" I didn't. By now, I knew: no one would intervene. The no-go zone was radioactive.

By the time the show began, I was so numb, I felt as if I was on Mars.

Rodney Price ("Glamour Puss"), *Séance for Sore Eyes*, October 1976

Vaguely, I could recall my lines, one word at a time. Afterward, people told me they thought I was fine. But even if nobody else thought that I'd fucked up, I felt that I had.

The Angels' Halloween shows were famously weird and this one was no exception, but in addition to a truly bizarre atmosphere, for the first time, Janice and Joe "Morocco," her lounge lizard housemate who sold heroin, were allowed to participate. Previously, they'd been banned due to the Angels' antipathy to hard drugs. Now, although they hadn't attended regular rehearsals, they marched in arrogantly, barking, "Where do we stand?" Even stoned on Valium, I wondered, "Who the hell do they think they are?" But there was little time to reflect; the show got underway.

The premise of the show was that, each time Phil did a séance, things went awry due to cosmic static. Instead of contacting Lance's dead mother, Phil resurrected Janis Joplin and Jimi Hendrix, followed by "Pimple Puss," one of Eunice's dead daughters, a morbidly obese child shaped like a human donut (in real life, a slim youth who stuffed a body stocking with foam until

Brian Mulhern and Indian, *Séance for Sore Eyes*, October 1976

his tiny head and hands stuck out of a virtual ball). Pimple Puss was a sugar-holic who would eat herself to death. Finally, there was "Glamour Puss" (Rodney)—Eunice's other deceased daughter, a good girl gone wrong who appeared in a 1950s-era flashback. Glamour Puss—a huge-breasted creature in a bouffant topped by a tiny bow—hosted a party that attracted rowdies (including Brian in a rare appearance). There was live music, of course; the musical number featured Victoria, stunning in a cobalt blue ball gown—*à la* Rita Hayworth's *Gilda*—with long, cobalt blue evening gloves and matching cobalt blue-dyed armpits. Tragically, the party got so raucous, Eunice called the cops. The teenagers took off in a hotrod, crashed it, and died.

Even for Halloween, *Séance* was flat-out peculiar. Squabbie, who was straight but adored the Angels, had brought some straight friends to see it, promising them they'd see something they'd never forget. They certainly had. Now they were regarding him curiously but he was laughing like hell. I just wanted to get out of there, away from Brian, away from Angel Dust people, away from Sandee and cocaine, away from any chance of encountering Sidney. Victoria was going off to join a yoga commune with Jillen, both now too fragile to endure pressure and in need of deep healing. Then Paul Aaron urged me to come to Hollywood, saying he wanted to cast me in a play and would have already done so if only I was there. So four months after returning to a home that wasn't home, I was on the road to Tinseltown.

Chapter 16

Aside from Paul Aaron, the only person I knew in LA was Bo, now Bo "Young," aspiring actor. But just as I arrived, he was moving in with a slab of beefcake. Alan Goebbels was apparently related to Joseph Goebbels, Hitler's sidekick, a fact he revealed proudly. I was dubious. Bo and I had drifted apart; I couldn't help seeing a bottomless pit in his eyes. We were both lost. The difference was that I knew it, whereas he didn't. Still, his now-vacated digs in La Fontaine, a much sought-after address resembling a French château, was a good place to hole up. I found it surreal seeing hustlers wearing cowboy hats and Gucci loafers showing up for "dates" with other residents, but this was mere prelude to the peculiar probing that took place during my first meeting with Paul as a Hollywood hopeful.

"You could be a big star," he said. "But LA is filled with actors willing to do *anything*. So? Let's say a director who could give you an important part invited you to Palm Springs for the weekend. What would you say?"

"I'd say, 'Have a nice weekend and I'll see you on Monday'," I replied.

Paul shared a story he'd written and asked me to try writing it as a novel because, if I could get something published, it would stand a better chance of being made into a film. In telling me the tale he wanted to film, he indicated that I would get the role. Or so went the operative theory. I got to work in February 1977 and, by March, I'd written *The Glass Arcade*, a novel that would be published three years later. The plot took place in a dark gay circus or cabaret world.

Outside, California was blighted by drought. People were asked not to flush unless necessary and not to wash their cars. But in Lala Land, people watered lawns in the heat of midday. Tinseltown was so bizarre that I rarely went out. At one party, glum wannabes stood around until a TV crew showed up, whereupon they launched into party mode, laughing and flashing smiles. But the minute the crew left, they took off.

Through mutual friends, I met *another* Peter, Peter Hartman, a delightful composer with the slanted blue eyes of a satyr. This charming new friend (to whom I dedicated "The Arterial Tribe"—see page 251) shared a chilling tale: he'd been in Nepal and he too had had an affair with Sidney, until he realized that *Sidney tried to murder him too!*

"Sidney and Sandee!" he fluttered. "Both of them were totally insane psychopaths and they were both after your head! My dear, I don't know how you survived!"

I didn't know either. My doubts grew as Paul prepared to direct his first feature film, *A Different Story*. The original story concerned two friends—a gay man and a lesbian—who have sex "accidentally," have a baby, then marry before coming to their senses and parting as friends. Progressive stuff for 1977. But to secure funding, Paul's revision had the pair *willingly converting* to happily ever after heterosexuality! It was a total sellout. But he theorized, "If all the rules are fair, anything goes." *If all the rules are fair*?!

Just hearing the words chilled me. This person who had talked so much about artistic integrity was now spouting the notion that anything that achieved a desired goal was legitimate. The ends justify the means: the exact opposite of my ethos. Considering my recent experiences, I started to suspect that putting any faith in the Hollywood system or Paul's big shiny promises was likely to be a dead end.

My doubts were confirmed when Paul and I discussed *The Glass Arcade*. Now that I'd written the book, suddenly the film role he'd first described as my part *wasn't* mine! According to this New Revised Version of Truth in a world where all the rules are fair, it was impossible for an openly gay man to be hired in homophobic Hollywood (notwithstanding the fact that he'd be directing and producing), even though the part was a gay role. No point bothering with the contradictions here. Or accountability. I knew what *I* thought as I flew to San Francisco for a visit.

It was August and muggy and there were strange currents in the air. Jim Jones and his cult, once inhabitants of the Haight-Ashbury, were moving to Guyana, claiming to be escaping "local persecution" for their new paradise in the jungle. Having been out of the loop in Lala Land, my goal was closer at hand: the Angels were getting ready to do another show. At a preliminary meeting at the studio, a conflict arose between a majority of those who wanted to stage a humanistic tale, and Janice, who advanced a science-fiction theme. Supposedly, the issue would be resolved at the next script meeting a week later. This gave me seven days to return to LA, pack, and move back to where I belonged.

Chapter 17

Seven days later I was home, but during my absence, Rodney and Beaver had appointed Janice to write the upcoming show! Such a decision should have been a collective one, but Rodney and Beaver co-opted it. Feeling undercut and shafted, I sensed something foul unfolding, not yet realizing that Rodney was using Angel Dust, which Janice sold.

The power play led me to withdraw from the group and the new show. It wasn't simply a case of injured vanity. The last thing I wanted after Sidney's attack and my parents' terrible betrayal was even *more* manipulation. I felt the Angels should go their way; I'd go mine.

San Francisco seemed lighter because, after three unsuccessful campaigns, Harvey Milk was running for the city's Board of Supervisors again. Those closest to him, like Dan Nicoletta, saw better days ahead. Perhaps this is why I, like so many others who wanted the city to represent altruistic ideals, felt a renewed sense of hope.

The Angels had moved to a house at 333 Noe Street. Rodney, Beaver, Brian, and Sham occupied the top floor. In the basement: the bedroom/sound studio of a new Angel, Tommy Tadlock, who resembled a skinny teenager, though at forty, he was significantly older than most of us. An avant-garde composer, Tommy achieved celebrity in the early 60s with an exhibition combining sound and light at New York's Whitney Museum.

Scrawny and temperamental, Tommy was resident genius and guru for packs of young, mainly gay, musicians. When aggravated, he had a tendency to smash sound equipment, erase tapes, sabotage tracks, and generally be impossible to be around. He and Brian often locked horns with pyrotechnical results because Tommy never backed down. But I never had any problems with him. I liked the fact that he was goal-oriented and not bothered with fussy detail. Hyper, wry, and opinionated, Tommy was a fount of musical ideas. Through collaboration with Steven Brown and Greg, the music shifted from rehashed Broadway songs to original compositions created for our shows. The result? Technically experimental and atonal scores that broke the sentimental tradition based on "tunes." The freedom from melody ushered in a new era.

Being back in a town as crazy as San Francisco had lots of unexpected benefits.

Early one day, I waited for a #24 bus at Castro and Market Streets with two suburban ladies who, obviously, wanted to get the hell out of the area. Down the block, two bedraggled drag queens were stumbling our way. When the women saw them weaving toward our stop, they gripped their purses.

Closer and closer came the tottering damsels, their shredded fishnets and morning stubble telling the rest of the story. They passed the bus stop without even noticing us, so the suburban ladies and I could hear one of the drag queens finish her particularly moving tale: *And girl, first it was two fingers, then three, then four, and before I could uncap the amyl again, that man was wearing my asshole like a bracelet!*

The women went cross-eyed with horror, but I had to laugh. Oh yes, I was home!

This was proved even more conclusively at the next Gay Day Parade. As it began, a conference of out-of-town Christians emerged from one of the nearby big hotels. Bibles in hand, they broadsided 400,000 gay people, gasping at the sight of the dykes on bikes, bare-assed men in black leather chaps and tinsel-covered tractors. One of the "Saved" was so aghast by the pagan festivities, she actually spoke to a man standing nearby:

"What is this?" she asked.

The sallow man looked her over slowly. "What is *what?*" he asked laconically.

"This! All this!"

"This?" he shrugged with superb nonchalance. "It's the weekend."

"Do you mean to say this is what you do on weekends?" she cried.

"Not every weekend," he replied with a straight face. "Only if the weather is good."

Yes, I was home. Sweet home. With delight, I wrote "After the Gay Day Parade" (see page 252).

Sharing a house in the Haight-Ashbury, with Peter Leone, Bo's ex and my former housemate from Polk Street, I focused on my writing while the Angels began rehearsing.

Jillen was in town, still working on a novel, still wrestling her demons, still wanting desperately to be rescued. As time passed and funds dwindled, she had little to show for her efforts. The stabs at meaning became increasingly disjointed, the downward spiral accelerated, and, despite her best efforts, her kids were following in her footsteps: dancing on the lip of a volcano. But being friends, Jillen and I started going to Cloud House, a weekly gathering of poets organized by activist-archivist Tony Kushner (not the playwright). These councils attracted writers whom I admired immensely.

Andy Hayes was a poet, musician, and ballsy politico, a good friend of Tede Mathews, and one who accompanied him on several journeys to Latin America where Tede helped establish gay liberation groups in Nicaragua. Andy, a heterosexual, had also created music for *Mind Kamp Kabaret* and was one of the foremost political poets of the era. Credentials aside, he was also extremely warm and authentic with a "can do" approach.

Another poet-phenomenon was so great he left me speechless: Anthony "Tony" Vaughan—a modern day Puck—was a poet/minstrel in the truest sense. A bird-like fellow who was thin as a shadow in a floppy hat and who wore his guitar slung over his back, Anthony created poems, shamanistic chants, and jazz based on diminished chords. Listening to him with rapt fascination, I felt I was witnessing the magna of creative genius that teetered between Celtic banshee madness, shamanism, and pure atonal music.

In November 1977, Harvey Milk was elected to the highest political office ever occupied by an openly gay person in the country's history. Meanwhile, the "Sisters of Perpetual Indulgence," queer artists who dressed as nuns, were zooming around town on Vespas. Outraged, the Vatican protested the insolence of our Sodom, but every time the Pope tried to visit the city, there were so many threats of rioting that he'd have to cancel.

Our community centered on a cozy "village green" of sorts: the Café Flore occupied one corner of a star-shaped intersection at Noe, Market, and 16th Streets. Here, in a potting shed-like structure with a corrugated tin roof, the extended tribe gathered over small tables inside or sprawled about the wide terrace and sidewalks. The Flore was a great place to see and be seen among the orange-clad devotees of Rajneesh, transvestite nuns, leather queens, and Castro clones.

One habitué, Robert Opel, was always clad in leather and had eyes like blue ice. Infamous for streaking the 1974 Academy Awards and, later, for outraging the LA Chief of Police by stripping nude at a city meeting to discuss rules banning nude beaches in Santa Monica, Robert was an exciting renegade. That canny cat and I saw one another as kindred spirits: bad-ass gay boys with lots to say and no problem saying it.

Robert wanted to open a gallery showcasing shocking gay art, a plan that I endorsed: the more disturbing, the better! In his Fey-Way Studios on Howard Street south of Market, Robert could function as community goad. How could I fail to be impressed?

Still, I stayed at home, writing and enjoying a new puppy, a red Chow called Woof. On foggy nights, it was lovely to curl up with him and listen to the foghorn moan from the south tower of the Golden Gate Bridge. But there were also signs of dissonance....

With 1978 looming, Jillen was all hyped up by her on-again, off-again use of medication to stabilize her thyroid. I was still looking for a safe and stable home, wondering if my save-the-world Quakerism might not be better served in a spiritual community than on the radical fringe until I attended a party on New Year's Eve, where a girl named Janet told me, "I know someone who looks like you. You two should meet." Janet studied film at the Art Institute; we had an interesting chat and I didn't mind giving her my number to give to her friend, though I never expected her to call a week later from the guy's apartment on Folsom Street. Would I like to stop by?

When I arrived, Janet was alone. This gave me time to take in the dungeon, complete with an iron cage, piles of debris, the white housecat dyed neon pink, and a few remarkable sculptures. One was a black wood and glass clock case that now housed a pile of ash, a half-burned Bible, and two dried gardenias, prefiguring Anthony Serrano's piss-soaked crucifix by twenty years.

Another piece was even more brilliant and macabre: a glass maze enclosed in a long glass box. At the center of the labyrinth was a dead mouse in the maw of a mousetrap still baited with cheese.

And then *he* came in.

How to be brief?

Well, okay, I knew he was a hustler, but for the first and only time, I actually debated paying. Angelic yet knowing, he combined the street smarts of an alley cat with the whimsy of an English schoolboy—so sexy, I felt dizzy.

Christopher N. was the offspring of missionaries who took their brood to Africa to save the heathens before returning to the Bay Area, a hop, skip, and a fuck to San Francisco where their sixteen-year-old painted dark circles under his eyes to get into bars and begin living "the life." At eighteen, of course, he knew everything. He proved it too: asserting that the highest form of art was to be a sniper and shoot people from a tower. I called him insane. He called me a prig. We argued for an hour before exchanging phone numbers. Unbeknownst to me, a girl he was seeing threw my number away later that night. And on the way home, I crumpled his up and tossed it out the window. I'd been with one whack job; I didn't want—and couldn't risk—another. But six weeks later, Robert Opel called to invite me to an opening. At this time, I was debating going to an ashram in India. But off I tripped to the exhibition, where everyone else was uniformed in black leather. Or denim. Or variants adorned with chains, cock rings, studs, key rings, and handcuffs.

Here, as fate would have it, I encountered Christopher again, now no longer hustling but working at a movie theater. We were studiously polite this time and exchanged numbers again. Later, as I chatted with people outside, he emerged, nodded at me, and walked off. But he only got halfway down the block when, for some incredible reason, I shouted, "Hey Christopher! Call me up sometime when you feel brave!" I couldn't believe I'd done that. Me—a hippie!—surrounded by the black leather studs. I was stunned. Christopher looked shocked too, but he nodded and walked away. As soon as he disappeared, I escaped and got home, asap. But the cat was out of the bag.

That's how all that deliciousness began, chocolate ice cream and MDA (a forerunner of Ecstasy), hickeys *everywhere,* coffee in bed, and the endless movies we trooped off to watch, movies that, no matter how hokey or clichéd, could not depict a finer romance. At thirty, I fell madly, madly in love. And at last, and for the first time, was loved in kind.

Christopher was as warm and sweet as a child. At ease in a superb articulated body, he was absolutely into sex: the more extended and experimental the better. Childhood gifted him with a black African soul in Caucasian form;

a pagan, he was an animist and tribalist for whom sex was a ceremony no less profound than any celebratory rite.

I still remember him coming up the street with roses to croon a love song to me, hopelessly off tune. That didn't stop him any more than a fear of heights would curb his nocturnal prowling, in which he even got *me* to scale the fire escape of a ten-story downtown city warehouse to make love on the roof at midnight under an enormous neon sign. Factor in his popsicles and drugs, of course, flights of fancy that rose up, up, and still farther up to greet the rising sun after a night of love—or plunging down and down farther still, spiraling on absolute trust that stop would mean *stop* if we got to that point. He was always there for me, as I became his religion and he became mine. Aside from my dog, we had no need for, or much interest in, anyone else.

It was 1978; I'd never had my own home. And never would. The price of a house that cost $25,000 in 1971 was now $120,000. But for the first time, I found an apartment. Aside from a small kitchen and bath, there were two rooms connected by French doors. Four-hundred square feet; $375 a month. All this on one of the quaintest tree-lined streets in the Castro. The address? 69 Henry Street. A teacup palace. And as events turned out, all my very own for the next five years.

Chapter 18

The scene: the future.

Dancing is illegal. Humans slave on behalf of a technocracy. Banks of grey computers are arranged in grim columns in steadily diminishing size, creating the illusion of a great hall in a futuristic factory. Synthesized music—eerie bubbles of sound tumbling in rises and waves—plays as red-masked figures appear and move in unison: the menacing mime sequence of integrated, interlocked steps is an oppressive combo of close order drill and Nazi rally. There is no redemption or empathy in this godless world. Nature has been extinguished by an all-conquering Machine.

Beaver created that scene for the new Angels show, *Sci-Clones*, and it encapsulated what the Angels of Light could do to perfection: create a stunning vision that literally leapt across the footlights to punch an audience in the gut.

The caption *Dancing Is Illegal* trumpeted posters for the show that opens in the setting of the garden of Eden—a favorite Angel locale—which is soon to be invaded, with the overthrown "Uma" purists falling into the maws of a gulag. But some Umas resist the totalitarian rule by creating a secret Tango Palace where they gather to dance. Ultimately, their underground is penetrated and wiped out by their Stalinist overlords. Even so, a few Umas escape, vowing to continue resistance. And such was the narrative plot that ended with humanity being extinguished.

But in the eerie way that art imitates life, the show ran a harrowing parallel to reality. The script was humorless and leaden, both overwritten and overburdened by space-age shorthand no one could possibly untangle. The opening paradise was exquisite and the mime piece was genuinely powerful, but aside from phenomenal sets, dances, and costumes, *Sci-Clones* was a plodding and joyless exercise, both onstage and off.

The drag queens were gone, alienated by an appalling dislocation best described both psychologically and spiritually. Out in the world, Harvey Milk was taking on big real estate developers as well as writing legislation to protect gay people from being fired on the basis of sexual orientation. Just as he was advancing the cause by fighting the good fight politically, the Angels were at the vanguard of San Francisco's gay community. But the takeover of

Beaver Bauer and Jessica Copen, *Sci-Clones*, 1978

the group was murky and numbing once Rodney and Beaver installed Janice as writer and de facto director. Once they granted her free rein, Janice displayed her true colors.

Her forte lay in tricking people into self-parody. But the last thing Janice cared about was heart. Or soul. To her, there were sharks in the water and, by dumping blood in, she could instigate a feeding frenzy, thereby exposing Angels as hippie-dippy bullshit and enjoying the mess.

"I will destroy the Angels of Light!" I'd heard her cackle at a party, stoned on Dust. I couldn't believe it but there is a certain type of person who enjoys defacing paintings or sneaking into zoos for the thrill of slaughtering caged animals.

Janice would never risk overplaying her hand by attacking Beaver, Rodney, Brian, or Madeline (now using a Hindu name, Radha). But everyone else was fair game. Thus, with a bully's zeal, Janice set about her malicious work.

Self-anointed radical feminists now, the alpha females—Beaver, passively, Janice, actively—encouraged less prominent Angels to go on the rampage. Lynne, a hulking lesbian with a low forehead and *issues*; Esmerelda—a self-professed local diva who was, according to Greg, "two gin and tonics away from coming out as a lesbian" and a walking, talking ad for a half dozen twelve-step programs; Jessica, a frustrated politico; and others seized their chance to vent. Not against each other, however. Nope, this sisterhood had one target, and one target only: *men*. And with Janice at the helm, fur would fly.

Janice got traction for several reasons. Rodney was smoking Dust on the sly, though in public, he maintained an anti-drug stance. Did Janice supply it? I can't say. And Beaver? Greg speculates that, by elevating Janice, Beaver ensured an ally and, not coincidentally, intensified her lock on power. Beaver wasn't gay; in fact, Greg asserts, "gay" was a barrier she couldn't storm. She'd never say such an "un-PC" thing aloud—she was too canny for that—but gay-ness victimized her by keeping Rodney from her.

Brian was another "straight victim" who never bonded with the gay men in the group. Though Rodney's lover, Brian was trapped. The idea of Janice, another nominally quasi-straight person, being in power, served his desire to escape a gay trap. And his collusion contributed to the atmosphere of misery for, at one point, every single guy in *Sci-Clones* (except Rodney) got so tired of being harassed and insulted, they quit after the harpies castigated the gay men for "not respecting" women *by doing drag*!

Consider that. These women had gravitated into what was, arguably, the gayest theater in the gayest city on the planet. In large part, and for whatever reasons, as "fag hags" or "gay widows," they subsumed their sexuality in symbiotic relationships with gay men; and just as they surrendered their femininity, a lot of gay men diluted their masculinity, identifying so strongly with women that they became self-parodies while, simultaneously, becoming close to, if not emotionally reliant on, women. Okay, that isn't exactly news, but for the women in the Angels to get their knickers in a twist over gay men doing drag was nuts. Even so, it provided justification for internecine feuding that led to people asking me to intercede.

It hurt me to deny friends asking for help but I was in love, happy, and writing (see "After Six Months" and "Song" on pages 253-55). And I was further insulated because, for various reasons—some born of possessiveness and others of his clear-sighted, no-nonsense outlook—Christopher *hated* the Angels of Light, wanted nothing to do with them, and was extremely wary of my having contact with them.

"They're vicious, selfish, mean people," he said. "I hate the way they treat each other. And I don't want you to get hurt."

Even so, I was in the crowd when the curtain rose for *Sci-Clones* in the splendid auditorium at Everett High School in the Castro. The Spanish-Moorish setting was perfect for a show with a climactic scene set in a tango palace. It had a Mediterranean Alhambra décor with balconies overlooking the stage and terra-cotta walls.

The first scene was a *Fantasia*-like sequence, with the spiritual Umas emerging from lotus blossoms in a celebratory invocation to the dawn. Watching, I felt intoxicated by the incandescent beauty on display. But after robots invaded, conquered and enslaved the Umas, I felt torn among my admiration of a thrilling tap dance, the fantastic mime sequence, and my depression over the unmitigated boredom of interminable dialogue. It was like watching Barbaro break a leg but still trying to run.

The last scene featured a wild, exuberant tango set to verbal histrionics. Playing an old woman in the only epic scene she ever did with the troupe,

Esmerelda exhorted her spiritual children to resist oppression by getting to their feet to dance!

Physically diminutive, Esmerelda had been around for years: I'd first glimpsed the dark Latina beauty with chiseled features before the curtain rose for *Paris Sites*, when she sang for the crowd. In an Angels show at last, after being sidelined for accepting money for performing, she found a perfect outlet for her conflict when belting out the finale. Her *crie du coeur* was astounding. If the Darth Vader menace of Beaver's mime was the best scene, Esmerelda's closing song was the show's most electrifying moment and gave the whole production dramatic resolution.

There were six or seven performances of *Sci-Clones*. I went to every one, half transported, half disgusted by its lack of soul. But there was no doubting the reason. One night, just before the curtain rose at one show, I got another close-up view of Janice.

"John Burroughs is dead! John Burroughs is dead!" she exulted, hopping up and down, clapping delightedly … at the news of a murder … yes, murder.

John Burroughs was a sad, tortured poet who had fallen in love with Sidney. They'd been living together and shooting up together in a hearse parked in the garage of a communal house. According to the story going around, they'd made a suicide pact, wrote farewell notes, hit up, and forty-five minutes later, Sidney came upstairs from the garage into the kitchen and "mournfully" told those who were there, "John is dead."

Yes, John was dead. Sidney lived. But everyone knew that no one who makes a serious attempt to overdose is ambulatory forty-five minutes later. Still, John had left a note so Sidney couldn't be charged for his crime.

Now, word on the street was that Sandee, with her gun, was looking for Sidney—he'd ripped her off in some cocaine deal—and someone told him that if he ever showed his face in the city again, he'd be killed. So he vanished. Others bailed too; half the cast of *Sci-Clones* never participated in another show. Many were the hippies who were sickened by the cruelty and infighting: Francine, Rose, Melody, and Much Obliged, the kindest, loveliest, and sweetest.

"People had to get out for their own survival," Teena told me. "There was such incredible cruelty between people behaving like zombies."

The company was in meltdown. Tony Angel went off to New York. And most of the remaining men were fed up, just fed up, with the complaints of the raging feminists.

But in San Francisco, one can never be insulated from such matters. Francesca was having a passionate affair with Mark Pieratt, a gay man and gifted artist. "It's so weird," she said. "We take separate buses to his place so that nobody sees us together! Imagine what people would say if they found out that a man and a woman were having sex!"

Still, I felt something dark was pending, as if wind chimes were stirring in a torpid breeze. I wasn't alone. Played out at forty-seven, Jillen moved back to her mother's place on Cape Cod as Victoria chased the constant vanishing point of celebrity with Tuxedomoon. Obsessed with a local puppeteer named Winston Tong (who went on to win an Emmy and brief acclaim), Victoria clung to the limelight before temporarily burning out, another casualty of the imploding scene that I described in a journal entry dated July 16, 1978:

> The glitter is off the tree. The party is over and I and my friends—
> my dazzling art freaks, whores, welfare dancers, guerilla street
> theater "personage" have got to find new ways to survive. Welfare
> is not enough. The Underground is non-supporting so it's time
> to select a life raft. I realize it sounds ridiculous but the 60s have
> *finally* ended. In SF, they held out for years. Now a country facing
> economic recession puts the squeeze to fabulous creatures who
> seem to have shucked glitter and tinsel for a new austerity.

In August, Anthony Vaughan (the poet) invited me to help with a conceptual art piece for Gay Day: painting Castro Street in the color lavender to protest anti-gay zealots. Anita Bryant was turning her homophobia into a campaign—"Save Our Children"—while California State Senator John Briggs crusaded to fire gay teachers. Harvey Milk led statewide opposition to the Briggs Initiative. My "Gay Day/Art Project: Paint Castro Street" was a community broadside in August 1978, plastered on hundreds of telephone poles and buildings:

Bicentennial kiss on Castro Street, July 4, 1976

Let's paint Castro Street so San Francisco
Seen from the skies will dazzle her birds.
Let's paint the street so this city will sigh
Not sink in cement strips smothering earth.
Let's color/streak her mud face with berries
Apply her cosmetics so the rain may wash
Ultra-violet down her iron pipes and drains.
Let's paint our street, re-consecrate ground
"Caucasoids" chose to own/divide/keep bleak.
Until stone was set to stone, this undulating
Country valley pocked by berry and lupen,
Jack rabbit, deer. Poor street, cut into shares,
Street of tea and bourbon and cruisey trade.
Paint our village street so when, at last, it rains
Her rouge will kiss the beach and grey Pacific.
Until then, birds will see more than beasts here.

Chapter 19

On November 18, 1978, Jim Jones of the People's Temple prodded his 900 followers into mass suicide in Jonestown, Guyana. Perhaps because of that, Harvey Milk wrote a note to be opened only in the event of his assassination: "If a bullet should enter my brain, let that bullet destroy every closet door."

On November 27th, I was at the vet when I heard that Harvey had been murdered. My dog Woof was getting a shot. A shot....

Dan White, an ex-cop and member of the Board of Supervisors who'd resigned before demanding reappointment after Mayor George Moscone named his successor, sneaked a gun into City Hall. Once inside, he assassinated our mayor. And Harvey Milk.

Like so many others, although I didn't know Harvey well, his murder took on far more than personal consequence. It was as if our collective efforts had imploded. As gays and lesbians, our first successful steps to gain legitimacy had led to slaughter. We were used to the cruelty of the American Psychiatric Association's diagnosis of homosexuality as mental disorder, to right-wing fundamentalist condemnation from whack jobs like Reverend Jerry Falwell, to the institutionalized denial of equal rights; but these murders would once again mark us as victims who deserved no better.

The bloodletting had not stopped. The night of the murders, after a candlelight procession that began in the Castro and moved in silent tribute all the way down Market Street to City Hall, Mark Pieratt, Francesca's lover, was spotted by some thugs who realized he was gay. And cut his throat.

The fatal slash also severed Francesca's lightness. Hearing the news, I rushed to her house with vodka and she guzzled down a drink, devastated. She then withdrew into skittish mourning, fulfilling in some strange way the social coda of Sicilian women: girls for too brief a season, then consigned to tragic widowhood. It was eerie. She kept writing—wildly gifted—but I felt her style-conscious prose lacked the ruthless, nervy romance of her hard, glittering poems. Certainly, her prose guarded her once so open heart.

In retrospect, I think the murders provided us with the impetus for mounting another show. For not only did the Angels grieve for martyred friends, the city was traumatized. Tragedy can be a great motivator. Whatever the cause, a year after *Sci-Clones*, many Angels felt ready to try coming together again.

Harvey Milk and supporters walk from Castro Street to City Hall, Inaguration Day, January 9, 1978

I wasn't certain where it would lead when I wrote in my journal on January 1, 1979:

> Today, hung over, and this city rolls over its own hills as if it's a trashed-out whore at home, in bed, with no one booked till six ...
>
> Today, the residents & friends of this city of St Francis's survivors huddled at outdoor cafés—as if shipwrecked or fed thru blenders ...
>
> Today, the holiday ends—exiles return from flight, Joy is overthrown and life is life again, not a merchandizing bull's-eye ...
>
> Today, San Francisco keeps going; the party shifts into Cruise, up all night, drunks go out for beer and long distance runners run ...
>
> Today, I give up on the 70s; it's been useful, I guess, tho' pale and compromised. Let it stagger around and collapse and die....

José Saria, Harvey Milk, and Mavis (presenting anonymous donation for Gay and Lesbian Freedom Marching Band), Beaux Arts Ball, October 28, 1978

Although I was insulated by love and my writing, there was a sense of peril brought about by changing demographics because the crazy quilt of San Francisco makes strange bedfellows. The Castro occupies the high ground of Eureka Valley that spills from a high ridge toward the Bay. Going east from Dolores Street, a magnificent palm-lined avenue, the Mission District remains essentially Hispanic, although it has been gradually gentrified by white gay residents, and escalating property values caused racial tension. Factor in a collision of social norms and cultural values from 14th Street south to 24th and one predictable result was street violence.

Muggings, robberies, and murders were escalating. For the first time, I felt imperiled when gangs of Latinos drove through the Castro shouting "faggot," and "cocksucker," and "queer." The Angels' studio on Valencia was right in the nexus of the developing Valencia Street Corridor—the new hip spot for second-hand bookstores, funky cafés, and the poetry scene at Cloud House. Among other traumas, Harvey's murder served to escalate an increasing sense of personal jeopardy in the Castro.

THAT SUMMER, I'D read poetry for 200,000 people at the Gay Day Parade from a stage in front of City Hall. That sounds like some big thing, but *nobody* listens to poets, *especially* at an event which opens with bull-dykes on Harley-Davidsons. Even so, performing again felt wonderful. And after a year trying to describe *Paris Sites* to Christopher, I made a decision.

"I'm going to do another show with the Angels," I told him. "If you and I weren't together, I wouldn't. But I can't spend the rest of my life trying to explain that group. So when it all happens and the hoopla begins, remember: this is for you."

My other reason for getting involved was because, like everyone else in the aftermath of the killings, I wanted to help heal our community. I made only one stipulation for rejoining the group: Janice had to be banned (although ultimately, she was allowed a walk-on role for thirty seconds). Everyone agreed, including Beaver, Rodney, and Brian. And if they hadn't acceded and I hadn't come back, I doubt other people would have agreed to participate. In any case, there was no opposition. Once again, democracy appeared to be the modus operandi, although the true locus of power would remain obscured. So, in January 1979, I rejoined the Angels.

Chapter 20

The show *Holy Cow!* (also called *Chakra Treatment*, another of Ralph's puns), grew out of classes that some Angels took in South Indian dance: highly stylized movements accented by ankle bells, the stamping of feet, and rolling eyes, all accompanied by music and vocal cues similar to a "caller" in a square dance. Through this format, ancient Eastern traditions provided impetus for a show.

Drag queens were back in. Tony Angel returned from New York. Slowly, the Angels were healing as people began to re-establish comfortable and trusting bonds with one another.

Having starred in big shows, I decided to do no more than provide structure and stability and move the plot along, as in *Mind Kamp Kabaret*. But I wanted to remain as detached as possible because writing is nothing like performing live, and I was happier maintaining a distance from the Angels. I rarely attended their parties, usually only on opening and closing nights; even so, I always left early because, after one or two o'clock in the morning, the vibe changed: the drugs were kicking in, the drunks were in overdrive, and I'm told that some parties still devolved into orgies. Not for me.

Meanwhile, the Castro was seething. Mayor Dianne Feinstein was well-intentioned blah blah blah. It was time for political statements. I felt I was succeeding in part because my novel, *The Glass Arcade*, was finally going to be published in 1980. I wanted the Angels to be more political, too, and I believe everyone in the group felt the same way.

In India, while officially denied, 10,000 women a year were immolated when their husband's family decided (sometimes years after the wedding) that the wife's family hadn't paid enough dowry for the honor of marrying their son. And if his wife failed to satisfy them, she may be murdered. Protesting "bride burning" was certainly a potent theme.

Script meetings got underway. At the studio, thirty-five of us sat around with burritos or cups of blueberry kefir as we shared ideas. It's worth reiterating: it's *not* possible to write a great play to please a collective. But with all due respect to the bard, scriptwriting is *not* the thing: *the show is*. Even at their best, the Angels never performed great plays, we staged stupendous events. I saw my task as the facilitator of that goal and to balance, compromise, harmonize, synchronize, integrate.

Outside our tiny world, Dan White was on trial. Inside, we developed the tale of a spiritual girl in love with a carving on a temple wall, awakened into human life by her devotion. The girl is obliged to wed a cruel Rajah. When she flees, he pursues her, laying waste to the countryside but ultimately meeting death at the hands of the god Shiva.

The format paralleled *Paris Sites*. In both shows, the first scene took place in the streets before a betrothal. In *Paris Sites*, people planned revolution after a child killing; in *Holy Cow!* dramatic action begins after a girl is killed. In both, young lovers are outside the realm of prevailing social and imperial power. In 1975, it was young Nostalgia and a Pierrot. Now, the silent dance was between young Kamala and a spirit lover. In both, girls are forced into arranged marriages in palaces where menacing mothers reign supreme. In *Paris Sites*, the Countess Flushette wore a toilet her head; in *Holy Cow!*, the Queen Mother sports elephant ears.

The entertainment depicted in both shows was eloquent. In *Paris Sites*, it was a ballet; in *Holy Cow!* it was an exquisite show-within-a-show (created by Rodney) similar to the Uncle Tom's Cabin sequence in *The King and I*: a politically charged dance-drama insulting a tyrant. What followed was chaos in the palace—the overthrow of the despots, revolution, flight, and eventually, spiritual fulfillment; in *Paris Sites*, the quest traveled to the North Pole before plunging under the sea for a cure for the plague. In *Holy Cow!* the quest leads to a rural village and the Forest of Death. And in a parallel to the absolution promised by the rose in *Paris Sites*, in *Holy Cow!* Shiva embraces the devotee/lovers. *Paris Sites* ended with a joyous victory celebration; *Holy Cow!* ends in joyful spiritual resolution—one led to political triumph, the other to mystical union.

The main roles also ran parallel: Beaver was the (asexual) martyr heroine; Rodney, the (nonsexual) hero; Radha, the romantic; Tony, the devilish traitor, and I the comic villain. All of us playing polar opposites of our actual selves.

As spring ripened, our studio on Valencia Street got too crowded so we rehearsed at the gay community center on Grove Street a few blocks from City Hall. We had access to a huge loft on the third floor, but it was seemed eons away from the trial in which Dan White was claiming that eating Twinkies had unhinged him and caused temporary insanity.

LET ME TAKE A MINUTE to draw your attention to Beaver sitting cross-legged on the floor, a large piece of gold lamé in her lap. She is patiently separating the fabric, one thread at a time. The job demands infinite patience. When finished—and yes, she will actually complete this obsessive task—she will have a thick and realistic-looking tail of gold. The reason for this labor of love is that, in one of her twin roles, she will play a unicorn. The mythic beast—so close to fantastical horses and her highest dreams of freedom—has provoked her imagination and engaged her yearning heart. Thus, she spends hour after hour creating a tail that will appear as a splash of pure gold.

MAY 21ST: We stayed late rehearsing, and it was about eight o'clock when we heard noise outside. Then the news: Dan White had been acquitted of first-degree murder. His jury accepted the Twinkie Defense. Subtext: it's okay to rub out a leftie mayor and pinko fag.

City Hall was ringed with helmeted policemen in riot gear when Tony and I joined the furious demonstrators filling the enormous esplanade. Rocks and bricks bounced off the plastic shields of the police, black truncheons in hand. The hail of stones was inaudible, however, due to the sirens; a long row of police cars were in flames. As plumes of dull orange and black smoke curled up into the maroon sky and a livid mob smashed in the glass doors of City Hall, Tony and I withdrew.

Christopher came in late, his head split open by a police officer's club. While I tended his wound, the police retaliated, counter-attacking a Castro bar—the Elephant Walk—randomly pulverizing innocent bystanders. Eighty were hospitalized.

"Dan White got away with murder," Mayor Feinstein said the next day. She inherited a city seething with rage and mourning its dead heroes. Against the background of the White Night Riots, *Holy Cow!* steamed toward its debut at Lone Mountain College, a medieval-looking institution set on top of a hill overlooking Golden Gate Park.

Fires from burning police cars, White Night Riots, San Francisco, May 21, 1979

Helping to prepare the show were new talents who contributed mightily to its reception.

Kevin Gardiner was a technically trained actor who'd appeared in many Bay Area productions. Pale, auburn-haired, and wolfishly handsome, he played the lead romantic role and directed(!) smoothly and professionally. Kevin deserves full credit for the heightened focus, better voice projection, blocking, and choreography; and Rodney gets a gold star for bringing him into the Angels after they met as students of Tai Chi.

Almost *too* heterosexual, Kevin was word perfect in his expressions of humility, but he made all the right moves so smoothly, I often wondered if he saw our group as an adroit career step or saw its female cast members as ripe for the pickin'. Whatever his ulterior motives (or the ensuing offstage kootchicoo), there's no doubt that this fey Lothario showcased our multiple and varied talents to superior advantage. But he couldn't possibly have untangled the *realpolitik* of the Angels; no newcomer could. Thus, like others gulled into believing that they *did* fathom the lie of the land, Kevin felt empowered. Acting on faulty assumptions, he strutted his stuff like a bantam cock. I found him self-serving and disingenuous, but—hey!—if everyone was happy and making solid progress, *and we were*, why express personal

Lenore Vantosh-Howard, Kavita Jonopolous, and Coco Vega,
October 11, 1981.

reservations?

Philippe Ruise was a multi-talented jack-of-all-trades: a dancer, prop maker, performer, carpenter, painter, and sculptor. The muscular, curly-headed Mediterranean was a creative dynamo who, like Tony, had a take-no-prisoners approach to visuals; his larger-than-life personality was another thing; this warm-hearted yet vulnerable man was the child of a mother burdened with a large brood and an alcoholic father. The foul-mouthed "Filthy" handled Life's chaos by slapping it into Art.

At the studio on Valencia Street, Philippe took a huge gorilla mask that he'd made and, using a *papier-mâché* technique, transformed it into a massive Chinese dragon head that became the signature image of the show. This somewhat shy, funny, and abrupt maestro labored like a fiend in tandem with Tony, turning out props and masks in a torrent.

Lulu was a rare soul, too flamboyant, too dishy, and too "too" to be believed. It's not easy to portray one so diverse and talented; he was a plethora of contradictions. As an artist, he was a belly-dancer, like Philippe, a tap dancer, a costume designer, and a gardener. The lively, blue-eyed, blond man made props too. But his readiness to assist extended far beyond that. Lulu was always willing to pitch in and perform the humblest, least glamorous scutwork. He had boundless energy. In the Angels, he saw a chance to represent his high ideals; he seized it and blossomed.

And last but by no means least ...

Even amidst a full raft of phosphorescent divas, Coco Vega stood out: a ballsy, unpredictable, neurotic, desperate, hilarious, whacked-out, and sordid character of the first order. Others wangled their way into the Angels to find safe haven, however precarious. Not Coco. By 1979, he was the only one left with the nerve-shredding outrageousness that compelled the drag queens at Compton's and Stonewall to take on the cops. But fashions change; all-American boys were "in." Still, like a one-person Statue of Liberty, Coco raised high the torch of tatterdemalion authenticity.

Imagine a hairy, pudgy, unshaven Puerto Rican junkie—massive five o'clock shadow pushing through a slather of rouge—clopping along in shredded fishnets, a tawdry leopard coat, and a jangle of plastic bracelets on tattooed forearms. There are chopsticks in the hair more or less gathered on top of his head; smooshed mascara streaks his bleary eyes. He's lost another tooth. His high heels are splitting, the gold lame purse is looped over one elbow; he is tottering yet still waving gaily at passing cars, his raspy voice bellowing across the street: "*Girrrlllllll!!!!*" A third-generation heroin addict from New York, Coco is on his way to the docks. You heard me: *the docks*. A French navy ship is due in port. "And when they hit the dock, I'm gonna get me some!" Coco confides. Yes, he's after French sailors. Just yesterday, he made wild eyes at construction workers who couldn't believe what was prancing around below their cranes, waving and cooing.

Skittering on a razor's edge between overdose and Goddess consciousness, Coco weaved and bobbed between welfare checks and the newest batch of opium to hit town. Yet, this brown-eyed dervish who considered himself a woman was a kinetic poet. Sometimes he came by for coffee or asked to borrow money (which he'd always pay back). Sometimes I'd run into him with a man on his arm.

"Mama got fucked, honey!" he'd shout, indicating the dimensions of the cock involved.

Sometimes he was articulate and focused, wise and sensitive. Other times, I found him sitting on a curb, weeping as he fished through his purse, trying to find even more lipstick to apply to the red abstraction slapped onto his mouth. But whatever the manifestation of the moment, Coco was an original and I adored him for his gallantry, although I knew he was far past the point of anyone being able to get through to him; the best anyone could do was to care for him and try to help out when possible.

IT'S JUNE 1979. As the lights dim, the curtain rises on *Holy Cow!*. A street in India is clogged by a throng of devotees, acrobats, tumblers, and jugglers. A snake charmer removes the lid of a basket and a cobra undulates up—tongue flicking—with deadly eyes. The extraordinary creature weaves and curls around the snake charmer's shoulders. As the festival moves on, leaving the street deserted, Kamala and her sister Sita perform a devotional dance, then Sita leaves Kamala onstage for a romantic interlude with Kalir-va, reawakened to life from frozen slumber as a temple sculpture by Kamala's devotion. But when Kamala's mother interferes, hectoring the girl to prepare for her bridegroom's arrival, Kalir-va returns to stone, apparently.

The Rajah enters with great fanfare. Kamala is brought forward to meet her moronic groom, but a slave driver whips a group of prisoners toward the market. One catches the Rajah's eye: Sudama, who once led an insurrection. He selects her for himself then turns to Kamala. She rebuffs him but, reawakened by her fear, Kalir-va intervenes to rescue her. During a sword fight, the Rajah accidentally stabs Kamala who, mortally wounded, calls for Shiva. Entering astride a bull (dyke), Shiva prevents the spectral figure of Death from claiming Kamala and offers the combatants a choice: "If you wish to spare her, one of you must take her place. The other will live and have her for his bride."

Realizing the Rajah is psychotic, Kalir-va gives up his life; Kamala is restored to the Rajah. He leads her away as Death claims Kalir-va, enveloping him in her veil. But a mysterious woman appears: Kali, the Goddess of Destruction, is Kalir-va's mother. She calls on all the gods to avenge his death and vows she will have justice.

At the palace, the conflicted Rajah summons his Demon, a deliberately oblique pet who speaks in riddles. Kali appears in disguise, warning the Rajah of impending ruin; he brushes her off when the Sultan of Beirut arrives;

(*l–r*) Adrian Brooks ("Rajah"), Tony Angel ("Demon"), Coco Vega ("Kamala's Mother"), *Holy Cow!* (I.2), May 27, 1979

(l–r) Ralph Sauer ("Eunuch"), Beaver Bauer ("Sudama"), *Holy Cow!*, May 27, 1979

The dragonettes in the Forest of Death, *Holy Cow!* (II.3) May 27, 1979

The tap-dancing dragon in the Forest of Death, *Holy Cow!* (II.3), May 27, 1979

Shiva (Rodney Price) and cast in the finale of *Holy Cow!*, May 27, 1979

FACING PAGE: Original drawing for *Holy Cow!* program, created by Rinaldo Iturrino, 1980

the angels of light in

holy cow!

or 'chakra treatment'

Street festival, *Holy Cow!* (I.2), May 10, 1980

FACING PAGE: Robin Bowen ("Cobra"), *Holy Cow!*, May 16, 1980

Tony Angel ("Demon") and Tommy Pace ("Kamala's Mother"), *Holy Cow!*, May 16, 1980

Tommy Pace ("Kamala's Mother"), *Holy Cow!*, May 16, 1980

Dragonettes, *Holy Cow!*, May 16, 1980

Randall Denham ("Eunuch") and Constance West ("Queen Mother"), *Holy Cow!*, May 16, 1980

Robin Bowen ("Death") and Beaver Bauer ("Unicorn"), *Holy Cow!*, May 16, 1980

Radha Bloom, ("Kamala"), *Holy Cow!*, May 16, 1980

FACING PAGE: Lenore Vantosh-Howard ("Kali"), *Holy Cow!*, May 16, 1980

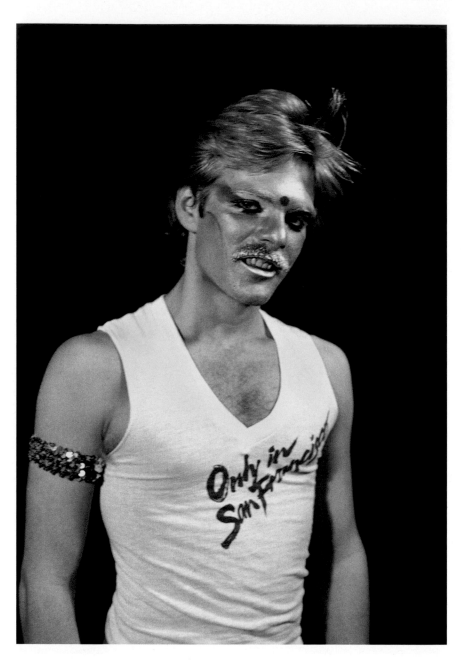

Rob Hichborn, *Holy Cow!*, May 16, 1980

Curtain call, *Holy Cow!*, May 10, 1980

FOLLOWING PAGE: Adrian Brooks ("Rajah"), *Holy Cow!*, May 16, 1980

the rulers soon quarrel, triggering the intervention of the mother-of-all-fag-hags: the elephant-headed Queen Mother. Teasing "little boys with big toys" and grabbing their crotches, she averts a war.

The presentation of gifts culminates with Kamala's performance with the court dancers. She plays a peacock princess who falls in love and escapes from her husband. When he pursues her, the cuckold is destroyed by Shiva. At this, the Rajah storms off; the Queen Mother—oozing sweet venom—offers Kamala a choice: provide an heir or else.

> QUEEN MOTHER: You will prepare a meal for your husband. There
> will be an accident. Your sari will catch fire, and it will all be over
> before you can say, "Bon appetit!"
> *When the Queen Mother leaves, Sudama suggests that Kamala*
> *escape.*
> KAMALA: *(shocked)* Leave my husband?!
> SUDAMA: Think of what it would mean.
> KAMALA: What are you suggesting?
> SUDAMA: What are you accepting?

In a palace garden, Sudama helps Kamala escape, saying that the people of her village will shelter her. The Queen Mother discovers the truth and tries to summon guards, but Sudama and a eunuch poison her. With her dying breath, she tells the Rajah everything. He summons a Torturer. In a delicate but grisly mime sequence, the Torturer teases and taunts Sudama before drawing a blade across her throat almost tenderly. Slain, Sudama sinks to the ground, veiled by Death as the lights fade into Intermission.

As the lights come up in Act II, Sudama lies lifeless beneath Death's veil. There is slow movement until the veil is lifted to reveal a beautiful Unicorn. The reincarnated soul of the butchered Sudama, the emergent Unicorn tests its first steps before galloping off.

In a rural village, peasants celebrate harvest, but when Kamala appears, they're torn. Should they protect her or send her back? There is scant time for debate; the Rajah's troops approach. Sending Kamala off, the peasants prepare for battle—a rapid sequence set to drums that melds Kung Fu, Shao-lin, tumbling, and acrobatics—but all the villagers are slaughtered except a baby whom the Rajah polishes off. Accompanied by his Demon, upon whom he's grown increasingly dependent, the Rajah spots the Unicorn. Believing that it will lead him to Kamala, he and the Demon give chase.

At the center of the cosmos, Lord Shiva realizes that his devotee is in peril. Thus is the great god stirred to intervene.

Kamala enters the nightmarish Forest of Death where she appeals to Shiva. Instead, a dragon appears. Thirty feet long, the snaking form sheds its skin, revealing twenty "dragonettes" tap dancing in Busby Berkeley-like syncopation. They drive Kamala to the edge of madness; the dragon withdraws and she's reunited with Kalir-va as the Rajah and Demon arrive to kill them; as they advance, self-revealing Shiva, flanked by Kali, makes His presence known. All prostrate themselves to receive Judgment.

In recognition of her merit, Kamala is transformed into spirit and reunited with Kalir-va. The Rajah and the Demon become a mouse and a toad. Thus does Shiva deal with those who offend Him. And thus is Kali placated. The finale is meditative: the cast strikes yogic positions to the accompaniment of gentle chimes and bells until the lights fade.

DEDICATED TO George Moscone and Harvey Milk, *Holy Cow!* presented a vision of healing, the blessing of Spirit, and the importance of the individual. As such, it was what our badly injured community needed. Perhaps that accounted, in part, for its enthusiastic reception.

But one of my favorite moments during the show happened backstage when Sham—now six—and one of his friends entered the men's room where I was making up because the dressing room was too crowded. The boys saw me as they breezed by and went into a stall to pee together. As that moment, someone came in but went out, the squeaking door giving the children the impression that I had left when, in fact, I was still there. Now, Sham had grown up surrounded by bearded queens and the little blond clear-eyed sprite was nothing if not cool with it. But as was clear, his sidekick was from another planet.

"That man was wearing *lipstick,*" he said to Sham. No reaction. "That man was wearing *lipstick!*" he repeated, louder this time. Again: no reaction. Then, more urgently, "Sham, that man was wearing *lipstick!*"

"I don't know what you're talking about," Sham replied. And meant it.

CONFESSION: I WASN'T wild about *Holy Cow!* I'd have preferred something even more political. Still, if one function of art is to address community needs, the show came through in spades. From opening night, it attracted big crowds. But from opening night, there was a problem. In our usual "damn the torpedoes" fashion, we'd opened without sufficient funds to pay for our second week, let alone six more weeks. So we faced a decision: close or devise a way to raise cash. Pronto. There was no one to borrow from, as we'd put every cent into mounting the new show. So we met to hash out our options.

After we rejected several ideas, I proposed putting out a donation box. At that, Beaver tongue-lashed me for this heresy. The fact that we all shared an ethos and had worked for free for years was irrelevant. The roles of Accusatory High Altruist and Defender of the Faith were as dear to her as Noble Victim and Misunderstood One. But I wasn't proposing charging admission. Nor was I responsible for booking Lone Mountain College. So we had two choices: shut down or let people give us money if they wanted to. If we wanted to continue, it had to be the latter. But this meant that someone had to accept the un-enthralling job of explaining this to the audience. Not surprisingly, no one volunteered to be the one to announce that the era of glorious free theater was over.

I bit the bullet. Every night before the curtain went up, I went onstage to speak to the audience and tell the plain truth, emphasizing that we weren't *asking* for contributions but, for those who wished to offer support, there was a donation box in the lobby.

Lulu tended that box, tap dancing nearby to draw attention to its presence as well as running a concession stand. A local bakery—Just Desserts—contributed its delicious wares. Contributions poured in. Night after night, we managed to cover our rent.

Over the course of the next five weeks, thousands came to *Holy Cow!* The response was visceral and deeply gratifying. Another wonderful benefit was that the show attracted many Asian people, who comprise one-quarter of San Francisco's population.

During the run, the Angels received help from Bill Bathurst and Ron

Blanchette, who videotaped many Bay Area art events but recorded our shows for free. The tapes were an invaluable tool for self-criticism and streamlining. Bill and Ron were *our* Angels.

After making it through our run, closing night was dedicated to the audience, whose support had made our survival possible. Then the curtain rang down on that incredible tap-dancing dragon, Shiva, the exquisite scene between the Unicorn and the Torturer, and the Unicorn and a resurrecting spirit. These were the finest moments of the show, and, I venture, the apogee of Rodney and Beaver's careers. They'd been poetic and eloquent.

When the show closed, I was happy to disappear, as being onstage again meant being in the public eye; every time I went to the bank or market involved acknowledging praise and compliments. People were just being friendly, but it wasn't easy to shake off a relentless attention that I found intrusive. And with so many people so excited about what we'd accomplished, invisibility just wasn't an option.

But eradication was. In early July, I ran into Robert Opel, the Fey-Way gallery director. I'd been doing the show and he was busy with Fey-Way and also dealing drugs. Two nights later, robbers entered his gallery and tied up Robert, and colleagues Camille O'Grady and Anthony Rogers. Before departing, they shot Robert in the head.

While mourning Robert in a series of untitled poems (see page 256), I was also caught up in a bitch's brew of leather, MDA, and darker, rougher sex with Christopher, all to the strains of Billie Holiday. Outside, so many people were so jealous of us just for having each other and being so happy, but there was a firewall between us and the world. Remote again, safe again, I was happy to write in my journal on June 2, 1979:

> Gold palm fronds/beer cans in the trash/flash bulbs and cheers
> from the crowd ... donations. The circle comes full/the same, not
> the same/I am myself again/of course/ wiser/I expect nothing/do
> my best to applause/compliments/bizarre confetti/still, I glimpse
> my Shadow/in public, loved/liked, admired/adored/despised. This
> time I watch/the oohs, the aahs. The show reorients the city/in-
> jects streets & cafes too recently riotous with infectious visions.
> Galaxies implode/the circus creates/its living epitaph. /Calm

before my cue/deep breaths/and then ... using space/sound &
silence/Creation! Like a lion onstage/I confess: I look for Love in
the crowd/search as if I might find a key to a maze and, so, complete myself through this. One lens falls to another. O! Grace and be
blessed by this city.

San Francisco started to feel vibrant again. But larger things were in the
works as recorded in an unsettling journal entry on November 15, 1979:

The Angels are at each other's throats. There's a move to do *Holy
Cow!* again but I don't know. I can't understand what's in it for me
at this point. I've accomplished that circuit. It seems almost better for them as well as myself *not* to jump in, pull it together, get
the group all organized. Actually, there's so little caring, so little
support within the group. Why should I give up any more blocks
of time? It seems better to let it be. As things stand now, it was a
perfect cycle. Perhaps the Angels need to inflict more pain on each
other before they can grow up and deal with the real world? I don't
mean to be unsympathetic or harsh, but the crosscurrents and psychological logjams within the group are so severe I think it's almost
better for them to take a dose of their own collective crazy-making. In a few years, they'll probably have grown up, but not at the
expense of my sanity. I'll go to the next meeting, but I hope they
decide not to do it. It seems just as well to let it pass.

Chapter 21

I agreed to participate in a restaging of *Holy Cow!* for four reasons: First, the show had a clear, beneficial effect on our community and city. With Harvey's murder, the Castro lost its champion. The Angels were the gay community's most visible artists. As such, we had an obligation to function.

My second reason stemmed from Bill and Ron's videos; for the first time, we could critique our own work. I wanted to use that technique to find out how great we might be if we edited, retooled, and refocused ourselves.

When I became involved with the Angels in 1974, they already had all the elements of greatness, but were still chaotic. Certainly, one crucial aspect of being a revolutionary is to be visible, and the Angels excelled at that. It takes courage to hit the streets and make a spectacle of yourself when you represent an unpopular cause. But aside from that, and the fantastical subject matter or the undeniable punch of drag queens, genderfuck, and outrageous imagery, I felt that we'd assembled all the elements for greatness and for uniqueness; we'd also long since ceased being objects of fascination because of our offstage personas or onstage antics. We needed to graduate from being Angels-as-freaks to Angels-as-artists.

My third reason was that I didn't see any way I was ever going to become self-supporting unless I "made it" as an artist. In the three-and-a-half years since my father had reneged on his pledge, we'd remained estranged. I would not back down or just forget it. Nor would he admit to having made the promise; in letter after letter, he denied it while castigating me for being unrealistic and having no business sense. Meanwhile, in the city and in Inverness, prices had doubled yet again, houses that cost $25,000 in 1971 were now $250,000.

Reason five was that, although I'd gotten back into the Angels for Christopher's sake, I was addicted again: not to the offstage acclaim but to the intoxicating bond with the audience. It's difficult to explain white-hot fusion, but the Angels enjoyed a double blessing: doing what we did out of love, and being repaid in kind by our fans. To be an Angel during *Holy Cow!* was to become something larger than our individual selves. But no matter how exquisite the show, there was a mesmerizing magic in the dreamy backstage netherworld. I was hooked.

EVERYONE WANTED TO cut the talky first act as much as possible, but this proved only partially successful. Because so many of the Angels played multiple roles, they required extra time for costume changes. The original show ran over four hours on opening night. By closing, it was three. To streamline, we cut the role of Sita, a part played by Janet Sala, who'd brought luscious Italian beauty and passion to the role and the group. Janet was—wonder of wonders!—a happy wife and mother, one of the juicy heteros who had enriched our world. Rodney's multiple dances were considered inviolable, however. This often made effective scene-cutting impossible because whole scenes or *mis-en-scènes* revolved around his dances or costume changes: another hurdle for a scriptwriter.

"People aren't paying, they shouldn't complain," Rodney said when anyone mentioned trimming his numbers. Left unsaid was the fact that, after Lulu gave all of the donations of the first run to Brian a week after the show opened at Lone Mountain College, Rodney suddenly appeared in new leather pants that he could never have afforded on his monthly stipend. Was he skimming off the top? Probably. There was never any accounting. Well, no one was still claiming the Angels were a democracy. Now, for the first time, we'd have a box with a suggested donation of three dollars to cover expenses.

Our six-week run was at Project Artaud on Florida Street, a huge warehouse divided into lofts, including a huge airport hangar-like one where *Holy Cow!* would be revived: an enormous space about fifty feet wide and 100 feet long where Brian and his tech crew would have to start from scratch. All he had to start off with was access to electrical power. Under his direction, the space became a fully developed theater with a 400-seat capacity.

In a new development, the Angels decided to install a board of directors. The belated admission of a need for clear authority was sensible but stood in marked contrast to the longstanding crazy-making pattern wherein the actual power imbalance was masked by a prevailing assumption of equality. Now, because we were aiming at wider exposure with serious intent, our self-defeating illusions were dropped for a healthy *realpolitik*.

The board consisted of Rodney, Beaver, Brian, Radha, Tony, and myself.

Kevin was also included, albeit temporarily, and only for decisions pertinent to the show.

In addition to a board, for the first time, the Angels would mount a publicity blitz. Being used to Xeroxing manuscripts and having finessed our way into the MOMA's calendar, I volunteered to handle the task which included creating press kits and sending out announcements. With dozens of media photos at my disposal, I chose pictures of the dragon, Rodney as Shiva, Beaver as the Unicorn, and Kevin and Radha as the lovers (but none of myself), laying the groundwork for our first "legitimate" performance.

Because we were going public with no other way to safeguard the script, I copyrighted the document. Hibiscus owned the rights to the name "Angels of Light." Granted, he was in New York, but the San Francisco Angels didn't exist as a legal entity. To protect us from having our story or ideas ripped off (as had already occurred, both in the city's popular stage phenomenon, *Beach Blanket Babylon* and *The Rocky Horror Picture Show*), we needed legal control of our material. I emphasized that I was ready to transfer copyright to any appropriate name or authority *at any time*. But this was irrelevant. Once again, Beaver acted as if I'd raped the group by "ripping off the script."

Bernard Weiner was the theater critic for the *San Francisco Chronicle*. Having received broadsides announcing *Holy Cow!* was being restaged "by popular demand," he invited us to his office for a pre-show interview. On that day, I had to undergo a minor surgery so I couldn't attend. When Kevin, Radha, Beaver, and Rodney showed up to meet Bernard, they never mentioned my name, my history with the group, or the fact that I'd written the show! As a result, I was ignored in his coverage. I was stunned; therefore, when Robert Chesley, a playwright and journalist for the *San Francisco Bay Guardian*, called me to ask if he could interview me about my upcoming novel, *Holy Cow!*, and my role in the Angels, I agreed. His interview quoted me (correctly) as stating that my scriptwriting had brought order to chaos and that my role in the group was central. Predictably, Beaver went thermonuclear, but I was glad to have set the record straight.

As the publicity campaign steamed ahead, Rodney painted a huge proscenium arch to frame the production and he and I designed a poster and program, the first ever to list each member of the troop and what they did (see page 224).

Out there, in America in 1980, Ronald Reagan was running against Jimmy Carter for President. We dreaded the idea of a Reagan victory, seeing his candidacy as a rightwing power grab. Just as the first *Holy Cow!* took place against the backdrop of Dan White's acquittal, its revival seemed to be framed by an even larger battle of cosmic forces.

This was true on a personal level too. My brother Squabbie adored the Angels, but from 1978 on, he became increasingly irrational. I thought he was depressed; trying to talk to him proved useless, but one day when he interfered with our rehearsals by appearing with a sword and making veiled threats, I had to ban him from the studio.

Squabbie wasn't the only irrational one. By 1980, life at the extreme edge of the radical fringe was getting tougher and tougher. And no one could possibly have been more vulnerable than Coco Vega.

The preceding year, lacquered and hairsprayed into a gorgeously vulgar pastiche that was part Hindu, part Jewish mother, and pure Puerto Rican drag queen deluxe, Coco nailed the role of Kamala's mother. Groaning with jewels and slathering ambition, he was in his element: admired and acknowledged for his slum-glamour and, touchingly, truly moved by his maternal role. Despite wracking addiction and homelessness, Coco was a star. He'd adored being in the show just as much as we'd all adored having him.

Now, however, he was on the skids. Missing rehearsal after rehearsal led to the inevitable: we had to offer his role to someone else. Tommy Pace was a hilarious queen with a different approach to the role. His conniving stage mother was a "pleaser," oozing collusion and glee over her social coup. Blessed with brilliant comic timing and deadpan humor, Tommy was subtle where Coco had been screechingly abrasive and shellacked.

There were other changes. In 1979, Ralph had played the eunuch and done it brilliantly. Now, he quit when Irving denounced the presence of a donation box. His role went to a newcomer: Randall Denham. Randy was weaker but there was no choice; Ralph was never predictable and he was unable to extricate himself from the high palooka. Another critical switch concerned the part of the Queen Mother. Previously, a fellow named Rinaldo Iturrino had played her; now, Connie West (thereafter "Constance") took over the role, and shone as a controlling bitch which may well have reminded herself of her own mother, a famous actress whose name I'll omit for the sheer bloody hell of it.

Constance was lovely, tall, oval-faced, fine-featured, talented, and a trained actress and costume designer. This Hollywood princess had been adopted to suit the career of a big star too busy for children. Joan Crawford once learned of an insidious woman named Georgia Tann who took poor, blond, pregnant girls under her wing, then telling them their newborn infants had died before selling the babies to eager well-heeled clients. It's how Crawford got her children, how Constance's mother got Constance, though she was basically raised by nannies and so had the classic insider's view of show business, something her role allowed her to skewer with her over-the-top portrayal of a power-hungry bitch. We had a similarly jaundiced view of our high profile "perfect" families, so I enjoyed the brilliant way she played her part to the hilt—zooming into view on roller-skates and flaunting elephant ears. She was hilarious. In private, Constance was honest, funny, warm, creative, and generous. I liked her enormously. Thanks to her, I learned how to conduct a publicity campaign. It was she who provided me with a list of all the local major magazines, newspapers, television and radio stations. The incredible success of the PR blitz was due to her coaching.

As THE OPENING drew closer, I became alarmed about Coco. Not only was he suffering because he couldn't perform with us, he was experiencing the horror of finding he was disposable. Having lost his role and his sense of belonging to our magic circle, he went into freefall, staggering around the Castro drunk, mascara streaking down his unshaven cheeks, I knew, we all knew, no one could save him. In the hard, fast rules of the game, departing the Angels of Light equaled social Siberia. Time was running out fast. People who'd just recently clamored to pick up his bar tab now turned away and told him to beat it, rolling their eyes and snickering as he hobbled away like a wounded dog.

In stark contrast and as a perfect symbol, I found a treasure while driving to a rehearsal. The American Conservatory Theater (ACT)—the city's major traditional repertory company—had a workshop nearby. They'd discarded a prop. The gold throne was perfect for my Rajah. I stopped and plucked it out of the trash, naturally. Enthroned!

June 2, 1980:

I want to create a magic mirror, a perfect forum where people can see their most beautiful fantasies come into being. A place where, instead of having to break their backs or sell twenty years of their lives to have a chance to shine, it'd be there for them—without having to kiss ass or lose their uniqueness to satisfy some idiot producer. And instead of having to watch someone else do their dream show, they can do it for themselves. In a town like San Francisco, there are literally thousands of talented performers. LA is where the industry is, but SF is the magical vortex.

Chapter 22

Holy Cow! reopened on April 11, 1980 to a packed house and rave reviews. "Easily the most beautiful show I've seen since the Royal Ballet," gushed the *Berkeley Gazette*. "Huge, outrageously splashy, delightful," raved Robert Chesley in *The Bay Guardian*. "San Francisco has something truly unique with the Angels and we should treasure it."

The critic for *The San Francisco Sentinel* wrote: "Certainly one of our greatest municipal treasures ... the liveliest, wittiest, and most colorful show in town. I also had the feeling that this was why I came to San Francisco. Long live the Angels of Light!" And in the *San Francisco Chronicle*, Bernard Weiner wrote: "A 'must-see' show. Stupendous visual and aural experience as only the Angels can provide. Scene after scene unfolds of theatrical complexity and great visual beauty, each one seemingly better than the last."

Within days, we were turning away 100, then 200, then 300 people a night. Only 400 could be admitted; crowds started lining up hours early, hoping to get in. Finding seats became increasingly difficult when the *Chronicle* published not just one or two of Bernard Weiner's rapturous encomiums, but four. Each trumpeted *Holy Cow!* as one of the most stupendous achievements ever staged in the city, an experience not to be missed.

Equally important, the mood backstage was just as harmonious as it had been during our first run. Without Janice, there were no fights. Watching the performance and the audience from "my" throne, I felt an almost guilty pleasure to be the tinsel prince of this harmonious dream world. It was mine in those moments and I shivered with the thrill, even if performing *Holy Cow!* seven times a week was physically exhausting. Many Angels were perfect in our streamlined version. Night after night, the audience roared approval as Robin Bowen slithered into view as the cobra; equally thunderous applause greeted Philippe's dragon and the tap dancing. Meanwhile, Bill and Ron again videotaped each performance so we could analyze our work as Tony, Lulu, and Philippe created new props and masks so the show's visual elements were constantly expanding and morphing.

As was now clear, there was nothing static about the Angels. Properly inclusive, the group had access to an endless array of talent. We epitomized an underground now bursting out into the open. But the biggest surprise was still to come.

In 1980, the American Theatre Critics Association met in San Francisco for a conference. Enthralled by *Holy Cow!*, Bernard Weiner persuaded seventeen attendees to see our show. Overnight, rave reviews appeared in newspapers and journals throughout the country. The pros were dumbfounded as they attempted to describe a show the likes of which they'd never seen.

After Dark magazine said, "Awesomely hot, a jam-packed success; an amazing show! A jamboree razzamadazzle that deafens and delights!" In the *Los Angeles Times*, Sylvie Drake compared the Angels to the great cultural treasures of the world, like the Moscow Circus and Beijing Opera: "The most typically untypical San Francisco experience, the uncontested highpoint.... Almost impossible to describe. Unlike anything I have ever seen. Entrancing, dazzling, splendid, first rate! Something for LA to look forward to!"

And Bernard Weiner wrote a fifth review: "Tightened up, there is no stopping this show from being the blockbuster local (and later touring) success it deserves to be."

This time, no fire marshals, news crews, helicopters, or squad cars surrounded the theater. The Angels had scored a second monumental success.

In June, my father, an experienced theatergoer, came out west. It was the first time we'd seen each other in four years. "I never saw anything like that," he marveled, although unlike my mother in 1975, he did not join us onstage. But his reneging on his promise now underscored our entire relationship. Still, something had happened before his arrival that I consider almost like divine intervention.

I always prepared for performances by getting my life in order. In the course of organizing *Holy Cow!*, one day I was filing letters that concerned the publication of my forthcoming novel when I came across something I thought I'd lost in the chaos following my return from Nepal: the letter my father had written in June 1975, in which he'd made his pledge to me after visiting San Francisco: "While I wished you had worked to save up down-payment money and not had to ask me, it is a moot point. It seems that what you need is capital to go into business. That is certainly reasonable and a $10,000 loan for ten years is something that I, as your trustee, would look favorably upon. Let me know when you want the check. The loan is interest free, of course."

Esmerelda and Lulu, August 1976

Now, I handed him back his own letter and watched as he read it. He said nothing. Nor did I. With a hit show on the boards and a novel about to appear, I felt my star was rising.

But stars were setting too.

For me, the sweetest moments of doing a show came from mingling with strangers after the performances. On one such occasion, I met two young gay men, one of whom held a pink quilted box almost reverently. I asked him what it was.

"Ashes," he said.

"What kind of ashes?" I asked.

"Remains," he said, opening the lid. The ashes of his loved one were adorned with tiny pink seashells and pink glitter. "He loved the Angels of Light. Tomorrow, we're going to scatter his remains, but we wanted to bring him here first."

Such delicate moments were the points of connection and intimacy that I loved most.

GIVEN OUR SUCCESS, there was huge pressure to keep the show going, and we managed to extend the run. But when the board of Project Artaud told us they needed to renovate the space, our circus came to a close in June. Almost immediately, fissures appeared.

At the closing night party, Brian got drunk, suspected Beaver of flirting with someone, and beat the hell out of her. At home, he destroyed her unicorn costume, an act of symbolic murder, for he knew what that represented to her. Even before *Holy Cow!*, if Beaver was late or stayed out with the girls after rehearsal, Brian would destroy her costumes, or take a knife and stab her bed and rip up the sheets. Another time, he trashed her sewing machine. No one intervened, of course.

A month after *Holy Cow!* closed, my novel hit the stands. Though unadvertised and not promoted, *The Glass Arcade* sold briskly and made money. At a book signing on Castro Street, Tommy Tadlock told me about an empty theater that was available, one with a huge rehearsal hall attached. Roger Williams, a florid Englishman and "walker" for retired actress Ina Claire, owned an ornate theater on Geary Street, just off Union Square. An Arabian fantasy, the Alcazar Theater had a plush, 400-seat auditorium. If the Angels wanted to sign an open, long-term lease, we could have the whole thing. *With no money down.*

Consider what that meant: With *Holy Cow!* a nationally known hit and with the sets and props to remount *Paris Sites*, we'd have two shows ready to go and rehearsal space to create new ones, and we'd have a magnificent downtown theater as our showcase, one whose Alhambra-like décor complemented the fantastical quality of our shows. There was no reason why the Angels couldn't attain worldwide acclaim. We often discussed becoming a repertory company; but without a stable home base, the concept had seemed impossible. Until now.

In addition to rotating the two works in repertory, I wanted to do a version of *Beowulf.* Influenced by Mark Thompson's interest in radical faerie and Wiccan energy, I began outlining a script which paralleled *Holy Cow!* and *Paris Sites*. Like them, it was to be a morality tale and a warrior contest between the Vikings who worshipped the god Wodin and the Celts, a horse/spirit culture, who worshipped the Goddess.

An opening scene would feature Celtic celebratory rites. The Vikings would invade and abduct the maidens; the Celts would have to regroup. I envisioned a full-moon midnight dance in the fog-shrouded dolman ring of Stonehenge by deer-headed dancers wearing pelts. Afterward, the Celts could journey to the fjords, where a battle against the Vikings might culminate in a titanic face-off with a dragon guarding a cave or a sacred symbol. The finale would feature priestesses performing sacred rites. Such was my idea for a new show to rotate with *Holy Cow!* and *Paris Sites* once we were in our glorious new home.

Now that our success seemed assured, my father offered to lend the Angels $10,000, interest free. If he kept this promise—and God knows if it was another switch-and-bait routine—we'd have funds to move into the Alcazar. All we had to do was say yes.

But Rodney complained that the proscenium arch he'd painted wouldn't fit the stage of the Alcazar. Although we didn't even have that arch when we performed *Holy Cow!* at Lone Mountain College, he objected to scaling down the sets by three feet.

I suggested delaying our reopening by a month to make new sets. But Brian, Beaver, Radha, and Rodney rejected the idea of moving into the Alcazar and continuing the show. They outvoted Kevin, Tony, and me. Of course, with no show to provide income, we couldn't afford even nominal rent. That meant rejecting the offer, scuttling our hit, and starting from scratch. Again. But our debate around this vote caused far worse damage.

When I warned them they were throwing away the chance of a lifetime, Brian snarled, "You're only interested in promoting yourself at the expense of the group!" Revolted by a slur that was not only insulting but dead wrong—and stunned by the arrogance of what they were doing and what it meant for the group's future—I quit.

Why? Out of pride and hurt vanity, certainly. But there was more to it than egotism.

Lulu recounts a fascinating story of asking Rodney how he could take on larger, more exciting roles in Angels shows. After years of selfless service, Lulu had certainly paid his dues.

"This is our theater and we get the best roles," Rodney said curtly. End of discussion.

Later, Chuck Drees put it differently: "The triangle (of Brian, Beaver, and Rodney) was the core. If you didn't kiss their ass, you were shunned or ignored until you backed out." And Constance West said: "Something was erupting and it frightened me because there were two energetic levels involved and I didn't know where to turn."

Since 1974, I'd been a tinsel prince of the Angels. These had been glorious years. Now foreseeing an undertow that guaranteed renewed spates of infighting and the restaging of aesthetic crap, I wanted nothing more to do with it, even if I was one of the "main Angels" or "*the* Angel," as our videographer Bill Bathurst told writer Robert Chesley. So I resigned, knowing that the group would soon be self-destructing.

Of all the sad, decadent things I ever saw, seeing the Angels of Light go off the rails was the worst. My friendships with geniuses were rare. Some were world-renowned, like Warhol—but Peter Sopagee (the rock singer from Syracuse) and Alex Bratenahl (the painter) hadn't been able to stick their landings; too fragile to withstand the non-negotiable demands of genius, they committed suicide. This willful ruin deprived our city, as well as the wider world, of something so marvelous that words fail.

Teena Rosen-Albert said, "The Angels of Light cannibalized their victims." I agreed. So did Tony who went back to New York where the *New York Times* celebrated him as a theatrical genius. He was, but without the forum provided by the Angels, he'd never again shine as brightly. As had been the case with Tihara, Tony's departure was an irretrievable loss for the Angels. Shorn of his masks, props, and muscular vision, the Angels lost much of their verve—Tony didn't give a flying fuck about personal glory, but he *did* care passionately about using art to communicate to a planet hurtling into the abyss. For Tony, the solution to life's challenges lay in devotion to a humble life and honest simple work whereby the Divine was invoked. Called by any name, this lay at the heart of spirituality. Through his work, Tony wanted to convey a simple message: *Stop killing, get over yourself, and love each other.*

Everyone pays ready lip service to that doctrine. But who lives by it? The freedom that once flowed so swiftly had congealed. Thus, the second cycle of the Angels that began with *Inferno Reason* in January 1975 screeched to a shuddering halt in August 1980.

Chapter 23

"We think you'd better get out of San Francisco," my mother told me over the phone. She sounded nervous. "Squabbie is threatening people. He may be dangerous."

I wasn't completely surprised by the call—Squabbie had looked really weird recently—but I wasn't going to flee. Besides, Christopher and I were flying east in two-and-a-half weeks, to celebrate my father's sixtieth birthday at a costume party with a sports theme. I was dubious about introducing Christopher to my family, but we'd been together for three years and he understood the situation from his uniquely African point of view. No one could have predicted what followed.

Just days after my mother called, Squabbie was arrested in New Orleans while trying to break into a high school. He'd been incarcerated for a two-week period of observation at the Louisiana State insane asylum. Against that backdrop, about which no one in Philadelphia would say anything, of course, the family circus took center stage.

As we dressed for the occasion, my parents received a shocking call. Squabbie's period of enforced observation was up; he would be deposited on the streets of New Orleans at ten o'clock the following morning.

"Someone has to be there to get him," my mother said fretfully.

"Are you asking me?' I inquired. "I'll go if you want me to but …"

"No, no. Dad will go but he's got to get up at five to catch a six-o'clock flight which means he's got to be in bed by ten sharp."

"But it's already eight," I said as the first guests arrived. "How in the world can he …"

"I've given instructions to the caterers," she interjected. "We've got to get these people in and out in two hours! Just don't start any interesting conversations over dessert!" And with that, she hurried away to welcome her guests.

IMAGINE A FILM playing in fast forward: caterers pressuring people to wolf down their food, bewildered guests giving toasts before being herded into the living room for a brief moment of chitchat before being handed their coats suddenly, thanked for coming, and shown the door. All in two hours flat. Naturally, none of them had been informed of what was actually going on. Why should they know? This was high society. No one *talked*.

Shortly after dawn, my father flew off to Louisiana. He returned that afternoon with Squabbie, tranquilized out of his ever-lovin' mind. He looked ghastly. For three years, I'd assumed that he was depressed. The diagnosis was incurable: paranoid schizophrenia. I felt so terribly sorry for him—as a child, he'd been the only sibling I'd been close to—but there was nothing I could do, nothing anyone could do. Squabbie was mad.

On the plane back to San Francisco, I turned to Christopher. "I told you so much about my family. Do you think I exaggerated?"

He gave me a baleful look. "No one could *possibly* exaggerate that."

I wasn't sure. Given my history over the past fifteen years, it was hard to know what was real and what was pure insanity. As far as I could tell, they were the same thing. But how could people not be confused? Christopher said that, on recent forays to the baths, he saw gay men prowling around with syringes tucked into rolled up towels. And though he'd always loved those places, the last time he went was for another purpose entirely.

"I went to say goodbye because I'm not going back again. It's too weird," he told me, describing a nightmare scene: junkies in dungeon cells suspended in leather slings. Then, one night, a fire broke out south of Market. The Bunkhouse was one of several buildings incinerated. Rumors flew that several men handcuffed to beds perished in flames that leapt sixty feet into the night sky.

Then one of our own adoring fans, James, jumped off the Golden Gate Bridge. Another casualty. And the toll was mounting.

Poor Coco was still suffering from his fall from grace. One night the Angels appeared to applause at the Café Flore and people elbowed him away from the in-crowd's table. I went home and wept. But there was no way to stop the momentum or the strange sense of hurtling toward some unknown reckoning. I personalized it: sooner or later, the Angels would mount another show without me; I had to face facts: I'd proved expendable.

Sensing deadlock, Christopher and I discussed moving to New York. I wanted to escape, but didn't even know what I was escaping as 1981 approached. I only knew I felt the city was losing its edge. Aside from the Angels and

Julie Petri and Ralph Sauer, Valencia St. storefront theatre, April 4, 1981

a really endearing all-female company called Les Nicklettes, the only edgy performing group really pushing the envelope was the highly political and satirical company, the San Francisco Mime Troupe, which richly deserved the praise it reaped, far and wide. But even they had settled into a predictable motif. I felt a wholesale lack of outrageousness in the local scene.

Peter Hartman opened a wonderful little performing space on Natoma Street. Community-oriented and generous, he put his money into a state-of-the-art place for experimental shows. 544 Natoma became a fixture in the SoMa scene, and I was happy to participate in its opening night. Still, it remained a fairly specialized location where one went to see art events such as Mark Chester mummifying men in plastic, then hoisting them into the air with ropes or chains and leaving them suspended.

Agitated by a sense of impending dislocation, I pretty much stayed huddled at home, devoting myself to my work. But it wasn't possible to avoid scrutiny. Everyone who starred in *Holy Cow!* had been trapped in the glare of the spotlight, and as one of its stars, I couldn't walk my dog without being stopped, congratulated, and otherwise mauled. It was so annoying, I made a decision to torpedo my good reputation and, after swearing him to silence and managing to keep a straight face—I told the biggest whopper I've ever told to a dishy queen who couldn't wait to spread the horrifying news: *that I'd had sex with my dog!* Within days, my star had fallen. I was so pleased and so relieved.

Out there, President Reagan was slashing funding for mental hospitals and halfway houses. Patients were released to wander the streets, obviously unable to care for themselves. There was fear in the air. Things were getting tougher. At home, things were getting tougher too. Christopher and I were abusing MDA. One night, stoned out of my head in the lobby of a local grindhouse, I collapsed, my swollen tongue protruding from my mouth. Incredibly, or in some symptom of his own state of denial, when I regained consciousness Christopher didn't tell me what happened for over a year. When he did, I was shocked. Of all my friends, only Mark Thompson had the guts to warn me about the amount of drugs we were doing. He was right. But I was heedless, reckless, even when Christopher bumped into a freestanding mirror propped up in the bedroom to better to observe our sexual gymnastics. As it fell, shattering to pieces, the mirror sliced my left leg clean through to the tendon. No problem. Off we went to the hospital, where we had a wonderful time in the emergency ward with a lovely lady doctor who stitched me up while we discussed Passolini and Rimbaud and Leni Riefenstahl. Then back home with Christopher for more sex. No need to apply the brakes. Brakes? What brakes?

By May 1981, the Angels had not done much since I left the group. I'd sensed something awful building. It was in my poetry—that sense of impending doom. My feelings were complicated and I was still psychologically engaged in the grand notion of saving this beautiful dream world, living in it, and seeing it thrive. So I wanted to save the Angels of Light but I also wanted to save myself. Knowing that the Angels wanted to do a show, but that if Janice wrote it, it would be a mess. I wanted to help them. With me at the helm, we could save the company. I was naïve. Still gullible. Still hooked. It was my own very special obsessive-compulsive disorder. So I called for a meeting.

> May 22, 1981:
> On Wednesday, the Angels will have a board meeting to decide
> on a proposal I plan to make about revising *Holy Cow!* And doing
> *Beowulf* as a follow-up. If they approve, we're in business. If not,
> I'm going to think seriously about leaving SF. It's been a wonderful
> decade, but I don't see any reasons for staying unless they want to
> go for it. I'm tired of waiting for them to grow up. I don't want to
> play parent, but if there isn't a mature process and realistic agenda,
> it will drive me crazy.
>
> I want to nurture, integrate, see things grow, be part of some-
> thing whole and healthy. I don't want to leave SF, but our commu-
> nity feels flat and listless. I want to see the Angels achieve success.
> I want to be part of it too, but they've got to meet me halfway and
> want to make it. If they do, I know we can make it work, but I need
> certain guarantees. I want them written down. I don't want to be
> accused of promoting myself at the expense of the group when my
> efforts will be to see the group make a name for itself again, make
> money and proceed logically and with clarity and grace. If this can

come about, great. If not, it's time for me to go for the years are passing without a sense of being where it's happening. I get tired of missing seasons, feeling I'm in the wrong place. If the Angels won't grow up and see that there's got to be order and that certain opportunities only come once in a lifetime, I doubt they will ever understand that their elitism constantly undermines the group and interferes with its progress. Well, as I say, I can't sit and wait.

At the meeting, I offered to raise money to re-stage *Holy Cow!* (a friend would put up the funds necessary for production) if I was reappointed to the board of directors and assured the right to continue our inevitable success by writing the next show. But my proposal was rejected. Instead, Rodney and Beaver (and Madeline and Brian) told me that they were going to get Janice to write their next show, using Tony's cherished concept of a welfare hotel. Once again, they were plunging off a cliff. Once again, I withdrew.

Chapter 24

"From Magic to Tedium with the Angels of Light," trumpeted Bernard Weiner's review of *Hotel of Follies* in September 1981. His critique of the new show took no prisoners. The debacle that opened to a packed house following enthusiastic publicity was another convoluted fiasco. Based on an idea Tony had promoted for years, that of the residents of a welfare hotel, it was a forerunner of the Broadway smash hit *Rent*.

After the first weekend, an average of eight or ten people filed into the 400-seat theater at Project Artaud to see the legendary Angels of Light. And their verdicts were identical: "Great sets and costumes and dancing ... but boring as shit." Condemnation of the dull, endlessly talky script was universal, unanimous, as it had been for *Sci-Clones* in 1978.

Tihara told me, "Janice felt she wrote wonderful plays, but the Angels failed her by not being good enough actors to deliver her lines."

I waited weeks before going to see it and when I finally did attend, I felt ill. It was worse than I expected. Not only was there was no humor, no drag, no political content, nothing positive or uplifting, once again, under Janice's influence, all the performers became self-parodies who looked worse than clumsy or amateurish; they looked cheap. Almost sleazy. And how Janice gloried in exposing people to ridicule.

Every beautiful element was there: the colors, the gorgeous light. The dances Rodney performed with Madeline (Radha no more, Hindu chic now being *passé*) were fine. But it was all wildly mishandled. Watching the company I loved struggle in the tarpits was heartbreaking—and worse, because I knew they wanted me to be proud of them and approve of their work; I could see they were busting their asses to make the show work. But no one could enliven such an embarrassing mess. At the end, I departed without a word. What could I possibly say?

Of all the participants, I felt sorriest for Scrumbly Koldwyn, a composer, pianist, songwriter, and performer who'd once been in the Cockettes, where he'd distinguished himself as the kindest and easiest person to work with. After their bust-up, he became an independent cultural force: a dapper, russet-haired fellow with warm blue eyes and a gentle smile. Quiet, agreeable, and brilliant, able to synthesize and improvise all sorts of music, Scrumbly could snatch a ditty or melody out of thin air and turn it into anything. In a scene notorious for backstabbing and dish, he was never cruel or an egotist. I admired his talent enormously and liked him too. So it hurt me to see that, never having been part of the Angels, he'd come into the group only to create an original score for a disaster playing to empty houses. The show was a hideous waste of his time. And his phenomenal talent.

At home, I lay in Christopher's arms and grieved. I wanted to escape. I wanted to fix things but there was nothing I could do. Something beautiful had been driven into the ground. I felt as if I'd just watched a magnificent crippled horse in a futile struggle to stand up on ice.

THE NEXT MONTH, in October 1981, I got very ill with a high fever. Drenched in sweat, I was unable to move for three days. At last, the fever broke and I was feeling much better, actually sitting up, when Christopher came home from work, a thermometer in hand.

"I don't need that," I told him. "I'm fine."

"Let's just see," he coaxed.

My temperature? 104!

A few days later, I was in a weird mood. I felt edgy, angry, trapped and fed up with our poverty: for years, we'd had *just* enough money to pay the rent, eat, and pay the bills. One day, I saw an old globe at a street sale for twenty-five dollars. It was the first time I'd bought myself a present in over a year.

When Christopher came home, I told him I wanted to take acid and have sex all night.

"I don't think we should," he said, looking dubious. "You seem pretty up-tight."

"I am uptight!" I agreed. "Because we never go anywhere and I'm working all the time and I need some fun."

Over his objections, we dropped acid, neither of us knowing that, after an extraordinarily high fever, people go into depression. Acid exaggerates experience. In this case, it made me implode. Ever loyal and loving, Christopher tried to help, but he couldn't.

In a crazy coincidence, as I was skittering into an abyss, an old church across from the Café Flore burned down. So I was going to hell as a house of worship went up in flames. And in LA, it was reported that five men who'd attended the same orgy had died of an extremely rare form of cancer, Kaposi's Sarcoma. What could possibly explain it?

I couldn't go outside after my breakdown. If necessary, I could make it to the corner to buy food or walk my dog. Mainly, I stayed inside writing a play about Leni Riefenstahl while television and newspapers carried more and more stories about more gay men dying from a mysterious disease that wrecked their immune systems, and according to the craziest paranoia of all, was rumored to be sexually transmitted.

Gradually, the apprehension that those we loved might be instruments of death began uncoiling like a cobra slithering into the bedroom. I recall an afternoon with a playwright friend who partied and partied hard: C.D. Arnold. After he left, I washed out the red mug he'd used and stared at it. Then I put it on the top shelf of a cupboard, hesitant to ever use it again. Such was my confusion in the first days of the new plague, when I wrote "Guided Tour" (see page 258).

STILL, THERE WERE positive signs on the horizon. At the Bay Area Critics Circle Awards, *Holy Cow!* garnered five important honors, including Best Original Show. Beaver won for Best Costumes, an accolade that would launch her new career.

Rodney created an entirely new group that made its debut at the Castro Street Fair: the Wasp Women was comprised of Rodney, Teena, and a lovely, dark-haired woman named Julie Petri who lived in the neighborhood with her extremely sexy boyfriend, Craig. The trashy vamps with black bouffants and brazen 1950s style vulgarity were a scream. Though they petered out pretty quickly, by dint of their existence, they proved that the Angels might be successful again if they would just re-embrace their inner drag queen.

But any sense of cohesion was fading away. Tuxedomoon drifted off. Careening into view again, Victoria performed with them briefly before throwing a fit and walking offstage in the middle of a performance, after which she disappeared from the scene.

Then, on January 8, 1982, Coco showed up at Lulu's. He wanted to score some smack. Would Lulu give him a ride? Off they went. On the way, Coco

(*l–r*) Janet Sala, Julie Petri, Ralph Sauer, Beaver Bauer, Lenore Vantosh-Howard, and Justin McCarthy, October 11, 1981

needed to make a stop, to pick up something from a man he knew. Lulu took him there and waited. After a few minutes—and a blowjob?—Coco emerged, waving some bills.

"I've got it, girl!" he cackled. "Let's go!" In the Fillmore District, Coco went inside to score. When he came out, he said, "Lulu, I know you've never tried this stuff and that you like weed but tonight I wanna take you where jazz comes from!"

Lulu declined. So knowing the next day was Lulu's birthday, Coco gave him a book and inscribed it.

"You have to kiss it too," Lulu said. "Otherwise, I won't take it."

Ever-obliging, Coco kissed the page he'd just inscribed, leaving the impression of his lips. Then Lulu dropped him off at a friend's house.

Early the next day, Lulu got the telephone call.

Coco was dead. He'd overdosed on China White, heroin so strong that eight users in the city died from it in one week alone. His heart stopped and he was revived by an ambulance team, but his heart stopped again and the battery on their defibrillator machine failed.

Characteristically thoughtful, Lulu arranged a memorial service/perfor-
mance on January 10, 1982, at the Stone Club on Broadway. Proceeds would
cover the cost of Coco's cremation. I was still reeling from my breakdown and
afraid to leave home, but I couldn't ignore that occasion, so I agreed to open
the midnight show with a eulogy.

The Stone Club is a dingy upstairs nightspot. The crowd was very uneasy
and there was desperation in the air. If I'd understood what was going on
backstage, I would have left right away, but I only found out later: incredibly,
the same dealers who'd sold Coco the lethal China White were offering it *to
the performers*, at times claiming that it was coke, but simultaneously offering it as smack to heroin users, until Lulu freaked out and drove the ghouls
off. Unaware of what was going on behind me, I went onstage to read:

Foolish bird of paradise, Coco, with smooshed mascara and
too much rouge. Too much of everything for the broken glass
and granite which afflicted you. How many times did you taunt
Death before she proved she was serious? That she could—and
would—close her jaws? Warnings were meaningless, stubbed out
with cigarettes and overwhelmed by orders to bring another beer,
another prescription, another batch of opium—ah, yes—that was
always coming into town.

My mind backpedals to Manhattan, to Spanish Harlem, where
you hid in graveyards while your mother put down the first month's
rent before the landlords learned too much. Oh Coco! Third-generation junkie! What strange aristocracy was injected into your
veins and genes? What spell pervaded you, clinging like a narcotic
to each phase of each moon?

The sequins and plumes have been incinerated. Now, the boys
look butch and slum royals have traded fishnets for plaid. Only
you remained: fierce and devoted to your mystic eye, your rituals,
your Goddess. I think you were the last great San Francisco queen
in a line of immigrants holding out arms decked with bracelets,
beckoning to the others to get here, to find their way home. There's
been a succession of pretenders to the throne, abdications, bum
trips, and role reversals, leading most of those canny birds to aban-

don drag and work out camouflage. But not you! Oh Coco! Spanish grandee! Black lace, roses and chopsticks in your hair, you made wild eyes at construction workers and pranced through slums on your way, where? Even when you staggered, you never lost your footing. Dead drunk, passed out, pale blue, you never surrendered. One day, at the bar at the Flore, you shuddered in my arms. Heroin had you between her teeth, giving you a preview, sanding down your skin, and I held you as you cried, "Oh Adrian! It hurts! I just want to die!"

"Don't die," I whispered, unable to disinfect you but unwilling to fund the next fix. "You have a great destiny."

I always believed in that last-minute rescue before the sirens. I never believed you'd slip and lose it before crashing through to a new plateau where there were no tracks on your arms, no probation officers, no need for excuses or even explanations. I believed your destiny was love, not seasonal praise from people with free drinks as long as you were "on"—amusing them and making them feel like stars. You were the star, Coco, and now you've left us like cast-off pearls in your wake. What's become of the bracelets and the fake leopard coat? Did those evaporate with your last breath? I never guessed your tightrope was a razor cutting through your feet, working toward the heart. Idealistic, romantic, I put my faith in your Gorilla Woman, your pride, your uproarious defiance and that discipline which drove you to maintain, never yield, never quit. Now I, like others, stare blind—left in the trail of a comet that glittered the night skies of San Francisco and seared its mornings. In an ideal galaxy, you'd have been born in a land of noonday moons or in an endless night of bright stars and men with dark eyes. You made do with what you got even though it was hardly ever enough, for you were intended for glory. You had it as an Angel of Light—sprayed and lacquered into Hinduism. You had it on the streets. You had it with your candles and incenses and, yes, drugs too—those strange brides and grooms ushering you to alters where you knelt to worship.

Now it is over and we're left like good souls, stout friends, and

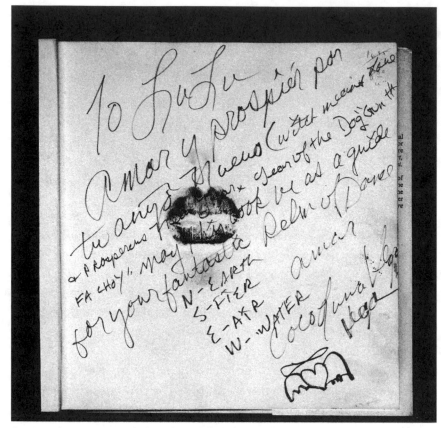

Coco Vegas's inscription to Lulu the night Coco died, January 8, 1981

ever-so-slightly-jealous lovers who wonder where you've gone and if it's better there. We've come to pay respects, late at night, to raise money for you to burn—our eyes showing a little more white than usual, stoned or in need, not only of you but of each other.

Here we are then, friends and children of that Goddess you observed, Coco, your leftovers, your collection of noble hearts. But what do we do now? There are no words to illustrate your fandango. There was no choreography to you who made each moment life as well as art, you who skated the thin ice above addiction, who sank, rose again, and flew off until you flew off. Nothing remains now. Only love and pride. The love you shared or inspired. And, finally, the pride you know we all feel, all who rightfully claim to be outcasts, wanderers, and members of the tribe.

I don't know what to say. I don't know how to mourn or what to do with words that blow off like ash. In endings, we boil down to ourselves, I suppose, but it's Love that draws us close, love that knits and binds. It's the reason we gather in this place tonight— yearning, needful and flawed: birds of the same feather. So go your way in peace, Gorilla Woman, and rest. We heal your wounds with love and memories that will not burn when you burn.

The next day, Coco's ashes were collected by friends who took them on a procession, visiting his favorite spots, then continuing out to the beach where the last physical traces of that dear and tender heart floated into the air and out to sea. The last great drag queen was gone, and the end of an era, for AIDS was nibbling at the fringes.

Initially, no one suspected the degree of the devastation. How could we? At first, rumor had it that the incubation period was six months. Then, two years. And while no one knew if was really sexually transmitted, certainly the wisest policy was to curb random promiscuity. Ever helpful and intent on encouraging safe sex, the *Chronicle* published reviews of the best city intersections for enjoying performances by exhibitionists!

Meanwhile, Beaver had fallen in love—really in love—with a heterosexual (at last!). Lars was Swedish. After several months, he had to go back to Sweden. Shortly thereafter, Beaver brought Sham over to my flat. In itself, this wasn't unusual; I often had the tow-headed sprite with deep laugh lines and an almost medieval cheeriness for the night if Beaver was busy. In this case, however, after telling him that she was going away, she flew to Sweden, leaving the Angels in a tizzy of doubt: Would she return or not? Would the Angels fall apart? But that was out there somewhere; I had a confused and frightened child to comfort and reassure on the night she left.

Although out of sight, Beaver kept me in mind because of her desire to secure the title role in a play I was writing about Leni Riefenstahl, a play and a part we had often discussed. The filmmaker's spellbinding 1934 documentary of the Nazi rally at Nuremberg equated Hitler with God. *Triumph of the Will* remains the greatest piece of film propaganda ever made, but also a fright-fully dangerous work of artistic genius that damns Riefenstahl as a malig-nant narcissist complicit in the Holocaust that ensued after she made the film (albeit reluctantly) and enabled Hitler's lock on power.

The notion of casting Beaver intrigued me; like Riefenstahl, Beaver was frighteningly single-minded in pursuit of her ambitions. She might be truly convincing as the multi-talented and seductive opportunist who put con-science aside (if she ever even had one) for her romantic and solipsistic vi-sion. Beaver was no trained actress, but since she could move to Sweden to be with the man she loved and return to San Francisco as often as she liked, the critical determinant in this case was the degree to which she'd honor her own stated ideals (stated to me, about Lars) at the risk of jeopardizing her secure status in the Angels. It was a core decision about core values that would imbue her performance as Riefenstahl with an edgy integrity. Or ex-pose it as a bald lie.

From Sweden, Beaver conducted a veritable charm offensive to land the role she wanted so badly. In a letter that surpassed all prior intimacies. She shared her sense of wonder at waking up with her passionate true love, add-ing that, in this moment of revelation, she felt imbued with Riefenstahl's spirit. Being in love myself, I felt happy for her, hoping she'd follow her heart. After all, she couldn't lose custody of Sham. Brian had no legal rights. Beaver hadn't put his name on the birth certificate, a fact that must have haunted him.

But upon returning to California, Beaver withdrew, keeping Lars on ten-terhooks as she became harder and harder to reach by phone until, at last, tortured and desperate, the poor guy called me to implore my honest opin-ion.

"She won't leave San Francisco," I told him, convinced that this was yet another case of Beaver playing both ends against a hard-to-pinpoint middle. And she didn't. Nor did she get the coveted role of Riefenstahl. Once again, stasis had triumphed. Or codependency.

Within weeks, I completed my play, which focused on the 1945 US Army inquiry of the director. As a war baby, I'd always felt confused by my attrac-tion to the electrifying Nazi rallies until, through Riefenstahl's sexy docu-mentaries, the central event of the century *vis à vis* the issue of individual ethos became clear. I was also fascinated by Riefenstahl's defense upon being arrested in May 1945—a week after the war ended—imprisoned and put on trial by three countries over a period of five years: is an artist ultimately responsible for the effect to which their work is used? Can an artist pursue a vision without restraint or responsibility for how it may be perceived?

In June 1982, I staged the play at a small theater at the Artaud. Christopher directed; I cast myself as an army officer. The script was excellent, but my performance was all wrong, Christopher's direction was sloppy, and the actress playing Riefenstahl ruined the play by skipping two pages of script (including the climax) on opening night, when all the major critics were in the audience: my fault entirely for hiring that dingbat. We limped along for the six-week run, somehow paying the bills and even turning a profit. Even so, the experience was a letdown.

Christopher and I moved to Mexico in the autumn of 1982—dog and all—to a village near Puerto Vallarta. Ten days later we were back. After five years, we were growing apart. Then my dog died of cancer. The Angels were in turmoil. Julie Petri told me that a woman beat her up at a party while Beaver, who had resented Rodney's attention to Julie and her sexy lover, stood nearby. Julie's voice shook as she told me how, as she was being attacked, Beaver-the-altruist watched. "She had a look on her face like, 'Too bad, bitch'," Julie said.

I felt nauseated by the whole goddamn sick and hypocritical scene; it was finally time to get the hell out of San Francisco (again), I told Christopher. Because he'd always hated the Angels, he agreed.

A few weeks later, the Social Security Office busted the Angels after someone turned them in for welfare fraud, a fact that thousands of people knew. "I can't believe anyone would resent us that much," Beaver told me, now under scrutiny because of a disparity between her claims for herself and those involving Sham. This had something to do with Brian not being on Sham's birth certificate. Had Brian reported Beaver when she went to Sweden? No one will ever know. But one thing is certain: someone of the many who'd felt ripped off by the Angels over the years did indeed resent them "that much." In the ensuing mudslide, Beaver's benefits got terminated.

The possibility of all the Angels being busted for welfare fraud, my own and Christopher's financial straits and my ongoing fantasy of resurrecting the theater were enough motivation for me to conceive restaging *Holy Cow!* under a new aegis: the Seraphim Theater. (Yes, I had already resigned from the Angels and could not get them to agree to do *Beowulf*. I meant to get the hell out of San Francisco. But we were so poor, and I wanted one more chance to restore the Angels.) We'd remount the show, albeit with several telling differences. In addition to making the new group a democracy where every member had a real voice, Janet Sala would be Kamala, not Madeline. And there was a reason for this.

Janet was a beautifully juicy Italian Mama with luminous eyes, luscious skin, and something that Madeline lacked entirely: charm. Moreover, knowing that Madeline would always play into Rodney's agenda as long as she was assured of personal glory, I wanted to shake up the ossifying status quo.

Everyone I asked—about twenty-five in all—approved the twin concepts of Seraphim Theater and restaging *Holy Cow!*. Janet signed on with reservations, but she too recognized that the triumvirate was ruining the company. They all wanted to initiate change. Now that the city was investigating welfare fraud, a new start was not only preferable, it would determine whether the group could reclaim its soul. But Rodney and Beaver could not, and would not, surrender their lock. Brian followed suit, obviously. So what had begun in anarchy and freedom hit the wall as totalitarianism, and the Seraphim Theater idea fell apart. And I distanced myself from the troupe again.

In October 1983, the Angels staged a third nightmare written by Janice: *True Tales of Hollywood Horror*. Like the *Hotel* show, it opened to a packed house and averaged ten or twelve people a night from that point on. Bernard Weiner wouldn't call it complete shit—the visuals and dances deserved some mercy—but his review savaged the script, and the show belly-flopped.

Parallel proof of dead ends surfaced when Tony called me. He was getting off heroin cold turkey and was out of his mind. I ran over to Haight Street and was shocked to find his small daughters there; Ananda and Kavita were untended and traumatized. A doctor had told him that if he ever had another drink, his liver would fail and he'd probably die. I couldn't give him a bottle and wouldn't go out and score smack for him, but seeing him being eaten alive was nightmarish.

Determined to quit San Francisco for good in October, I gave up my apartment, then sold my car. A friend in London invited Christopher and me to stay. But one day before our flight and just hours before the phone was disconnected, I got a call from someone named George Kovach, who'd gotten my number from Rodney. He was a local theater producer. He wanted to take *Holy Cow!* to Broadway. Was I interested?

I couldn't believe it! But now, I had to weigh my commitment to a new life with my lover, something I desperately wanted, against seeing my highest aspirations realized. It felt as if I was spinning on the corner edge of a razor blade with only minutes to decide my future. Our mail was already being forwarded to England; the plane was leaving in less than a day. And yet, this dream was a dream come true. Could there be time in the future to catch up to whatever we'd miss out on if we stayed? I knew I wanted to, this is what I had dreamed....

After Christopher said he understood why I wanted—or needed—to stay, a decision that speaks volumes about his character, I called the Angels to say I'd remain in San Francisco if they'd appoint me to head a board of directors and handle negotiations. When Beaver, Rodney, and Brian agreed, I put the Angels before my lover and, with his support, I canceled the trip and devoted myself to remounting the show.

My first move was to transfer the copyright of *Holy Cow!* to an appropriate new legal entity, as pledged. After we chose a name—The San Francisco Angels of Light—an airtight copyright would protect us from any showbiz sleight of hand. Realizing that they needed a lawyer with expertise in entertainment law, Brian, Beaver, and Rodney appointed *me* to find one without ever telling William Lee, their longtime attorney, who was also a friend and a fan, that they were firing him. When he learned that he was being dumped, he felt hard done by and, as we were friends, he blamed me for not alerting him.

I felt as sorry for him as I did for everyone who wound up being savaged by the Angels, but I was busy. From the start, it was clear that George wanted to assert total control of the group, although he had no knowledge of the intricate alliances that made it possible for the Angels to function. Being neophytes, how could we protect our integrity? Or keep from being exploited?

Within weeks, however, George started crying poor. I was surprised; his projected production budget was only $30,000. But as he seemed stuck, I secured a $15,000 loan, then offered to co-produce on one condition and one condition only: that no one would be replaced by a "big name." In short, as long as no one in the Angels got shafted, we were ready and willing to go to Broadway and go for broke.

Instead, he dicked us around for two months, then bailed, claiming that he was unable to raise the remaining $15,000. Bullshit. Obviously, he quit for other reasons. In hindsight, I now realize that I could have raised the rest of the money and been the sole producer, but the idea of having sole vested authority in the Angels never occurred to me. I wanted to see power flow in the other direction: back to the company.

Anyway, reinvigorated by seeing a way to shepherd the Angels to larger success, my focus was on creating a repertory company and either developing a new show at once, or restaging *Holy Cow!* or *Paris Sites*. But at the next meeting of the board, Rodney dropped a bomb: before I canceled my trip, he'd been flirting with a writer named Daniel Curzon. I'd never heard of him and he had nothing to do with the group, but rather than demonstrate loyalty or thanks to me, the Angels were going to do a show with him!

The entire scenario fell into place. Of course, George hadn't just *happened* to call me the day before my departure. He and Rodney must have been in touch for awhile. Certainly Rodney would want to go to Broadway so he'd be eager for a deal that would ensure his stardom. But as a producer, George must have told Rodney that no one could restage *Holy Cow!* without me. Even if they junked every word of dialogue and kept only Rodney's part of the written text, his excellent show-within-a-show, intellectual property rights were involved. I'd conceived the story and narrative, so even if someone jettisoned every line that I'd written and reworded the whole play, if the work was staged, I'd be able to sue.

They'd delayed revealing George's interest until the last minute—hoping I'd leave them free to do whatever they pleased. As ever, it was all about "the moist quivering triangle of desire"; they felt no commitment to come through for anyone else. Without realizing it when I copyrighted the script, the worst threat to the Angels came not from outsiders, but from within. Utterly disgusted, I felt I was seeing Rodney, Beaver, Brian, and Madeline for the first time. What I saw was *not* pretty. I quit. Again.

THE ANGELS' NEXT offering—*Cinderella II*—can be summarized simply: at the end, Prince Charming (Rodney) becomes an accountant. As in their previous two flops, a show that opened to a packed house was a wash. Having manipulated Daniel Curzon to write *for them,* Rodney and Beaver hogged every scene in a show that *Chronicle* critic Bernard Weiner pounced on for its lackluster script. The thing hemorrhaged money, forcing the playwright to borrow heavily or close down while the Angels went hog wild with greed and staged a strike ... *for money!*

Craving a hit, this *naif* not only cast Janice as one of the evil stepsisters, a blunder roughly akin to the Trojans requesting that pretty gift horse from their Greek pals—she got the cast to strike!—Curzon went bankrupt. Emily Dickinson says, "Fame has no Arms—And but one smile—that meagers Balms—." Well, he learned that lesson the hard way: mounting, then trying to ride the tiger disguised as the Angels of Light.

Tihara reports that Daniel came backstage in a white rage on closing night. But if he sought consolation, he was in the wrong place: there was no mercy for the fallen. "We didn't ask you for money," Rodney shrugged. Outraged at having been exploited for all he was worth only to be spat out like garbage, Daniel threw a knife with such force that, though he missed the target of his wrath, the blade stuck in a nearby wall.

The unfortunate author was not the last to be exploited and ripped off; rented lighting equipment vanished, purportedly stolen. The leasing company warned the Angels that if they ever staged another show, they'd be sued. But with three flops in the four years after *Holy Cow!*, the final verdict was in.

Exit Angels stage left; enter AIDS stage right; lights fade; curtain; blackout.

Epilogue

At the onset of "the gay plague" in 1982, Christopher and I became monogamous before volunteering for the Bay Area Men's Health Service, one of the earliest, if not the first, centrally organized monitoring system for gathering data and tracking the virus. When the first HIV test became available in May 1985, as volunteers, we were eligible to take it. Going in for our results, I assumed we'd have the same status, but no such luck.

"Adrian, you're HIV negative ... but Christopher ... *you are positive*," the doctor said.

"That's what I expected," Christopher sighed. And we left. At home, I swore I'd never leave him and feeling so sorry for him because he was younger, I said, "I wish it could have been the other way around."

"Well, it isn't," he said quietly.

Passion had long since left our relationship, but because HIV meant AIDS, and AIDS meant death, I wanted him to know I wasn't afraid to make love with him. He didn't want that, and so we lay together tenderly and listened to jazz.

We spent the next night at the movies, coming home to an urgent message from a doctor, insisting that I call no matter the hour. When I did, the doctor said, "I'm horrified to say this, but there was a mistake because you and Christopher were tested at the same time and you live together. We had it backwards: You, Adrian, are HIV positive. Christopher is negative. I'm sorry!"

Hanging up, I turned to Christopher, who stood in the door inquiringly. "Guess what?

I felt almost relieved. If Christopher had been positive, I'd have felt obliged to stay with him. Now, I was at liberty, even if I carried in my blood a lurid afterburn of the young man who'd hit town in 1973 to participate in gay lib, establish himself as a poet, and find love.

All my dreams had come true but leaving Christopher meant beginning a new life. That didn't scare me and there was no drama to parting, but nothing is deader than a dead love. On September 20, 1985, I stepped into a new life, one I saw as surreal by Thanksgiving Day in London:

In Waterloo Station, I met a blond angel, twenty-three, traveling on an expired ticket. We got to talking. As a teenager, he'd been a hustler but quit before marrying two years later. His wife knew all about it. They had a baby girl. One day—scandal!—one of his friends met one of his former johns. His friends dropped him; his wife stuck it out, then finally left too. He lost his job and came to London. Now he lives on welfare, wanders around, and considers jumping in front of a train. He didn't ask me for money. He says he doesn't want to hustle. Doesn't want counseling either. Just wants his family back. When we reached Paddington Station, he wandered away. I got a connection to a friend's farm: James—a cousin of Mark Phillips, husband of Princess Anne—owns 10,000 acres.

I didn't feel I was leaving much in San Francisco. That same year, Mark Thompson had left. In the spring, he went to LA to interview Christopher Isherwood for *The Advocate*. There he met Malcolm Boyd, a blue-eyed activist and ex-priest, thirty years his senior, who led the North American Episcopal Church to revise its official position on homosexuality. Malcolm was not only physically handsome, he had a serenity born of a lifelong commitment to true spirit.

Mark continued working as a journalist and wrote five fine books on gay culture. In addition to being a motivating force in setting up the National Gay & Lesbian Archives—the world's largest collection of LGBT materials—his shows of photography and sales of his books and DVDs have raised funds for a gay men's medicine circle. In 2004, he and Malcolm were married in a service presided over the bishop of the diocese of Southern California. In 2005, he completed training to become a Jungian psychologist.

Others from our culture had moved out into the "real" world.

Brian helped to light the opening ceremonies of Olympics at Los Angeles in 1984. But he wasn't the only ex-Angel to find success in LA. Chuck (now Charles) Leavitt, whom I recalled as a sweet-spirited musician, and Madeline Bloom, now his wife, were there too. Chuck became a screenwriter of note, among his works, *Blood Diamond* (2006).

Beaver deserved her many Bay Area Critics Circle Awards for best costume designs.

Neeli Cherkovski continued writing tremendous poetry and nonfiction as well.

Tede Mathews took gay lib and AIDS awareness campaigns to Latin America before succumbing to the disease. His life and his altruism were rightly honored by a memorial at the Modern Times Bookstore.

Tuxedomoon went on to international celebrity but remained based in Europe where they performed with choreographer Maurice Béjart, among others.

Dan Nicoletta continued documenting the local scene and preserving the history of the LGBT movement. A founding member of the San Francisco International LGBT Film Festival, he's also been involved in many projects concerning Harvey Milk, including the preservation of Harvey Milk's archive, the Harvey Milk–Scott Smith Collection at the James C. Hormel Gay and Lesbian Center at the San Francisco Library.

Many former Angels, such as Teena and Francine, had stable families and were raising beautiful children. Still, many others closer to the nexus had been scorched.

 Ralph devoted himself to working with homeless people, selflessly doing theater with them until in July 2007, he committed suicide.

Tihara worked with mentally ill people at the YMCA and, like Ralph, staged shows with them.

Esmerelda had a spotty career as a singer and costume designer but went on to create something new and ecologically sensible: burial shrouds for a movement to replace coffins with biodegradable materials.

Greg became a disk jockey in gay bars and worked for charity events like the Macy's Passport Fashion Show, an annual benefit that has raised millions of dollars to combat AIDS.

Victoria and Jillen acquired quiet stability far from the madness into which they had plunged so incautiously; recovery was hard won and tremulous. Like dewdrops at the tip of quivering leaves, they were ultimately obliged to curb their once-grand expectations and to learn to be content with modest lives.

AIDS brought out saintly qualities in Lulu. As the years brought death and devastation, he rose to the occasion splendidly, nurturing and nursing stricken friends, seeing to their needs when they went to hospital, coping with the paperwork, then later helping their families by overseeing the funerals and arranging memorials. Beautifully, lovingly, Lulu turned such ceremonies into works of art and celebration. He was an inspiration.

From 1985 to 1995 I divided my time between Europe and India. During those years, the meaning of the 1970s became increasingly clear. And at San Francisco's tiny Eureka Theater, Oscar Eustis and Joe Taccone developed and produced Tony Kushner's play, *Angels in America*. Thus, San Francisco not only midwifed the radical theater of gay liberation with the Angels of Light, it nurtured what might be the finest American play since the 1950s.

During my years abroad, I wrote novels and worked with a Dutch theater collective, the Amsterdam Balloon Company, a forerunner of Burning Man. At festivals in Holland and India, I developed solo shows combining poetry, storytelling, and live-action painting. Twice, I visited San Francisco. Once, I saw Rodney. He was a waiter at a gay bar; I was thin and brown from living in Asia. There wasn't much to say. I never saw him again.

I didn't see my parents for twenty years for reasons revealed in my forthcoming family history, "Dragon Hill." When we did meet, I did my utmost to show them forgiveness, generosity, and respect. All pointless. I'd failed to let them run my life. I was unforgivable. To be discredited, of course. Disinherited. I don't mind. The rewards of an honest life are beyond price. Or bribes.

In India, the central thrust of my life and my writing became increasingly clear, for I met many gay Indians who'd heard tales of San Francisco and the freedom gay people enjoyed in a beautiful city. Some had even heard of the Angels of Light and longed to hear about visionary, out-front gay artists. For them, the concept of life in a progressive community carried with it the hope of social acceptance and a dream of equal rights.

After time in various ashrams, I returned to San Francisco to study with a spiritual teacher. Back in a city I'd never expected to live in again, I learned that over seventy-five percent of the men in the Angels had died of AIDS. Many of those still alive had the HIV virus.

Others such as Daniel Curzon carried a different bug. He sued an Internet site that ranked the faculty at City College (where he teaches) for dubbing him one of the "ten worst teachers," and for being a pompous ass. Thankfully, the ACLU defended the website and, not coincidentally, freedom of speech. As a consequence of losing his lawsuit, the hapless man was forced to pay thousands to the victor.

The catalogue of horrors is too long to detail. But one macabre incident is worth noting: the Angel Dust dealer known as Miss Tiddy had a brain tumor requiring surgery in the late 1980s. While "she" was in hospital, another dealer took over the territory. When Miss Tiddy got out, "her" business had dried up. With a shaved head and scars and stitches clearly visible, he was now known as Zipperhead, a slur that speaks volumes about the always punchy yet vicious wit on tap. Destitute, Miss Tiddy begged drugs from a new kingpin who got so angry, he threw Miss Tiddy down the stairs; later that night, Miss Tiddy died of a brain injury. Whether or not the dealer actually caused the death, rumors flew that he had. People spray-painted his garage door with a simple accusation: *Murderer.*

Rodney died of AIDS. Wheelchair-bound for his last appearance during the summer of 1988, he sang a plea for love, "I've Got Less Time Than You." Later in the same show, Beaver's mime piece culminated with her kissing Rodney's tap shoes reverently before placing them in a trunk and closing the lid. Although the benefit raised $5,000 for Rodney's care, the money disappeared that same night. Brian was now using heroin. Apparently, he stole the money meant for his dying lover and used it to buy smack.

I think Beaver sealed up more than Rodney's shoes when he died, even as Brian's case of AIDS progressed. In 1996, I asked her if I could borrow her tape of *Holy Cow!.*

"My copy of the video is in Rodney's trunk," she told me, "and I can't bring myself to open it." No. Apparently she couldn't. But not for the implied reason. Greg confided that during one of his rampages, Brian destroyed the trunk and its contents. Either Beaver couldn't deal with that or she was concealing it. Either way, just as the Angels had been her province in life, it seemed that, as far as she was concerned, its memory became a sacrosanct and more-than-slightly-morbid domain over which she would reign supreme. Her taxidermist's outlook became clear in 1996 when I began this book, thus triggering another one of her wild insinuations. "Some people say that you destroyed the Angels of Light," she accused. We would never speak again.

Rodney Price Memorial Altar, September 18, 1988

I went to see Brian in 1997 at a Zen hospice. We sat in a garden, reminiscing gently. He was happy because, after years of estrangement over the abuse he'd suffered, Sham had visited. Weeks later, Brian died. But Beaver's progress to Golgotha had not yet ended.

While one of her friends knew that Sham was using heroin, in the familiar pattern of neglect and denial that characterized the Angels, the "friend" revealed nothing about it. Thus, apparently unaware, although they shared a little house, Beaver returned home one night to find him in a coma. She rushed him to hospital in time to save his life, but he'd suffered irreparable brain damage. Only thirty years old at the time, Sham will be institutionalized for the rest of his life.

Half-blind as a mole, Irving lived virtually alone. He was in litigation with Mary Hyssen, who had bought him the warehouse for Kaliflower, over title to the building, and he railed against undocumented immigrants selling flowers without official permits. Thus do revolutions devour their own, as in the case of David Meadows now claiming he could cure AIDS, assisted by "visitations" from Zeus!

As Reggie Dunnigan, who was both a Cockette and an Angel, was dying of the dread malady, the kind and sweet Melody called on old friends, who donated thousands to help him fulfill his most cherished wish: to have a place of his own. The day after moving in, he died. At his memorial in Dan Nicoletta's studio, Tony Angel—riddled by substance abuse—remained funny. And adorable.

"We should do a show," Tony ventured, his brown eyes crinkling as he grinned.

"You bet," I said. "We'll take Viagra, go onstage naked, and try to achieve erections!"

"The audience will bet on who gets it up first!" he brightened. "Paid shows, *dahling*."

Reggie's memorial shed light on various interpretations of our history. Chuck Drees, now a fine painter, startled me during his tribute to Reggie by alluding to me as someone who brought people together in harmony while, in a private chat, Melody may have hit upon a deeper truth or, at least, acknowledged her own by saying, "You always wanted to go in a more professional direction than the rest of us. We just wanted to party."

Angels of Light and friends gather at a memorial for Reggie Dunnigan, Dan Nicoletta's photo studio, June 2, 2001

Really? Well, maybe for her. Personally, I was trying to survive a world that killed Harvey Milk, to create a society where right-wingers might not be elected, where early AIDS research might have been so well funded that Reggie might not be dead. Obviously, Melody and I saw it all very, very differently.

Either way, fun-time was over and, thirty years after leaving Inverness, I was a hermit. Stubbornly, I kept writing: poems, novels, plays, and nonfiction until, after twenty-six years of editorial rejection following the publication of *The Glass Arcade*, other works finally began wending their way into print. But no matter how gratifying, security would prove elusive. Bay Area houses that went for $25,000 in 1971 now cost $2,500,000.

Fortunately, gay liberation was neither out of reach nor "over," even if its aging denizens wore baseball caps backwards. New activists didn't need bearded drag queens to foment progressive change, although they surely owe those revolutionaries a debt. But even if history moves on, there is always hilarity in San Francisco.

A few weeks ago, for example, one of the Sisters of Perpetual Indulgence went to Grace Cathedral (in drag, of course) where, without realizing that this nun was '"none of the above," the archbishop of the diocese gave her holy communion. When the news became public, it shocked the hell out of the Vatican, but sent gales of laughter through our out-and-proud city.

As delicious as such moments are, the vanguard culture of the 1970s had vanished without sufficient testimony. And to lose our own history is crazy.

The Angels of Light had been the hub of a whirling wheel with radiant radial spokes. Not only had we been supremely visible—and visibility is the first critical step in the transition from dehumanized unreality to equality—we'd created a revolutionary theater form. The fact that we were also allied with a just cause, one to which some of us remain committed, gives it a unique standing in twentieth-century art movements.

Though a rainbow flag flies over the Castro, the revolution has moved on as is inevitable. But I find myself looking for some poignant image as if it is 1974 again and I'm at Oak Street, noting the cigarette butts stubbed out on cement steps, the savaged mannequin, the torn paper umbrella, a doll, arms akimbo, staring fixedly. In "Music for Limbo Palace" (page 244), I imagined performers staggering around at dawn; now, the terrain is uninhabited. Oh yes, there are people, but they are mainly far away now. Still, even now I feel involved enough to share these tales. How can we vanish without leaving ample markers? Art was our way to declare identity. Can we expect future generations to embrace their own uniqueness or avoid repeating our mistakes if we withhold authentic touchstones? Everyone should tell their story in their own words. If not, revisionists will squat on our legacy and culture vultures will pick our bones clean.

An example of such creeping crud happened a few years ago when *Vanity Fair* featured photographs of Hibiscus, who succumbed to AIDS in 1982, in an article about a hot new "return" to glittery hippie fashion. The gutsy angel had been turned into the deadest of all things: a commodity. I like to believe that the iconoclastic Hibiscus would have hated being used as a merchandising gimmick.

A sweeter accolade occurred in 2004 when the US Postal Service announced a contest to commemorate the 1960s with a stamp. Of the half dozen finalists, one—an image that I remembered from the era because I'd been so arrested by it and so turned on by it too—pictured Hibiscus at a peace rally in Washington, DC. Confronted by a row of National Guard troops, the shaggy-headed youth wearing a tatty Irish sweater is seen inserting a daisy into the barrel of a soldier's rifle.

That deserved to become a national stamp. Not only does it picture a gallant activist, it exemplifies an ethos to which many millions more than the Angels of Light were devoted. For beyond the flash and glitter, and issues of gender, sexual preference, race, nationality, class, origin, or age, at essence, the heart and soul of gay liberation was—and remains—nothing less than a dedication to love, not hate, and peace, not war, from people committed to life, liberty, and the pursuit of happiness. The daisy that Hibiscus placed in the gun became a lotus.

Holy Cow! Cast and Crew

Cast (in order of appearance)
Uday Sengupta (1979)—Devotional Dancer
Janet Sala (1979)—Sita
Radha Bloom—Kamala, Peacock Princess
Rodney Price—Snake Charmer, Shiva, Peacock
Robin Bowen—Cobra, Death
Kevin Gardiner—Kalir-va, Narrator
Coco Vega (1979)—Kamala's Mother
Tommy Pace (1980)—Kamala's Mother
Tony Angel—Chancellor, Demon
Adrian Brooks—Rajah
Lulu (1979)—Slave Driver
Janice (1980)—Slave Driver
Beaver Bauer—Sudama, Hyena, Unicorn
Lenore Vantosh-Howard—Kali
Ralph Sauer (1979)—Eunuch
Randall Denham (1980)—Eunuch
Lynne—Nandi, Sultan of Beirut
Rinaldo Iturrino (1979)—Queen Mother
Constance "Connie" West (1980)—Queen Mother
Honey Galeborg—Mechanical Doll
Judith Ogus—Mechanical Doll, Monkey
Andra Mitchell—Torturer, Spider
Nicole Sawaya (1979)—Raven
Julie Petri (1980)—Raven
Ed Barrow—Monster
Philippe Ruise—Dragon

(Note: Almost all of the above were also seen as villagers, soldiers, and spiritual devotees.)

En corps: Ma Anand Becky, Don Boone, Paul Dubois, Rob Hichborn, Marsha Hultberg, Noelle Olompali, Teena Rosen-Albert.

Choreography
Constance West composed choreography except for the following:
Indian dances—some traditional choreography, some choreographed by
Beaver Bauer, Radha, Rodney Price, and Uday Sengupta
Mime—Beaver Bauer, Robin Bowen, Honey Galeborg, Andra Mitchell, and
Judith Ogus
Fight—Louis Brill and Kevin Gardiner

Costume Coordinators (for group scenes only; individuals created their own costumes)
Ribbon Dance and Village Dance: Beaver Bauer
Rajah's Army: Constance West
Karanas (the yogic asanas in the finale): Constance West and Judith Ogus

Musicians
Composer for guitar and drum: Charles "Chuck" Leavitt
Composers for synthesizer: Justin McCarthy and Walter Black
Composer for tape and sound: Tommy Tadlock
Invocation (vocal) and percussion: Yassir Ashaadly
Piano: Bob Drewry
Sitar: Eric Davis
Zither, flute, percussion: Yosuf Fanun

Sets (in order of appearance)
Street scene: Ralph Sauer
Throne room: Adrian Brooks
Garden: Selma Brown
Village: Beaver Bauer
Forest of Death: Rodney Price
Proscenium arch: Rodney Price

Puppets and Masks
Philippe Ruise, Tony Angel, Lulu, and individual cast members who, as was
customary, created their own props and masks.

Technical Crew
Mark Ciano, Paul DuBois, Brian Mulhern, William Poy Lee, David Waldren

Stage Lighting
Brian Mulhern

Exterior Lights
Bill Bathurst

Stage Directions; Rules of Engagement

To make a doll: to make a three or four inch doll, first find a face no longer than one half inch, sufficient to be a queen. Cut it out carefully leaving a long stem to serve as a backbone. Wrap and bunch tissue paper so the head sticks up out of a tight torso. Find nice material. Using straight pins, wrap fabric around the doll. Leave enough skirt for support. For arms, cover small coils of tissue and affix them onto the shoulders using straight pins passing down, through the center.

To make a place: old books, especially leather ones with gold binding, make excellent palace floors. Fold tissue for beds, spools of thread for tables, whatever tiny furniture you have.

Note: As the queen is always in captivity, her circumstances don't have to be appropriate to her station. Note: no kitchens or bathrooms. Just entrance halls, receiving rooms and secret passages. Note: It is good to use connected books so, if there's a knock at your door, you can quietly slide the palace under your bed and return to the necessary orbit.

Important: The Queen must not lie just anywhere. Find a nice box for her or a special cloth. The soldiers must never physically abuse the Queen when she is arrested or deposed. Her person is inviolate.

This is a game for only one person.

Personal Feelings: Queens should not be smiling. They should be thin, in their mid-thirties. I always used pictures of Garbo.

November 1973
San Francisco

228 ⊚ Adrian Brooks

How Long Has it Been Since the Circus Began to Win?

In the first booth, the Queen of Sheba. Look at his legs: black hair covered with black net. S/he carries a fan and sings from a cardboard balcony. S/he falls in love and gives a fur vest so real you'd swear it's true. With a vial of pills among the cosmetics, somewhere on the dressing table, a blond child runs across summer, somewhere between the red kimono and that cowgirl outfit with white leather fringe. Notice: cigarette stubs in a jar of cold cream. The beard comes through makeup.

In the second booth, the Fat Lady performs with her husband. He is a dwarf. She pours honey on her breasts. He tries to lick it off but he is too short. He jumps up and down. He is too short. Look at her eyes—painted blue. Look at her half closed eyes. She wets her lips. Observe the black spot on her cheek and see how many layers of fat roll over her silver bikini. Today is her birthday. Now watch the dwarf! He climbs her like a rubber ladder. See his little boots? He puts them against her thighs. She opens her eyes. He holds her breasts and makes small noises like a child. She pretends to be alarmed but they are both satisfied. They will be paid.

In the third booth, a beautiful boy. He has gold hair and green eyes like a God. He thinks everything is tin and the sun, a light-bulb. If you want to know more, ask, but I can tell you: he came to the city to be a poet but stayed too long on the street, an alley cat with one too many cups of coffee, one too many strangers telling the Truth all the way to bed where they fucked him and gave him a buck to go home. I'll tell you a secret: this kid is rotting with VD. He thinks the sun a light bulb. He thinks the sky is tin. He passes Death.

In the fourth booth, "Face to Face,"—a favorite of mine—where the nun is tied to a naked African and the priest, bound to a nymphomaniac. They have all been told their parents are here. See? When the nun tries to confess, the Ethiopian licks her nose. The priest feigns ignorance. I like it when they all talk at once.

In the fifth booth, this woman cannot get ready. She is frantic. She's in a rush. Look at her pile of wigs and costumes. Look how fast she moves! No matter what she tries on, it's never right. A little too much of this or that she'll improve with a slower, a ribbon or comb, perhaps, another strand of pearls. No! You see? She decides "it's too much," and begins again. Soon, she will begin to cry. She'll tear at herself, rip the cloth, then repair the damage. But it's never right for her. All day and all night she prepares to have it just so. When she was young, her Mother combed her hair. Her Mother told her, "A prince will come for you, one day, a prince and you will be perfectly happy...." Ah! She's stuck on her own needle! She bleeds!

In the sixth booth, you find our philosopher. He took drugs of the mind. He thinks in twos and threes. He tells you one side of the mirror. It makes sense. Upon reflection, he shows you the other side. His words are calm. His eyes are calm. He doesn't eat meat. He is a deconstructionist, a martyr to twos and threes, a fractured brain never fits pieces together. He continues an Oriental interpretation followed by The Western View. He has gone mad in sets and versions but he is articulate certainly, he is everything a man is desperate in his cave of mirrors. Sooner or later, if you listen long, he swallows his words like a snake, his tail. He thinks of wisdom. He dreams of nothing.

In the seventh booth, an older couple dresses up like royals to receive company. She's understanding; he's heard it all—nothing is new. She dresses as a crab, sometimes a spider. They have a secret: unless you confide, they die of themselves.

Here is my booth and my coat; I put it on. Look at the pockets. One—for unpaid accounts. In the other? Measurements on paper, dreams and other poems. This is my secret: both pockets have holes so I can feel myself as I hold you. Here is a bill for Reliance. Here is a dream to claim: I am a moth bewitched by the moon. Now you have seen it all. As you leave, let me put my camera in your eye. As you depart, I return to the world of uncertain arcades.

San Francisco, October 1974

(Published in *Voices of the Seventies*. Edited by Paul Mariah. Manroot: SF, 1977)

Portrait of a Room

Adrian lies in bed
—sheets sticky—
Adrian should be out cold
but his hangover won't wait

Oh yes, he should be asleep
being stamped, marked, bruised
from last night's pastiche
of rhinestones and remnants

In white satin and silver
Adrian danced
with Egyptian hookers
and acrobats

Riding in the back of a truck
—an oyster on a half shell—
he came home at three
but now it's six

The star on Adrian's door
never meant to see morning;
the star is paper and door bats—
hinged to intrusive dawn

Words fall
tumbling
drunk gymnasts
on flimsy trampolines

Adrian in disrepair—
a white moth struck
by the moon, by the moon
all gone, all gone;

He leaves a note:
"If you want to find me
1- sweep up the sequins
2- multiply to bodyweight"

San Francisco
October 1974

Untitled

A young man moves in a crowd
Eyes dart from masks
Go belly up

He's heard a hundred times
A thousand, "You're beautiful!"
Willing plunder—
Cuts requiring iodine

He feels his face from inside/out
Sudden silver in blue lights
A hook

San Francisco
December 29, 1974

Untitled

Here is the queen getting ready for a party. He stands in the bathroom pinning a flower in his hair. It is a silk rose. He touches his collarbone—ascertains its definition. He will wear something with a low front. At the mirror, he powders his face and surveys it like virgin land ripe for development. He pencils thin brows and views his progress. There's a lot to do. Our queen must leave in five minutes. He adds green to his eyelids, finds the rouge and colors the white base, then stands back. He darkens the lips, decides the rose is too much and adds rhinestone clips. It's starting to work. The eyes smolder. Lines are extended. Quick dabs of sandalwood at a wrist, elbow and neck. It's getting hot. One minute to touchdown. The queen slips into a white satin dress and brushes his hair away from his face. Transformation complete, a creature of the night is ready to enter the neon arena. He picks up his raincoat and trips out the door on his way toward the glory of sidewalks and the light of passing cars.

Out on the street, the queen moves between lamplight and shadows as if drawn by a magnet invisible to the naked eye. Listen carefully and you may catch the rustle of the gown on castle stairs, the wheels of carriages rattling along cobblestones towards a fatal rendez-vous. The queen cruises past the donut shop. Inside the satin dress, his legs are coming alive; his body is electric again; he is living cinema, only distantly related to this century.

San Francisco
January 1975

(Published in *Angels of the Lyre: A Gay Poetry Anthology*. Edited by Winston Leyland. Panjandrum Press: San Francisco, 1975.)

Look Twice Before Crossing America

"Hail Mary full of Grace, forgive us our trespasses as you would have our Father who art in Heaven give us this day and Jesus Christ, His only son, our Lord, Allah Akbar. Blessed art thou among women, hallowed be thy children come on earth, as it is in heaven and to the country for which it stands to assume thy will be done and obey the Scout Law. Pray for us sinners till we pledge allegiance to the flag, the fruit of thy womb, forsaking all others on the right hand from whence He will come to judge the republic for which it stands with liberty and justice for all. Shalom."

1975

sHe

When a man becomes a woman
he does so slowly no one might
notice the way he pauses on stairs.
Suddenly all time in no time at all
just put down to sleepy afternoons

If a boy grows fe/male
the game is rained out.
In porchlight spilling onto grass
sHe grows acutely conscious
of music in silence

When a woman inhabits a man
one might miss the ways wherein
she pauses to gaze out a window
considering who and when
not how and why....

Morocco
1975

Backstage Angel: Incandescent Under Blue

Behind the curtain, at a remove—
concocted plumes and moonlight
inseparable from swans, willows
and lanterns in deserted arcades.

As it rains softly on a world of silver foil
a harpsichord grazed, a forbidden chamber,
taffeta rustles descending curvilinear stairs
brushes cool shadows on midnight lawns.

A serpent glides across wet grass.
A full-bellied moon appears to linger
on a marble abduction of Persephone
who never returns from where no one knows....

San Francisco
June 12, 1975

Daydream—Color in Dissolute Blues

This is not a world of future plans
Everything is for sale, every hour
Good intentions
Evaporating vows

The pattern may seem familiar
Nearest measurement, approximate
Who understands this understands
The spell of no certain plans

Numbers, dates, names, even faces
Sometimes ... hard to recall.
One even kept black socks on
The rest ... like marble ...

Another with a roommate asleep
In the same bed (never woke)
But it's alright if boundaries blur
There's coffee ...

Today seems viable even if
A recent flirtation joined the Army
After a kiss on a moonlit balcony.
Do you still pretend to understand?

Oh! What goes on, what goes on
When grey days stack into weeks?
Epidemics, infections
For which there is no cure

For this moment
In a world of no future plans
We eat lunch on the edge
And dinner at the brink

Each moment, the last before eviction
On days that kick in at 2 p.m., or so,
Scrounging food stamps and coupons
On the terrace of an abandoned house

This is a constant end
To guide the Way
No matter what, I'll claim
"I should have known...."

San Francisco
June 13, 1975

More Justifications; Absolute History

We do what we do to survive,
credit steps that work.
Others get it second hand
but we must amuse the troops!

So welcome to way beyond Beyond
past the point of being Past the Point.
It's home turf, baby, don't look down.
It's what you want, where you belong.

San Francisco
June 1975

Rubble

Saint Innocence of Contraband
Scores smack for his new love.
Poet of last days and countdowns
Bewitched poet of the double take—
Kitchen witness to coffee sacrament.

On the one corner he can tolerate
He declares every spot Center—
Talking like he could always quit—
Too far gone to get out
Not far enough to get off.

San Francisco
June 1975

Life on the Cutting Edge

Day begins at 2 p.m. in an abandoned house
where a lover fills the rooms with flowers
lifted from graves. Day starts buck-naked
then draped with a deco French robe

In sienna light, I ruminate
over brown velvet laced with gold.
So it goes: cocaine, silver and turquoise—
beads strung on wire, gifts for friends ...

Hashish, black coral, amber ...
"Ex/es" blow in from Mexico; a coke lady too;
the Joker doesn't show so ... off to rehearsal—
a rising tide of Thai grass and California beer

Later, home again: first time in days
The silent flat like a doctor's waiting room.
Phone a way back to confetti and sawdust.
"Free champagne" always works. *"Dress up!"*

Night begins with a ride
to a party in rhinestones, sequins and fringe.
I drag a spangled net, the glittering boy
dancing to applause

from debutantes with Dutch lovers
in a bistro of red candles
the warm smoke of Samoan men
and startled tourists stare.

Sorry, Peggy Knickerbocker, sorry
I love you but this is just too straight
Next up: a birthday/cake/candle/joints
primed with dust

Night rages on, queens puking in the loo.
Night won't quit; ex-loves manage a light
as night winds down—mute green orphans
stoned on pig downers, immobilized

Central to action I swore to compose
I negotiate my way across bodies
trip down long straight stairs
to a door and out to the street

Midnight. Home; a pile of scarves,
narcotic and sensual pleasures:
oils once banned in France; a whip;
I dismantle the Painted Boy

Weary of the cardboard world
with no reprieve from blue lights and crowds
suddenly needing five minutes of country air
not afterburn or flashbulbs

Nothing will remain but fantastic photos.
No one who isn't here could believe this.
Even I can't be sure. Oh thousands know
who I am now but this is not my desire.

San Francisco
June 1975

Testimony and Stage Notes

1—Testimony

I left the circus by the back door—
Bailed out at 9 a.m.
We all know how the movie ends

Connect scars to a black dance
It ends in thin white ribbons:
Stone rubbings on tombs.

2—Stage Notes

A poet's exposure; tables alone
A floral arrangement of stems

I will die of young men on bicycles
Climbers. Skiers. Blondes.

San Francisco
June 1975

Music for Limbo Palace

Hot trumpet and steady drumbeat, the fog blows smoke over windowpanes and first love. Well, goodbye you city of yellow sunsets and cypress silhouettes. Goodbye you city of endless nights alone. Goodbye midwife of scarlet and sequined dreams. The circus is moving on.

Let morning be grey. Let dawn uncloak striped tents in a pocket of fog. Tomorrow (just hours away) could come with steam rising around cages and wagons. Let half-costumed dancers and tightrope walkers stagger across a roped-in enclosure hoping for coffee but scoring something to smoke while water boils.

Pink silk ballerinas listen to rain on a tarpaper roof. Let the circus begin where it left off—red wagon wheels hubcap deep in green weeds. Finally, let the wagons be drawn by one great lion pulling carts and tin cans towards the open road, the route to go to cross country.

A few ostrich plumes in a clenched fist, a strand or two of artificial pearls will be the only tangible evidence of nights that really did burn off black lacquer until the gold of sunrise and early morning.

Then goodbye, city of countless rodeo queens and all night cowboys. Goodbye to the unmarred blossoms of your public gardens. Your post adolescent daydreams all came true. Goodbye to your endless virgin. Goodbye to foregone conclusions.

Philadelphia
September 1975

Between Three Worlds, Maybe Four

Grey day on the wide lip of monsoon
Somewhere in green paddies of Asia
A poet and tinsel prince chooses life.
He takes a guitar to the temple of Kali.
The children cannot grasp the sorrow
In the song, or opium ...

Black spangled nets and ermine
Pink pearls in goblets of champagne
Taxi windshields 4 am; take me home
After windmill kisses on balconies
and a year in and out of hotels
I return to uncertain arcades.

Kathmandu
June 1976

Untitled

Mr Right and Miss Can-Do got married
Had babies and saw the babies grow.
We grew, we grew—nice boys and girls.

But thunder struck a cradle at morning
Cold wind the dark ride of our star.
We live in groups, as a rule,
And, as a rule, die simply.

Kathmandu
1976

Back On Stage with Angels

1

Once again, the flaming night bird rises and flies
with glittering wings against a gypsy fandango.
Once again, we pull a tinsel chariot of sweet madness
into men's room polished airports of straight minds.
Once again, electricity ripples up the spine of visible
night Goddess moaning split-legged pleasure coming
milky white over the city as we go on again, blazing
frenzied street corner glory—princes and princesses
promising the wide tropic brim of panorama.
Once again, we flex invisible wings and predict
stormy weather.

2

Full moon! Full moon! We did a show!
San Francisco storefront grey
on otherwise night of no stars.
Full moon! A show of beautiful boys
and winsome ladies in sawdusty floor
dancing bars of hot rhythm and blues.
Full moon over trees by the water
over lives still not yet quite sure ...
Full moon, August, ripe full moon
skirting Aquarian ochre medallion
above flabbergasting Pacific blue.

Full moon naval over San Francisco
as Angels orgasm—another eruption
of confetti against all odds of technical
land-rover junked and metal arm-claws
scraping Mars at this very moment/high
above weekend canyons of this city
which may momentarily all fall down
go boom. There's still time, though!
Sixty, eighty, one hundred thousand
guys are out on the prowl right now.
It's 2 am, baby, and bars are closing!

San Francisco
September 1976

Cocaine Love Charade

White powder breakfast
Chipped on blue glass
A late afternoon in bed

You and I crisscross
A river of stones
It is your glass bridge

I am a forest
Felled
By a white axe

You smile Sacrament
To the quick chip
Of a razor

San Francisco
October 1976

Autumn

Winds shift and coins declare: it's Fate.
Drift ... Abandon safe base. Move on ...

The shape at horizon is a messenger.
Someone said he speaks your tongue.
You hope you'll remember the words.

Choices melt before a golden key
Yielding secrets, treasures, hearts
Acquired in the qualifying rounds.

San Francisco
October–November 1976

The Arterial Tribe

—for Peter Hartman

1

I have always known you
Known from first hearing
Now I cast my nets.
Watch and listen well

As words spiral into poems—
Visas in strange passports.
Wait! I changed my mind.
No letters, no emissaries ...

2

The lantern light is umber, then green.
It grows dark, darker than Chinese ink.
This poem-in-a-bottle floats your way.
Pick it up. Keep it....

West Hollywood
Spring 1977

After the Gay Day Parade

The day's review tumbles from confetti,
Sweat stained t-shirts and suntanned necks
Of humpy mechanics braving a haunting jeer.
The day's review glistens: 3,000,000 beer cans
Crunched by restless boots and automobiles
Driving thru the litter of 400,000 gay crazies
Crushing overflow juice, fruit pulp, rind, corks,
Bottles, butts and wrappers. With half the sea
In abalone, puca shell, with silver and bone
Bronzed glory- the young melting waxen hearts—
Dance, stomp, blissed-out, stoned, tripped-out
All American boys and girls in torn faded jeans
Shred inhibitions, lusty and ready to fuck.
And I wonder if we know what draws us in—
to crowds, torsos, lean and sun-kissed brown
or what lies behind this finding...?

San Francisco
June 1977

After Six Months ...

One perfect moment, loving a man.
One perfect day in the life,
not a letter, song or very good poem.
Maybe it's the work I do or season?
At home alone, or in his arms, yes,
I agree ... it's corny, a cliché, passé ...
I know all the Reasons Why Not.
Still, I'll take a perfect day doin' nothin'
at home, just relaxing in bed, lazy,
hanging out, talking, just being together.

We talk plain talk, make love like coffee
spend days at the movies. Intermission
or previews, plot, gossip, lose ourselves
in sudden hugs, kisses warm with sweat.

It might go on like this forever.
It may have ended ten minutes ago
when he went to work but, at last, at last,
who cares? It has nothing to do
with beginnings or ends;
the Blues stay unemployed
on mornings of nectarines and peaches
on afternoons of news and calls
on nights of flick or intricate depictions
of another working day

Now I type plays; he sells popcorn;
I plot novels; he charts art outrages;
I rewrite; he goes off alone
to his one room cheap hotel.

A bird's eye view of love
might reveal no more
than two men, same height,
similar build, same color hair.
A telescopic lens may not show
an extraordinary ordinariness
of how it is to be him or me
these days. It's no spectator sport
though heads turn and calls affirm
he and I look good … fuck it;

in the end, what won't show
what no one knows is: these days
for him and me the way things are
it's no visual thing or visible show.

Now critics may argue or cynics agree:
it's easy to have fun if you're young
sharp and artful.
But we fell in love when I was fat
sick with a cold, coughing up pus
sweaty, in bed and pale.
Now let me ask you, sir:
Is that any way to begin a romance
me being thirty
and him nineteen?

San Francisco
August 4, 1978

Song

—for Christopher

I wondered who you'd be
if I let go and loved you.
Called up friends, said I knew
how we'd end, you and me.

Seen the film, knew the score,
played each role, swore I knew
more too. Much too much too
risky too: came to your door

later, both being alone.
Rainy night nimbus,
when I asked you home ...
to fire then wine, then us ...

Fold me in and take me
impatient and I need
crave—this—love—will kill
white lights and empty nights

1978

For Robert Opel

Your death stays with me
Lingers at the cafe
And haunts my street
The street we walked
Two days ago as you said
I'm ivory faced and rare
To be courted, wooed, desired.
You added you liked my Act

I laughed, kept walking
But you tagged along
To a line at the bank
To say you *saw* me
And wanted more ...
I laughed again,
Still in line
Called you a child.

"Kiss me," you urged,
"Kiss me."
I complied. Once ...
Without losing my place
Or my tongue.
We knew the odds: so it was
A kiss before a glance
Before a bullet in your head

I wouldn't draw too close
To your scene, Tough Stuff;
Oh, whips, chains don't faze me.
But I knew your Artdream only—
Cementing city streets to skies
In time for one collective fuck.
Now the way I laughed/sticks
Like thick cock in a sore throat.

San Francisco
July 9, 1979

Guided Tour

Let me change before one may/be man arrives.
The unspoken query and pending reply is "yes."
Don't worry; I'm prince and prisoner,
Sage, hermit and ghost. In short: *I live here.*

Begin in the maze, the conveyor belt
to gardens, facades and iridescence.
Windows shuttered behind scrolls.
Rusting balustrades; neo-classic halls.

Each symmetric room opens on a gallery.
Other doors, other chambers, past lives.
Chandeliers collect dust, delineate space.
It's best to quit each room forever now.

Across hedges and weeds, construction sites
zig-zag back to colonial lamplight, connecting
front doors. I don't mind admitting: all doors
intersect. Domes and walls dissolve ...

In this part: you find no trap doors, just stairs
to turrets. A litter of applications below,
notarized letters of intent.
Uniformed attendants; lost luggage—

Locate the owners by names on tags.
Oh yes, some go/occasionally/wander off
ignorant of the fever chase, big chance or payoff.
Telltale clues? Bags of groceries and small coins.

Here, we adorn ourselves with ribbons or stones;
They imply immortality, a wiser gamble than war.
A poet wrote, "A skull grins beneath even the chic
and pieces of the True Cross are *never* resold

so long as armies publicize the drama of blood."
Current wisdom holds all human life is layered.
Word travels fast on the jungle telegraph:
"All art is referential'" Anyway, we're still alive.

In the attic, a piano covered with black cloth.
In a corner, mice emerge from a round pink box.
The bonnet is a memory, the family *émigrés*
Still, we sense a drift in the medina

and those who cannot fly receive the news:
Someone did something! Prick up your ears!
Word comes: none will arrest Death this year
but they—the Great They—hawk likely cures.

Someone cries, *"Give it up! God lied!"*
Passersby cluck and carry bacon
in carts, barrows, wagonloads
home to bed and sex.

Kathmandu
1975–76

Birthday 59

Here am I at fifty-nine, then.
My father (eighty-six) plays prophet:
"This is your last year of middle age."
Really? Fine. So be it.

In my room, alone, a pile of books—
my dog (Vashti) deaf and restless
unsure how to guard me now
senses she's failed

But no ... Never ...
We inch over a glass bridge,
blood test to blood test,
X-rays to illusionary flight.

We shift to hand signals—
pat the car seat,
wave to the door—
(new tricks for old dogs.)

Summer is gone with its deaths.
Today was first rain, due south,
a hint of welcome fall.
Any change would do.

Vashti pads down the hall
and into bed.
I check to be sure
she hasn't wet ...

Old dog, aging man, friends.
Grey wind down my valley.
where someone burns leaves
as I count: one to sixty.

Vashti goes to the roof
To lie there and supervise.
I lie here in my spidery web
of words and thin black lines.

Fifty-nine, sixty, sixty-one ...
like clicking gears of a bike
heading uphill slowly,
slowing   and   slower   still

and soon, so soon, Vashti goes
and no words, then, no none,
as numbers themselves turn
toward some final reckoning.

Shall I measure in books?
Poems? Kings? Saints?
Loves? Losses? Collections
or simply Posts Abandoned?

They make scant difference
As Vashti trundles in again.
Cars pass on my quiet street.
I'm tranquil in this instant all.

San Francisco
October 2, 2006

Thirty Lines Finish in Silence
—for Ebony Brown (d. 2007)

SBF; Thirty-something
Singer, living in Berlin
lost both breasts in May
now your doctor/friend
predicts a month or two
six at most, no more

6', 240, charismatic
What's a key for Blues
If a clock ticks 3 ... 2 ...?
One single second splits
leucocytes; a blind date;
rsvp; regrets only

Artist Unknown
ex-pat lionized by the "ex"
who didn't pierce your tit
confused now How to Act
when you visit before you
end. Cut. Wrap.

Adrift in liquid time,
a poet lulls a chanteuse
unable to harvest thirty
flimsy hinges to half-lives
barren/colonized by virus
obscure ... absent record

as if, *almost*, as if platinum
albums boost t cell counts
or resurrect you/in flight—
sky-borne crane on a night
of no moon; Ebony Brown
fade to black

San Francisco
February 2007

Composed in a November Dream

Midnight. Diamond garter torn
the liner lists in her mute bridal
thirty-five boilers smothered.
Up on deck, a fair Welsh hymn
tails off ...Women and children
stand clear ... Lifeboats dispatch
men in drag.

All hail Attila! He reins in, cuts
his mare's neck, drinks blood
from a vein and rides on/Rome.
Noon. Termites infest ghostly
facades. Doric porticos implode
and crows confirm the Oracle:
Sacrifice or die.

Dusk. Regicide breech births
panic; wagons, litters and carts
evacuate stricken cities
but a risen ogre dwarfs retreat:
the hairy-backed Neanderthal
strums his phallus and swivels
a milky eye West.

San Francisco
May 2007

Footnote or Epitaph

From birth—
Unloved and alone;
Twenty to forty—
Adept and engaged;
Forty to sixty—
Apart yet Awake.
And after?
Useful, hopefully....

San Francisco
January 21, 2007

Acknowledgments

Heartfelt thanks are due Mark Thompson for his lucid introduction, and Dan Nicoletta for far more than his beautiful, essential images; to cite only one example of dozens, it was Dan's idea to invite Billy Bowers to create the cover art—an inspired fit—for Billy isn't simply a visionary artist or honored member of the community; his jackets and collages were part of the glittering pastiche throughout the 1970s. Our sincere gratitude to Billy.

Mark enjoys the benefit of objective distance, but Dan was, and is, so bonded with the Angels that this book presented challenges. Our memories and perceptions differ in places, so let me emphasize that my text represents only my opinions. For all of these I'm happy to assert responsibility.

The issue of names was touchy. As most of the Angels, including myself, changed names, initially I included both given and chosen names, but if people asked to be mentioned solely by stage names, "street" names or first names only, I honored their requests, of course. This may sound picayune but some people had two names or more, or went back and forth, or veered from given name to stage or spiritual name and back. The shifts are noted accordingly with apologies for unintentional blunders.

As conceived, *Flights of Angels* was a history of the era when the Angels were the outrageous vanguard of underworld gay culture. The editors of my fledgling hometown press told me they couldn't handle such a massive project, so with their blessings and backed up by Jonathan Katz, then head of the Larry Kramer Center for Gay Studies at Yale and who could not have been kinder and more supportive in his warm endorsement, I began submitting an early draft to the best-known and purportedly the most forward-leaning publishers in the United States. All praised it heartily. And turned it down. At times, their rationale was truly absurdist: one opined that the story would be best served by a writer "with strong academic credentials," as if a scholar without direct inside knowledge could untangle this scene. Then a big university press offered to publish it *without photos!* The rationale? Doing the book justice would be too expensive. Stubborn thing that I am, I refused, opting not to have the book produced at all rather than to see it shorn of color.

Realization of this apparently unattainable vision did become possible, but only thanks to the courage and creativity of Robert Ballantyne and Brian

Lam at Arsenal Pulp Press. Brian urged me to make my history into a personal memoir. He and Bethanne Grabham chiseled my text into far more beautiful form than I'd ever imagined possible. This collaboration was like dancing inside a diamond. (*Note to self*: fine editing is *ART*). Shyla Seller designed the book. I'm profoundly grateful to all for their patience and kindness, although I find it telling and disgraceful that *Flights* could find safe harbor only in Canada, home to gay marriage, after being rejected by so many self-professed cutting-edge publishers in the United States. They should be ashamed of themselves for their fundamental lack of imagination, obsession with the bottom line, and resistance to risk.

I am beholden to marijuana, hashish, LSD, mescaline, peyote, and psilocybin, among other drugs. A time came about naturally, of course, when artificially induced adventure evolved into organic discovery, but I'd be a huge hypocrite if I failed to acknowledge such appropriate first passports into Pepperland, and to its beautiful inhabitants of all sexual preferences, the well-known and the obscure, the still-living and the departed, who contributed so much to my growth and, far more importantly, who addressed planetary issues in a holistic, inclusive way that might yet save the world.

Reverence is also due to the community that nurtured the Angels of Light in its heyday; I so appreciate Tony Angel and Chuck Drees for their friendship and keen input. I'm also indebted to Teena Rosen-Albert and to Lulu, for their forthright interviews in 1995; to Tihara, for his insights about so many of the Angels during the period before I came on the scene—without the benefit of his memory, I'd never have fully fathomed those first two years; to Greg, whose thematic overview was invaluable to understanding the same period when he was most involved, and also, to the intricacies of the triumvirate; and to those in the troupe who don't wish to be named as sources but who have honored me with their perceptions and trusted me with intimate confidences, I am deeply obliged.

To the miserable old dish queens who interfered with this work and deserve special mention. Without meaning to do so, they inspired me to finish my task with a delicious sense of purpose. I appreciate the jaundiced assist.

Finally, let me acknowledge my dearest beloveds whose lifelong care has anchored me in stable, unchanging circles and provided a wholly different kind of tribal integration. As none seek acclaim or participated in this circus, no need to name names. They know who they are. In completing this book and this cycle of my life, I withdraw to their fold.

So at last, the truth, ruthless as Truth always is, is out: in its glittering manifestation and the compost from which it leapt into being. It is yours now. Construe it according to your own heart.

—Adrian Brooks
November 15, 2007

Acknowledgments
by Dan Nicoletta

I want to thank my parents, Salvatore and Helen Nicoletta. Also, Joan Salerno, Michael Pinatelli Jr, Dee Dee Stout, Norm Halm, Marcus Ewert, Brian Lam and Shyla Seller at Arsenal Pulp, Bill Bowers, Snappy, Joey Cain, Kevin and Suzanne Dugan (Iris Photo), Steve Reczkowski (Robin Color Lab), Steve Bernzweig (Bernzweig Framing), and Jose Marco et al (Express Photo). I would also like to thank the mentors who inspired me, most significantly, Harvey Milk and his lover Scott Smith who, through their emotional support and great love of theater, helped fuel my early years with the Angels of Light.

I also want to thank Adrian Brooks for his encouragement over the years and for his warm endorsement of me and my work in the group in 1975. Thirty-two years later, our true and meaningful friendship remains strong. Although collaborators always have some differences of perception, we found common ground through full and lively discourse that remained unfettered by censorship despite our differences. As a result, collaborating on this project was not unlike the template of awakened perception and free expression that the Angels were famous for, and which this book sets forth to echo.

Most importantly, I would like to thank the Angels of Light. The years that I worked alongside the troupe remain some of the most poignant of my life. Their influence on me remains indelible; their significance as accomplices in leaving these strange markings on the cave wall of time cannot be overstated. They are the photos. I was simply a poor, scraggly haired twenty-something kid with a beat-up secondhand Pentax camera, the keen and lucky conduit who got to capture them on film. It is my hope that the way the Angels of Light captured my imagination will inspire yours.